LECTIO DIVINA WITH THE SUNDAY GOSPELS

Michel de Verteuil

Lectio Divina with the Sunday Gospels

THE YEAR OF MARK – YEAR B

the columba press

First published in 2005 by
the columba press
55A Spruce Avenue, Stillorgan Industrial Park,
Blackrock, Co Dublin

Cover by Bill Bolger
Origination by The Columba Press
Printed in Ireland by ColourBooks Ltd, Dublin

ISBN 1 85607 508 7

Contents

Introduction   7

Advent: The Mystery of Waiting   11
1st Sunday of Advent   14
2nd Sunday of Advent   17
3rd Sunday of Advent   20
4th Sunday of Advent   24
The Nativity of Our Lord   27
The Holy Family   30
2nd Sunday after Christmas   33
The Epiphany of the Lord   37
The Baptism of the Lord   41
1st Sunday of Lent   45
2nd Sunday of Lent   49
3rd Sunday of Lent   53
4th Sunday of Lent   57
5th Sunday of Lent   61
Palm Sunday   66
Easter Vigil   71
Easter Sunday   75
2nd Sunday of Easter   78
3rd Sunday of Easter   84
4th Sunday of Easter   88
5th Sunday of Easter   92
6th Sunday of Easter   97
Feast of the Ascension   103
Liturgical Notes for Pentecost   107
Pentecost   110
Trinity Sunday   114
The Body and Blood of Christ   119
Celebrating Ordinary Time   124
2nd Sunday in Ordinary Time   127

3rd Sunday in Ordinary Time 130
4th Sunday in Ordinary Time 133
5th Sunday in Ordinary Time 136
6th Sunday in Ordinary Time 140
7th Sunday in Ordinary Time 146
8th Sunday in Ordinary Time 151
9th Sunday in Ordinary Time 156
10th Sunday in Ordinary Time 162
11th Sunday in Ordinary Time 165
12th Sunday in Ordinary Time 168
13th Sunday in Ordinary Time 171
14th Sunday in Ordinary Time 174
15th Sunday in Ordinary Time 178
16th Sunday in Ordinary Time 182
17th Sunday in Ordinary Time 186
18th Sunday in Ordinary Time 190
19th Sunday in Ordinary Time 195
20th Sunday in Ordinary Time 201
21st Sunday in Ordinary Time 206
22nd Sunday in Ordinary Time 210
23rd Sunday in Ordinary Time 215
24th Sunday in Ordinary Time 221
25th Sunday in Ordinary Time 225
26th Sunday in Ordinary Time 230
27th Sunday in Ordinary Time 235
28th Sunday in Ordinary Time 240
29th Sunday in Ordinary Time 244
30th Sunday in Ordinary Time 248
All Saints 252
31st Sunday in Ordinary Time 259
32nd Sunday in Ordinary Time 262
33rd Sunday in Ordinary Time 265
The Feast of Christ the King 270

Introduction

Lectio Divina: A method of biblical reflection
The reflections proposed in this book are the fruit of lectio divina, a method of meditative Bible reading which goes back to the early centuries of our church, and continues to be a source of deep spiritual growth for many people throughout the world.

Lectio divina (a Latin expression which means sacred reading) is done in three stages:

- Reading: you read the passage slowly and reverentially, allowing the words to sink into your consciousness;
- Meditation: you allow the passage to stir up memories within you, so that you recognise in it your own experience or that of people who have touched your life;
- Prayer: you allow the meditation to lead you to prayer – thanksgiving, humility and petition.

The prayers given here, week by week, are intended to serve as models. You can use them as they are, but they will also suggest ways in which you can pray from your own meditations.

Now and then, prayers will be preceded by quotations from well known thinkers or spiritual writers. The quotations are there to remind us that through Bible reading we enter into the wisdom of the entire human family.

The basic principle of lectio divina is that Bible reading is a personal encounter with God, a communion which resembles (though different from) the communion of the Eucharist. This goes against what has prevailed in our church for some centuries: the text was seen as containing a message – doctrinal or moral – and once we got the message, the text had achieved its purpose. In lectio divina, we love the text, linger over it, read it over and over, let it remain with us.

When we approach the text in this way, we come face to face with the fact that it speaks to the imagination. A Bible text is not like a textbook or a newspaper, providing us with objective information. It was not written like that. Instead, it stirs up feelings; we find ourselves identifying with the characters – we feel for them, admire them or dislike them. We are caught up in the movement of the text, its suspense, its dramatic reversals of fortune, its unanswered questions.

Gradually, we 'recognise' the text; we find that we have lived the sequence of events ourselves, or have seen them lived in others who have touched our lives, for good or for ill. Reading the text becomes a homecoming – and a lifting up. We find ourselves caught up in the story of God's people, 'fellow citizens with the saints' (Eph 2:19); we are the lowly ones whom God 'lifts up from the dust and sets in the company of princes, yes the princes of his people' (Ps 113:7-8).

Lectio divina, like all imaginative communication – especially storytelling – teaches not directly but by changing the consciousness of those who practise it. By identifying ourselves with God's people – Jesus, the prophets and the great men and women of the Old and New Testaments – we find ourselves adopting their attitudes. We also recognise ourselves in the bad characters of the text – the Pharisees, Pharaoh, the apostles when they were jealous of each other – and find that we want to give up these attitudes.

The Bible, recognised as coinciding with our experience, reveals to us the truth about life – not abstract truth, but an ideal we hunger and thirst for and, from another perspective, an evil we recoil from. In the Bible text, therefore, we discover the double reality of every human person – a story of sin and a story of grace. They are not equally true, however – the story of grace is the deep truth of the person, their 'true name', the wheat which God will gather into his barn; sin is the chaff that will be burnt in a fire that never goes out (cf Mt 3:12).

Lectio blossoms spontaneously into prayer in three dimensions:

- Thanksgiving that Jesus is alive in the story of grace;
- Humility that the story of sin is alive;
- Petition that the story of grace may prevail – 'Come, Lord Jesus!'

In lectio divina we experience the true meaning of theology – entering through Bible reading into the wisdom of God or, more accurately, allowing God-alive-in-the-Bible to lead us into wisdom, humbly, gratefully and with awe, like St Paul on the road to Damascus. The wisdom of God gives us his perspective on every aspect of life: one-to-one relationships, but also economics, politics, agriculture, etc.

Lectio divina is best taught and practised with the church's Sunday lectionary as it was reformed after the Second Vatican Council. It has its shortcomings, but overall it is a wonderfully constructed three-year programme in Bible reading. By being faithful to the lectionary in this way, we experience ourselves in communion with the church and, through the church, with all humanity, sharing in the grace and the sin of our contemporaries. We can say of Bible reading what St Paul says of the Eucharist: 'We, though many, form one body because we partake of the one bread' (1 Cor 10:17).

This volume completes the three-year cycle of reflections on the Sunday gospel readings. Once again I would like to thank all who have helped me prepare them for publication, especially Elena Lombardi-French in Dublin and Brendan Clifford OP in Limerick.

Advent: The Mystery of Waiting

Advent is the liturgical season when we pay special attention to the mystery of waiting. We have a real problem here because most of us don't like waiting, we don't see it as something to celebrate. In fact this may well be one of the reasons why people don't understand Advent correctly – although it may also be true that not celebrating it as we should has led us to misunderstand the value of waiting.

Whereas waiting bores and often irritates us, the Bible teaches us that if we approach it in the right spirit, waiting is a creative moment when we grow spiritually. When we wait we are in touch with an essential aspect of our humanity which is that we are dependent on God and on one another. It is also an act of love since, by waiting for others, we pay them the respect of letting them be free.

Waiting is a mystery – God waits and nature waits – so that when we as individuals wait we go beyond ourselves and enter into a sacred life-giving process, experiencing that we are made in the image and likeness of God. This is why Advent is a time of celebration. It is the season when we remember with gratitude creative experiences of waiting in our lives or the lives of people we have known, the people who have waited for us at one time or another. We also remember the great waiting experiences in human history, in the Bible, and especially in the life of Jesus.

But we must also make Advent a time of teaching. During this season all those involved in the work of Christian education, whether as catechists or preachers or guides, should explore the mystery of waiting: true and false ways of waiting, the danger of not knowing how to wait, ascetical practices that will help us wait more creatively.

Finally, waiting can be, as we know from our own experience, a time of suffering and sometimes of despair. In Advent, we make a special effort to feel for those who are crying out in their agony, 'How long, O Lord?' – those we can name and the countless others 'whose faith is known to God alone'. Through our meditation we can let the special grace of the season flow through us to these brothers and sisters of ours, turning their mourning into dancing and their time of barrenness into one of abundance and fertility.

The liturgy of the word is a teaching moment. It is not abstract teaching, where truths are presented to be learnt, but teaching by celebration. We celebrate biblical stories which exemplify the spirit of the particular season, identifying with the persons in them. In the process we learn more about biblical values, experience repentance as we become more aware of how we (and the whole church) have failed to practise those values, and pray that we will enter more fully into God's plan for us – that his kingdom will come. The main person we identify with is Jesus himself. At each liturgical season we celebrate one particular stage of his life on earth, not as a past event but as a way in which he continues to live among us.

The grace of Advent is hope, the virtue by which we human beings can recognise and welcome God present in the world but not experienced with our senses. The corresponding stage in Jesus' life which we celebrate in this season is when he was in the womb of Mary. It was a time in the history of salvation when the Word was made flesh, but was not visible, his presence was real but an object of hope, like the tiny mustard seed which we trust will eventually become a great tree in whose branches the birds of the air will shelter.

The fruit of Advent then is that we grow in the virtue of hope that God is present even when he is hidden. We are undaunted by evil, do not give up on our dreams, face with confidence the present historical moment (ours, that of our society and of the modern world), welcome the people he sends us, and help them get in touch with the best in themselves – where God is present.

In celebrating Jesus in the womb of Mary we celebrate all the times, in the Bible and in history, when human beings have been invited by God to recognise his hidden presence in the world. The liturgical readings for the season then present us with biblical persons who are models of hope.

The Bible teaches this through stories, not abstract definitions. It does not attempt to define what hope is, but invites us to meditate on people of hope. We celebrate them and enter into their attitudes, how they interpreted the events of their time and how they related to their contemporaries.

By doing this we celebrate our own experiences of hope, in ourselves and others. In the process we experience conversion, renew our hope which had grown cold. We also pray that those in despair will turn to hope and we commit ourselves to bringing hope into the world.

First Sunday of Advent

Gospel Reading: Mark 13:33-37

³³*Jesus said to his disciples: 'Be on your guard, stay awake, because you never know when the time will come. ³⁴It is like a man traveling abroad: he has gone from home, and left his servants in charge, each with his own task; and he has told the doorkeeper to stay awake. ³⁵So stay awake, because you do not know when the master of the house is coming, evening, midnight, cockcrow, dawn; ³⁶if he comes unexpectedly, he must not find you asleep. ³⁷And what I say to you I say to all: Stay awake!'*

Although the passage is short, we can divide it up, as each section is different and we can meditate on each separately.

The key to understanding verse 33 is to take 'the time' as the time of grace, the time when a longed-for event finally comes to pass: Jesus is reminding us that if we are not awake we let those moments pass us by.

Verses 34 and 35 are a parable, although the emphasis changes is verse 35 so that even these two verses should be meditated on separately. In verse 34 the vocation of the doorkeeper is the focus, so enter into it. In verse 35 the delay in coming is the main point.

In verse 37 identify with Jesus, consciously making a distinction between 'you' and 'all'.

* * *

Lord, we remember the hard times:
- a relationship meant everything to us, yet we were just not communicating;
- a beloved child had turned to drugs or alcohol;
- the project to which we had given ourselves wholeheartedly collapsed.
Then, quite unexpectedly, something happened
and all was well again.
How true, Lord, that when we are dealing with people
we must never lose hope
but remain on our guard and stay awake,
because we never know when the time will come.

The future will depend on what we do in the present. Gandhi
Lord, the world today presents a dismal picture:
  - violence in families, in neighbourhoods, between nations;
  - famine in the midst of abundance;
  - money that is sorely needed for food and drink spent on arms.
It is enough to make anyone despair.
You tell us today that this is not your will for the world at all.
It is like when the master of the house goes abroad
and delays returning,
so that everyone becomes slack and undisciplined.
We pray that we Christians may be like faithful servants,
each of us with our own task,
and especially that we may be like doorkeepers,
a sign to all that this world is your home
and you will be returning soon to live with us.

Lord, we thank you for the people who have waited for us
– parents, grandparents, uncles and aunts;
– the church community;
– friends.
When everyone else had given up on us and gone to sleep,
they were the doorkeepers.
As we hesitantly made our way home,
wondering if we would be let in,
they were awake and welcomed us back.

Hell is not to love any more. Dorothy Day
Lord, forgive us for giving up too quickly
just because evening and midnight have passed.
But when we stop hoping
we miss the opportunities you send us:
  - a moment of reconciliation comes but we don't even notice it;
  - the word of encouragement that could have brought a community or nation to life remains unspoken;
  - we give things to people but we do not give them the space where they could grow in self-confidence,
all because we are not on our guard and have gone to sleep.

Lord, we watch today with all those who wait:
    - oppressed peoples throughout the world;

    - those who are trying to be agents of reconciliation in
    Colombia, in the Holy Land;
    - those who are working for solidarity between rich and poor
    nations.
Evening, midnight, cockcrow, dawn have all come and gone.
We watch with them, trusting that their time will come.

Lord, there are many in our country who have lost hope.
Say to all what you have said to us Christians
that we must not despair but must stay awake.

Second Sunday of Advent

Gospel Reading: Mark 1:1-8

¹The beginning of the Good News about Jesus Christ, the Son of God. ²It is written in the book of the prophet Isaiah: Look, I am going to send my messenger before you; he will prepare your way. ³A voice cries in the wilderness: Prepare a way for the Lord, make his paths straight. ⁴And so it was that John the Baptist appeared in the wilderness, proclaiming a baptism of repentance for the forgiveness of sins. ⁵All Judaea and all the people of Jerusalem made their way to him, and as they were baptised by him in the river Jordan they confessed their sins. ⁶John wore a garment of camel-skin, and he lived on locusts and wild honey. ⁷In the course of his preaching he said, 'Someone is following me, someone who is more powerful than I am, and I am not fit to kneel down and undo the strap of his sandals. ⁸I have baptised you with water, but he will baptise you with the Holy Spirit.'

On this Sunday and the next, the church gives us John the Baptist as the model of the prophet calling people to move from the wilderness or place of despair to a state of hopeful and trusting expectation. Jesus himself was someone who knew how to wait.

Like last week's, this reading should be read in sections. Omit verse 1 which is an introduction to the entire gospel of St Mark rather than to this part of it.

In verses 2 and 3 you can focus on the fact that the story of John the Baptist was already written in the book of Isaiah, or you can look at the content of the verses. The first two lines are from Malachi, and the pronouns must be interpreted correctly: they are saying that when God is about to come into the life of a person or a community he always sends a messenger to prepare the way for him. In the next part of the prophecy be sure to interpret correctly the meaning of 'cries in the wilderness' which means that God's prophets always announce confidently to those who are in the wilderness that they must not despair, but rather act as if God's grace will come to them at any moment.

Verses 4 and 5 summarise the mission of John the Baptist who touches a community or nation so that the people commit themselves to a renewed life, recognising their former sins.

Verse 6 speaks of the Baptist's simple lifestyle, in sharp contrast to the extraordinary success of his preaching in the previous verses.

In verses 7 and 8 we get a glimpse of the humility of John the Baptist, a model of waiting. John may have said these words
– at a time of triumph, showing that he did not let success go to his head,
– at a time when he was feeling frustrated and knew he must be content to wait for God's moment of grace.

* * *

By excluding death from our own life we cannot live a full life, by admitting death into our own life we enlarge and enrich it.
Etty Hillesum, a Dutch Jewess who died in Auschwitz in 1943
Lord, we celebrate today our conversion experiences:
- we turned away from drink or something else that was destroying us;
- we took up our courage after a bout of depression;
- we moved from self-centredness to a life of service.
We remember with deep gratitude the messenger you sent before you who was to prepare your way:
a sermon, a friend, one of our children, an illness.
At the time, we were in a wilderness, drifting aimlessly, not going anywhere.
Then, as it is written in the books of the prophets,
a voice cried out in our wilderness
that we were not destined to remain there forever,
that we could expect a moment of grace.

In the body there is a little shrine.
In that shrine there is a lotus.
In that lotus there is a little space.
The whole universe is in that little space, because the creator, the source of all, is in the heart of each one of us. Upanishad
Lord, we thank you for our John the Baptists:
- a Life in the Spirit seminar;
- a national leader;
- a new parish priest or a new principal of our school.

The whole community, all Judaea
and all the people of Jerusalem,
we made our way to him,
we let ourselves be baptised in the river Jordan,
reconising how we had become lazy, self-satisfied and grasping,
and we put the past behind us.

We pray for those who have given their lives
to making society more just
and who at this moment find themselves
becoming bitter and resentful, and are tempted to violence.
Keep them humble like John the Baptist.
Remind them that it is your sacred work they are doing,
that they are unworthy servants,
not fit to kneel down and undo the straps of your sandals.
If they feel they are not achieving much, you are following them;
if they feel powerless, you are more powerful.
They baptise with water,
but you will baptise with the Holy Spirit.

Lord, we thank you that in many countries today
your church is bringing hope to the lowly,
so that once again John the Baptist can cry out good news
to those in the wilderness:
    - those who have failed so often that they have given up hope
      of bettering themselves;
    - those who have been written off as unemployable;
    - those who are being deprived of the minimum resources
      necessary for survival,
announcing to them that they need not despair,
but can be full of hope
because they will now experience that you are in their midst
and they are free, creative members of the human family.

Lord, we are anxious that all Judaea and all the people of Jerusalem
should make their way out to us and be baptised,
but we think it can be done through money or earthly power,
forgetting that your prophets wear a garment of camel skin
and live on locusts and wild honey.

Third Sunday of Advent

Gospel Reading: John 1:6-8, 19-28

⁶*A man came, sent by God. His name was John.* ⁷*He came as a witness, as a witness to speak for the light, so that everyone might believe through him.* ⁸*He was not the light, only a witness to speak for the light.*

¹⁹*This is how John appeared as a witness. When the Jews sent priests and Levites from Jerusalem to ask him, 'Who are you?'* ²⁰*he not only declared, but declared quite openly, 'I am not the Christ.'* ²¹*'Well then,' they asked 'are you Elijah?' 'I am not' he said. 'Are you the Prophet?' He answered, 'No.'* ²²*So they said to him, 'Who are you? We must take back an answer to those who sent us. What have you to say about yourself?'* ²³*So John said, 'I am, as Isaiah prophesied: a voice that cries in the wilderness: 'Make a straight way for the Lord.''* ²⁴*Now these men had been sent by the Pharisees,* ²⁵*and they put this further question to him, 'Why are you baptising if you are not the Christ, and not Elijah, and not the prophet?'* ²⁶*John replied, 'I baptise with water; but there stands among you – unknown to you –* ²⁷*the one who is coming after me; and I am not fit to undo his sandal strap.'* ²⁸*This happened at Bethany, on the far side of the Jordan, where John was baptising.*

St Mark's gospel has only a brief section on John the Baptist, and so in this Year B the reading for the Third Sunday of Advent is taken from St John.

The passage is clearly in two sections: the first is an extract from the prologue to St John's gospel, and the second is from St John's account of the ministry of John the Baptist.

To get the full meaning of verses 6 to 8 it would be necessary to go back to the previous verse of the prologue in which St John affirms that light always shines in the dark and darkness cannot overpower this light. In this perspective the passage says that John was sent by God with the mission to 'speak for the light,' a powerful metaphor of a lawyer bearing testimony that the light is trustworthy.

Verses 19 to 21 give us a first dialogue between John the Baptist and the people whom St John calls 'the Jews', meaning those who are reluctant to accept God's word. Enter into the personality of the Baptist as he, with growing impatience, refuses to

allow himself to be put into any categories – a model of the great
person establishing his own unique identity, just as the messengers are like us when we try to fit God's new word into some
time-worn category, 'putting new wine into old wineskins'.

In verses 22 to 24 the story moves forward with John again
refusing to let himself be categorised and affirming his mission
humbly but courageously. He must reach out into the wilderness and let God's saving word be heard among those who were
neglected by the religious leaders of the time.

Verses 24 to 27 show us once more the humility of John the
Baptist, using the same metaphors we had in last Sunday's passage, although here we have in addition the contrast between
him and 'Christ', 'Elijah', and 'the prophet'. Let yourself be
touched also by the Baptist's conviction (not mentioned in St
Mark's account) that 'the one who is to come after' is actually
standing there even though the community does not see him.

Verse 28 is very symbolic: John is baptising on the far side of
the Jordan, far away from the religious centres of the time.

* * *

Lord, there is much darkness around us in society,
in our church community, in our family, in our own hearts.
Eventually it gets us down.
We become cynical and settle for mediocrity.
We thank you that someone always comes on the scene,
sent by you as a witness to speak for the light:
> - on the world scene, people like Gandhi, Martin Luther
> King, Mother Teresa;
> - in our country, teachers, workers, community leaders;
> - a grandparent, one of our children, a friend.
They bear witness to the rest of us that somewhere in the dark
a light always shines,
a light that darkness cannot overpower,
and therefore we can all believe again.

Lord, goodness is always small, very frail and vulnerable,
whereas evil is loud and self-assertive,
dominating the news and our conversations.
We pray that your church may always speak for the light,
so that through her people might believe.

Lord, we get frustrated when we see
the shortcomings of your church,
or our personal shortcomings.
That is because we have become self-important,
forgetting that we are not the light,
only witnesses to speak for the light.

Lord, when someone speaks your word to us,
we look for endless reasons not to respond,
we put the person into a category –
'the same old message,' we say, 'just another of those do-gooders,
we have heard it all before.'
We thank you for the times
when your word became something new,
a voice penetrating right into the wilderness we were in,
so that we heard it and entered into a new relationship with you.

Lord, forgive us for confining your word to some restricted areas
whereas we leave others untouched:
    - the world of economics and politics is cold and heartless;
    - the food policies of the wealthy nations are causing famine
    among the poor;
    - workplaces know only suspicion and confrontation.
Help us to be your voice crying out in those wildernesses
that you want to be present there too
with your love and compassion,
and they must open themselves to you.

Lord, we feel incompetent.
We ask ourselves how we can be preaching your gospel
when we are so far from being the Christ,
a great prophet like Elijah, or the promised Messiah.
Help us to be content to baptise with water,
trusting that you are standing with us
even though we do not experience your presence,
that you will come after us
and put right all we have done wrong,
and we are not fit to undo your sandal strap.

Lord, forgive us for becoming complacent in your church,
as if grace is at work among us only.
Forgive us too for becoming discouraged
when we find the church not doing enough.
Remind us that John is baptising on the far side of the Jordan.

Fourth Sunday of Advent

26*The angel Gabriel was sent by God to a town in Galilee called Nazareth,* 27*to a virgin betrothed to a man named Joseph, of the house of David; and the virgin's name was Mary.* 28*He went in and said to her, 'Rejoice, so highly favoured! The Lord is with you.'* 29*She was deeply disturbed by these words and asked herself what this greeting could mean,* 30*but the angel said to her, 'Mary, do not be afraid; you have won God's favour.* 31*Listen! You are to conceive and bear a son, and you must name him Jesus.* 32*He will be great and will be called Son of the Most High. The Lord God will give him the throne of his ancestor David;* 33*he will rule over the House of Jacob for ever and his reign will have no end.'* 34*Mary said to the angel, 'But how can this come about, since I am a virgin?'* 35*'The Holy Spirit will come upon you,' the angel answered 'and the power of the Most High will cover you with its shadow. And so the child will be holy and will be called Son of God.* 36*Know this too: your kinswoman Elizabeth has, in her old age, herself conceived a son, and she whom people called barren is now in her sixth month,* 37*for nothing is impossible to God.'* 38*'I am the handmaiden of the Lord,' said Mary, 'let what you have said be done to me.' And the angel left her.*

St Mark has no story of Mary's conception of Jesus nor of her pregnancy, so the reading for the Fourth Sunday of Advent this year is from St Luke, the famous story of the annunciation.

It is difficult to enter into the story because we have long been accustomed to read it as uniquely the story of Mary, and therefore outside our experience. This is clearly against the intention of St Luke who gave us Mary as the model of the faithful one entering into God's great plan for the world. Take her as model of a church community discovering its vocation to bring Jesus into the world, or an individual person discovering his or her personal vocation.

Take the story as a long journey during which God, through the angel, walks with Mary. He is accompanying her at every stage, until finally she surrenders herself to him and he leaves her.

Verses 26-28: The first encounter with God's word. Mary experiences herself deeply loved by God.

Verses 29-30: She is filled with awe but the angel reassures her, calling her by name.

Verses 31-33: The angel unfolds God's plan for her, a plan that is way beyond her own expectations for herself.

Verses 34-35: Mary is in awe again, and once more she receives words of reassurance.

Verses 36-37: The angel gives further grounds for trust by citing another example of God's power.

Verses 38a: Mary leaves herself humbly and trustingly in God's hands and plan.

Verses 38b: Mary is now perfectly at peace and the angel can leave her.

* * *

There is no pit so deep that He is not deeper still.

Corrie ten Boon, a Dutch Jewess in a concentration camp

Lord, there is something very wonderful stirring within your church:

- she in entering into the struggles of the poor for a more human society;
- voices within the church speak out fearlessly against all forms of injustice;
- lay people grow in holiness through their family commitments and their work.

It seems that you have sent your angel to your church in our time, with the good news that she is still your chosen one,

called to bring forth your Son into the modern world

and make the dreams of the ancient prophets a reality.

Naturally, we are confused and fearful,

deeply disturbed by this word.

We have become set in our ways, sterile even.

Tell us again, Lord, through your holy angel,

that we need not be afraid:

- that the power of the Most High will cover us with its shadow;
- what has been conceived within us will be your own child;
- that you have done wonderful deeds before, since nothing is impossible to you,

so that we may see ourselves as your humble servants,

letting you bring to fulfillment the word you have spoken to us.

Lord, we think today of all who are faced with a difficult decision:
- can they attempt a reconciliation?
- take on some new responsibility?
- engage themselves in a work of human liberation?
Send them an angel to walk with them
as Gabriel walked with Mary,
- to call them by name;
- to speak a word of encouragement – 'Rejoice, so highly favoured, do not be afraid';
- to assure them that what they have conceived will be great and a Son of the Most High;
- to remind them that nothing is impossible to you,
and finally, when they have accepted your will, to leave them.

Lord, we thank you today for those who have conceived a child
and received it as a sign that they are highly favoured.
Even if they feel deeply disturbed,
called to bring forth a holy child who is destined to live forever,
they see themselves as humble servants of this great mystery,
and give themselves trustingly to the fulfillment of your word.

Lord, we thank you today
for the many great women of our world.
They conceived a vision within themselves,
trusting that it came from you.
They struggled with feelings of infertility,
imposed on them by society,
but they took courage from knowing
that they were servants of a sacred work,
bringing to birth the rule of your Son.

Know that the pope stands united with the Black community as it rises to its full dignity and lofty destiny. Pope John Paul II
Lord, we thank you
for the precious moments of contemplative prayer,
when after a long journey with many doubts and hesitations,
with you at our side calming fears and answering questions,
we finally felt able to let the word you had spoken be done to us
and you could withdraw your sensible presence from us.

The Nativity of Our Lord

Gospel Reading: Luke 2:1-20

[1]*Now at this time Caesar Augustus issued a decree for a census of the whole world to be taken.* [2]*This census – the first – took place while Quirinius was governor of Syria,* [3]*and everyone went to his own town to be registered.* [4]*So Joseph set out from the town of Nazareth in Galilee and travelled up to Judaea, to the town of David called Bethlehem, since he was of David's House and line,* [5]*in order to be registered together with Mary, his betrothed, who was with child.* [6]*While they were there the time came for her to have her child,* [7]*and she gave birth to a son, her first-born. She wrapped him in swaddling clothes and laid him in a manger because there was no room for them at the inn.* [8]*In the countryside close by there were shepherds who lived in the fields and took it in turns to watch their flocks during the night.* [9]*The angel of the Lord appeared to them and the glory of the Lord shone round them. They were terrified,* [10]*but the angel said, 'Do not be afraid. Listen, I bring you news of great joy, a joy to be shared by the whole people.* [11]*Today in the town of David a saviour has been born to you; he is Christ the Lord.* [12]*And here is a sign for you: you will find a baby wrapped in swaddling clothes and lying in a manger.'* [13]*And suddenly with the angel there was a great throng of the heavenly host, praising God and singing:* [14]*'Glory to God in the highest heaven, and peace to men who enjoy his favour.'* [15]*Now when the angels had gone from them into heaven, the shepherds said to one another, 'Let us go to Bethlehem and see this thing that has happened which the Lord has made known to us.'* [16]*So they hurried away and found Mary and Joseph, and the baby lying in the manger.* [17]*When they saw the child they repeated what they had been told about him,* [18]*and everyone who heard it was astonished at what the shepherds had to say.* [19]*As for Mary, she treasured all these things and pondered them in her heart.* [20]*And the shepherds went back glorifying and praising God for all they had heard and seen; it was exactly as they had been told.*

This well-known story is very rich so we will focus on some aspects only, staying with Mary's perspective, especially in verses 6 to 7, and 16 to 20.

In verses 6 and 7 Luke tells us that Mary gave birth 'when the time came for her to have her child.' Contrary to the popular in-

terpretation, he indicates no regret that there was no room in the
inn. All happened as was foretold.

To understand the significance of verse 19, it is important to
note that the Greek word which we translate as 'things' is *rhema*,
means both 'word' and 'event'. Mary, through her interior attitude of respectful listening, turns the event into a sacred word.

* * *

'Nothing happens before its time.' Trinidadian saying
Lord, we pray for those who are involved in lofty projects and
are becoming impatient:
    - parish youth leaders who are not getting co-operation;
    - a new party that has won no seats in the elections;
    - parents who are trying in vain to dialogue with their
      teenagers.
Help them to remember Mary
and how when the time came for her to have her child
she gave birth to a son.
She was at peace,
felt no great concern that there was no room for them in the inn,
merely wrapped her child in swaddling cloths
and laid him in a manger.

Lord, these days we are all very busy.
At work or in school we have to expend much effort
to achieve success.
At home we are bombarded with information
from television and radio.
We have time only for the sensational
and we allow the ordinary events of life to come and go:
    - the signs of maturity in our children;
    - the life crises of those close to us;
    - new stirrings of resentment or of hope
    among ordinary people in our country.
Even in our relationship with you
we concentrate on the miraculous
and the extraordinary, glorify and praise you
because things turn out exactly as we were told they would.
Mary teaches us on the contrary

to see in every event a call to grow,
a sacred word you speak to us,
to be welcomed as a treasure and pondered in our hearts,
reflected on and integrated into our consciousness.
Lord, help us to be more like Mary.

'My cell will not be one of stone or wood, but of self-knowledge.'
St Catherine of Siena
Lord, we thank you for all the contemplatives in the world,
those in enclosed convents, and those called, like Mary,
to live in their families and in secular surroundings.
While others chatter and repeat endlessly
what they have been told,
these, like Mary, know how to be silent,
treasuring things and pondering them in their hearts.

The Holy Family

Gospel Reading: Luke 2:22-40

22When the day came for them to be purified as laid down by the Law of Moses, the parents of Jesus took him up to Jerusalem to present him to the Lord 23– observing what stands written in the Law of the Lord: Every first-born male must be consecrated to the Lord – 24and also to offer in sacrifice, in accordance with what is said in the Law of the Lord, a pair of turtledoves or two young pigeons.

25Now in Jerusalem there was a man named Simeon. He was an upright and devout man; he looked forward to Israel's comforting and the Holy Spirit rested on him. 26It had been revealed to him by the Holy Spirit that he would not see death until he had set eyes on the Christ of the Lord. 27Prompted by the Spirit he came to the Temple; and when the parents brought in the child Jesus to do for him what the Law required, 28he took him into his arms and blessed God; and he said: 29'Now, Master, you can let your servant go in peace, just as you promised; 30because my eyes have seen the salvation 31which you have prepared for all the nations to see, 32a light to enlighten the pagans and the glory of your people Israel.'

33As the child's father and mother stood there wondering at the things that were being said about him, 34Simeon blessed them and said to Mary his mother, 'You see this child; he is destined for the fall and for the rising of many in Israel, destined to be a sign that is rejected – 35and a sword will pierce your own soul too – so that the secret thoughts of many may be laid bare.' 36There was a prophetess also, Anna the daughter of Phanuel, of the tribe of Ashev. She was well on in years. Her days of girlhood over, she had been married for seven years 37before becoming a widow. She was now eighty-four years old and never left the Temple, serving God night and day with fasting and prayer. 38She came by just at that moment and began to praise God; and she spoke of the child to all who looked forward to the deliverance of Jerusalem.

39When they had done everything the Law of the Lord required, they went back to Galilee, to their own town of Nazareth. 40Meanwhile the child grew to maturity and he was filled with wisdom; and God's favour was with him.

The passage for this Sunday is very long, and we have to stay with some aspects only.

It is highly significant that when Jesus entered the Temple the priests are absent. Simeon and Anna are symbols of God's faithful ones, having no official status and yet – or perhaps therefore – free enough to recognise the decisive moment of grace for their people and for all humanity.

It is also significant that the Holy Family are among the poor who are excused from the more expensive sacrifices and are allowed to bring 'a pair of turtle-doves or two young pigeons' (see Leviticus 5:7; 12:8).

As throughout his first two chapters, St Luke stresses here that everything is done 'according to the Law of the Lord.'

* * *

Lord, we go through life just living day to day as best we can,
- bringing up our children;
- doing our jobs;
- socialising with friends, going to parties, playing games;
- going to church and doing our bit in the parish.
Then, every once in a while, you send us someone,
a distant relative, a friend, a spiritual guide,
who does for us what Simeon did for Mary and Joseph
welcomes us with enthusiasm,
blesses us for fulfilling a long-held hope for the world,
leaving us surprised and wondering
at these wonderful things being said about us.

'Do not suppose that I have come to bring peace to the earth;
it is not peace I have come to bring but a sword.' Matthew 1:34
Lord, forgive us for making the message of Jesus so comfortable,
a word that tells us we don't have to try and change the world
we live in because it will never be different.
We pray that your church will be like Simeon
proclaiming to all that Jesus comes into the world
to separate good from evil, to exalt virtues like humility,
generosity and trust where they are not valued,
and to confront arrogance, meanness and self-centredness
wherever they are found.
As for us who, like Mary, are called to bring Jesus into the world,
a sword of sorrow will pierce our hearts, because through our
words the deep-seated prejudices of many will be laid bare.

'The secular school explains things and creates knowledge;
the religious school teaches how to contemplate things and creates
wonder.' Anthony de Mello SJ
Lord, often those who follow our education programmes,
both in schools and in parishes,
are not taught to see the world with new eyes.
Like everyone else they are dazzled by power and wealth
and set great store by them.
We pray that these programmes will be temples
out of which people like Simeon will emerge,
able to recognise that a small group of humble people
coming to do what the Law requires
are the men and women who are the hope for the future,
the light of the world and the glory of your people Israel.

Second Sunday after Christmas

Gospel Reading: John 1:1-18

¹In the beginning was the Word: the Word was with God and the Word was God. ²He was with God in the beginning. ³Through him all things came to be, not one thing had its being but through him. ⁴All that came to be had life in him and that life was the light of men, ⁵a light that shines in the dark, a light that darkness could not overpower.

⁶A man came, sent by God. His name was John. ⁷He came as a witness, as a witness to speak for the light, so that everyone might believe through him. ⁸He was not the light, only a witness to speak for the light. ⁹The Word was the true light that enlightens all men; and he was coming into the world. ¹⁰He was in the world that had its being through him, and the world did not know him. ¹¹He came to his own domain and his own people did not accept him. ¹²But to all who did accept him he gave power to become children of God, to all who believe in the name of him ¹³who was born not out of human stock or urge of the flesh or will of man but of God himself. ¹⁴The Word was made flesh, he lived among us, and we saw his glory, the glory that is his as the only Son of the Father, full of grace and truth. ¹⁵John appears as his witness. He proclaims: 'This is the one of whom I said: He who comes after me ranks before me because he existed before me.' ¹⁶Indeed, from his fulness we have, all of us, received – yes, grace in return for grace, ¹⁷since, though the Law was given through Moses, grace and truth have come through Jesus Christ. ¹⁸No one has ever seen God; it is the only Son, who is nearest to the Father's heart, who has made him known.

This passage is the prologue to St John's gospel, a very deep teaching on the mystery of the incarnation. But do not let yourself be intimidated by the depth; remember that it was written for you; like the whole Bible, it was for you and for your salvation that it came down from heaven.

It may be helpful to divide the passage as follows:

Verse 1: The Word of God which was made flesh had his beginnings with God before creation. Identify what in your experience was an incarnation of the Word and then remember when you knew that this word was with God from all eternity.

Verses 2-5: The story of creation, understood as an ongoing process.

Verses 6-8: the vocation of John the Baptist; recognise in him the vocation of all great people.

Verses 9-14: St John's presentation of the incarnation. Recognise the mystery from your own experience, in particular the strange mystery of the one who made and sustains humanity being rejected by this same humanity.

Verses 16-18: A further meditation on the mystery of the incarnation. Note especially the process of growth 'from grace to grace', and the difference between Jesus and all others.

* * *

'To the end of our lives the Bible remains an unexplored and unsubdued land full of concealed wonders and choice treasures.'
Cardinal Newman
Lord, we thank you for the deep moments of Bible reading
when we knew that we were in the presence of a Word
which existed from the beginning, before time began,
which was with you before you created the world,
which was truly divine, with you from the beginning,
and which was made flesh and was living among us.

'In meditation I pass through my body which exists in time and space, and beyond my thoughts which reflect my body-consciousness. I discover my ground in the Word, my real self which exists eternally in God and with God.' Bede Griffiths
Lord, we thank you for the moments of deep prayer
when we know that we have life in your Word,
that Word which was in the beginning,
which was with you and was you.

Lord, humanity today wants to live independently of you,
and even Christians speak as if you created the world
and then left it to its own devices.
We thank you for the teaching of St John
reminding us that all things come to be
only because you speak a Word,
and that every single thing that exists today
has its being because that Word continues to be spoken in it,
and the only way that anything which has come to be
has life today is because your Word lives within it.

'Perestroika shows that there are some live cells still left in our society,
battling against the disintegration of the Spirit.' A Russian writer
Lord, we thank you that the human spirit is unconquerable,
it is a light that comes from you,
a light that continues to shine even when there is great darkness,
a light that no darkness can overcome.

'Far from being the ultimate measure of all things, human beings can
only realise themselves by reaching beyond themselves.'
Paul VI, *Populorum progressio*
Lord, how true it is that we can only find our dignity
as your sons and daughters
if we believe that there is more to us than a human birth,
the urges of the flesh and the human will
and that within us your love is at work.

'Of all the crimes of colonialism there is none worse that the attempt to
make us believe that we had no indigenous culture of our own.'
Julius Nyerere
Lord, we pray that as Christians
we may live the message of the incarnation,
that your eternal Word was made flesh,
so that in every culture you are at work,
and if we look at our past in the light of faith
we will see your glory,
Jesus at work in our history, full of grace and truth.

Lord, a conversion experience is always a home-coming:
- turning away from an addiction,
- being reconciled with our family,
- forgiving an old hurt,
- going to confession after a long absence.
Once we are there we look back and wonder at our resistance.
Here was something that we needed in order to live,
and yet we did not recognise it;
the truth of ourselves demanded it,
and yet we did not accept to do it.
Now, Lord, by your grace,
we know that your Word has been made flesh
and found a home in us.
Thank you, Lord.

'One of the deepest joys of life is to be used for a purpose recognised by yourself as a mighty one.' George Bernard Shaw
Lord, we thank you for times
when we have the deep satisfaction of knowing
that we are working for a noble cause,
one that we know is far greater than ourselves,
even though we are making a contribution to it,
so that we can say like John the Baptist that what comes after us
ranks before us because it existed before us.

'There is nothing in my former ministry that I would repudiate except my many sins and shortcomings. My becoming a priest in the Roman Catholic Church will be the completion and right ordering of what was begun thirty years ago.' Richard Neuhaus, Lutheran pastor, on entering the Catholic Church and asking for ordination as a priest; October 1990
Lord, we pray for all those
who are becoming members of our church,
that they may experience their life up to now as being fulfilled,
as having received from your fullness,
the grace of the present fulfilling the grace of the past.

The Epiphany of the Lord

Gospel Reading: Matthew 2:1-12

¹After Jesus had been born at Bethlehem in Judaea during the reign of King Herod, some wise men came to Jerusalem from the east. ²'Where is the infant king of the Jews?' they asked. 'We saw his star as it rose and have come to do him homage.' ³When King Herod heard this he was perturbed, and so was the whole of Jerusalem. ⁴He called together all the chief priests and the scribes of the people, and enquired of them where the Christ was to be born. ⁵'At Bethlehem in Judaea,' they told him, 'for this is what the prophet wrote: ⁶And you, Bethlehem, in the land of Judaea, you are by no means least among the leaders of Judah, for out of you will come a leader who will shepherd my people Israel.' ⁷Then Herod summoned the wise men to see him privately. He asked them the exact date on which the star had appeared, ⁸and sent them on to Bethlehem. 'Go and find out all about the child,' he said, 'and when you have found him, let me know, so that I too may go and do him homage.'

⁹Having listened to what the king had to say, they set out. And there in front of them was the star they had seen rising; it went forward and halted over the place where the child was. ¹⁰The sight of the star filled them with delight, ¹¹and going into the house they saw the child with his mother Mary, and falling to their knees they did him homage. Then, opening their treasures, they offered him gifts of gold and frankincense and myrrh.

¹²But they were warned in a dream not to go back to Herod, and returned to their own country by a different way.

In the Christmas story as told by St Luke, the Word made flesh manifests himself to the shepherds; in St Matthew's version, he manifests himself to the wise men from the East. Although at first sight the two stories seem different, they are in fact basically alike – as you will discover when you meditate on each passage – since there is only one God and he has one way of relating with us.

For this feast, then, make the journey with the wise men, as you did with the shepherds on Christmas Day.

The story is told in clearly defined stages, and you will find that each of these stages will touch you in your meditation, so that you need not include the entire story in order to do a good meditation.

Verses 1 and 2 tell us of the journey from 'the east' to Jerusalem, and the symbolism of the first searching which takes us some of the way, before we get lost and have to resort to a religious centre.

In verses 3 to 9 we have the meeting between the wise men and Herod – very dramatic, and so true to experience. You can read these verses

– from the point of view of the wise men, so humble and open to learning from religious leaders, even though these have bad motives;

– or from the point of view of Herod, typical of ourselves when we are in a position of authority and privilege and become insecure at the mere thought of a new religious insight.

In verses 10 and 11 we have the touching story of all moments of grace – the joy of recognition, the sense of homecoming, the simplicity of the presence of God. The mention of the 'treasures' is clearly meant to convey the arrival of other cultures doing homage to Jesus.

Verse 12 is very significant, indicating the new-found freedom of believers.

* * *

Lord, there comes a point in our lives when we finally discover what we want to give our whole lives to:

- a cause like racial equality, community development, women's rights;
- a spirituality which combines union with God and social involvement;
- the religious life or the priesthood;
- contemplative prayer.

We look back on the long journey that brought us to this point, from the time we knew in some vague way
that we wanted to change our ways
– like the wise men seeing the star as it rose
and deciding to follow it.
Then, as it always seems to happen on a spiritual journey,
we lost sight of the star and drifted aimlessly for some years,
until we realised that the only sensible thing to do

was to get help.
So we went to our religious leaders,
and though they were rather confused themselves,
they put us back on the right track
and the old enthusiasm returned.
The last part of the journey went quickly:
suddenly we knew that we had found
what we had been looking for,
and it was like coming home, so that we went into the house,
fell on our knees and opened our treasures.
Thank you, Lord, for guiding us every part of the way.

Lord, it is strange how we become attached
to positions of privilege
  - as parents or teachers;
  - occupying a position in the church;
  - accepted as one of the better educated members of our little
  circle.
When people come forward
who are from a different background,
or who are asking new questions,
we are pertubed,
as Herod was when the wise men came to Jerusalem.
We reflect on what to say, and may even give them good advice,
but deep down our main concern is
that we should continue to feel secure where we are.
No wonder those whom we help do not come back to us
but return to their country by a different way.

Lord, for many centuries now the church has been European.
We thank you that in our day
people of other cultures are looking for Jesus
because they have seen a star out in the east.
Naturally, we are perturbed by all these foreigners,
and so is the whole of Jerusalem,
for they will bring changes to the whole church,
and we will lose our special status.
So, though we give them the right instructions,
we tell them that once they have discovered Jesus

they must come back and tell us exactly what they have found.
But you are guiding them, Lord, and when they come to Jesus
they will open the treasures of their own cultures.
Furthermore, you will reveal to them
that there is no need to come back to us,
and they will make their own way home.

Lord, we sometimes think that we must spend plenty of money
to make Jesus more attractive, or that we must be very learned
so that our preaching of him can draw many to him.
But wise men are looking for an infant king,
and the scriptures say that he will come from Bethlehem,
the least among the leaders of Judah,
because people are tired of great kings who dominate them.
But if they go into a simple house
and see the child Jesus with his mother Mary,
even as they fall on their knees and do him homage
they will feel comfortable to open their treasures
and offer him gifts of gold, frankincense and myrrh.

Lord, we look today for instant results
and for the 'quick fix' in all things,
so that we end up looking for instant spiritual growth as well.
But before we can see Jesus
and fall on our knees and do him homage,
we have to make a long journey from the east.
We have to follow a star,
lose it and discover it again many times,
until finally it halts over the place where he is.

The Baptism of the Lord

Gospel Reading: Mark 1:7-11

7In the course of his preaching, John the Baptist said, 'Someone is following me, someone who is more powerful than I am, and I am not fit to kneel down and undo the strap of his sandals. 8I have baptised you with water, but he will baptise you with the Holy Spirit.'
9It was at this time that Jesus came from Nazareth in Galilee and was baptised in the Jordan by John. 10No sooner had he come out of the water than he saw the heavens torn apart and the Spirit, like a dove, descending on him. 11And a voice came from heaven, 'You are my Son, the Beloved; my favour rests on you.'

Mark's gospel was the first gospel to be written and therefore tells us some basic points about Jesus. Nowadays we are inclined to neglect some of them because we think they have little importance. We must however give them their full meaning. They will help us understand the mystery of faith as the church of the early ages understood it.

The passage is in two parts: verses 7 and 8, and verses 9 to 11. We will only look at the second part which tells of Jesus' baptism.

This incident happens very early in the gospel story. We learn in the introduction that Jesus 'came from Nazareth in Galilee'; it was there, in that small position, that he finally made the decision to enter his public life. He was led to his public role. He decided that he would go out there and assume his role as Messiah and Saviour of his people.

Jesus wanted to be baptised. The river Jordan was a great river in Palestine, near Jerusalem, and he decided that this was where he would be baptised. It was no ordinary baptism, it was 'a baptism of repentance and for the forgiveness of sins.' This was happening to many of his people and he wanted to join them at this point.

Clearly, this was an important moment in his life, when he accepted to be in fellowship with those who were receiving baptism from John. In the same way, he is today in fellowship with us – and it is important that we recognise this.

When he came up 'out of the water' something extraordinary happened – something that would remain crucial to him and to the rest of his ministry.

- 'The heavens were torn apart'. Everything else became unimportant. This was a real breakthrough in his relationship with God and with the world. For us today too there are things on which we need to turn our back if we want to live fully and in the present. Now we realise that they might have been important but could be obstacles between God and us. They prevent us from finding our true self and what we really want from life.

This often happens to us as a church community too. Unimportant things in the world – status, authority, the desire to be admired by all – become obstacles to our following of Jesus.

- The voice that came from heaven was 'in the form of a dove'. This was a communication which had been with God's people from the beginning of creation. In Genesis 1:2 we see it said of God when he came to earth to carry out his work there. It is the same right through, and in every aspect of life.

- The Spirit then 'descended on us'. This tells us that we can now find our true self by allowing the Spirit to come to us and take possession of us. We leave ourselves entirely in his hands.

- A voice 'came from heaven', and the words it spoke tell us three important things about Jesus, and therefore about ourselves:

a) 'you are my child'. You are someone very precious to me, someone I would be happy to be alone with, someone I can trust easily;

b) you are 'the Beloved', called to be important to me; I love them and they are one with me;

c) 'My favour rests on you'. This is a crucial phrase in the Bible. God's favour rests on us – whatever we thought about the world now counts for nothing; it is unimportant to him and to us.

Together these words tell us what counts between Jesus and God; they also tell us what happens between us and God.

* * *

Lord, we thank you for those times when we realised
that things we had considered important in the world
were really of no interest to us: they did not lead us to you.
We knew then how we must leave them on the shore
and go forward to be baptised by John.

We saw then that things we were attached to
were of no consequence to us.
It was a touching time.
We could leave the past, our own Nazareth in Galilee
and make our way to Judaea;
it was not fame or glory that we sought.
We must now ensure that we meet you as you are.
You would really manifest yourself to us
and tell us that this is what really counts and is important for us.

*'The other true purpose of school studies, of education, is to inculcate
humility, not just a virtue, but the condition of all virtues.'*
Simone Weil
Lord, help us to see the greatness of all you do for us,
our education as humans and as Christians.

*'Whosoever is at pains to read the psalm will find in it a sort of gymna-
sium for the use of all souls, a sort of stadium of virtue, where different
sorts of exercises are set out before us, from which we can choose the
one best suited to train us to win our crown.'* St Ambrose
Lord, we thank you that as we came out of the water,
something new happened to us.
the heavens were eventually what they now truly are for us,
the source of all we need in this world,
all that is worth our while to follow.

*'The best of all for the soul is what God wills at this particular moment.
Everything else must be regarded by the soul with perfect indifference
as being nothing at all.'* Jean Pierre de Caussade SJ
Lord, we thank you for the times when all that is crucial for us
is who we are and who you are.
All the rest is like nothing at all
and we thank you that we are now in that state
where everything else
are things on which we know that we must now turn our back
and leave them behind us on this shore.

Lord, we thank you for the great moments of prayer
when we finally become aware of how limited we are.

Things we sought with so much interest
now counted for nothing.
We thank you for the times when we finally realised
how unimportant they really were,
in spite of what we had thought .
What we used to set our heart on:
    - our status in life,
    - fame and what we really look out for in our lives;
    - our desire to be great and famous in your kingdom, which
    means being better and holier that those we live with,
we thank you that we see them now
as things that would keep us from you.
We thank you that we have now left them behind
and go for what is really important for us –
that we are your children, your beloved,
and that, no matter what we think,
these are the reasons why your favour now rests on us.

*'The religious life has the best of all messages, one that is presented in a
most boring way.'* G. K. Chesterton
Lord, we thank you for giving us the things
that are most important for us.
They may seem boring but we know
they are very deep and wonderful for us.
We can now devote our lives to them
and make sure that they are really what counts for us.

Lord, as we look around at what is going on in the world today,
we remember that these things tell us very little about you,
about our relationship with you,
and how we are to grow in knowledge with you.
We pray that we may turn our backs on them
and focus on how we can draw closer to you.

Lord, we thank you for the time when we really understood
that the only thing that counts for our community
is whether we are right with you and what we need from life.

First Sunday of Lent

Gospel Reading: Mark 1:12-15

¹²*The Spirit drove Jesus out into the wilderness* ¹³*and he remained there for forty days, and was tempted by Satan. He was with the wild beasts, and the angels looked after him.* ¹⁴*After John had been arrested, Jesus went into Galilee. There he proclaimed the Good News from God.* ¹⁵*'The time has come,' he said, 'and the kingdom of God is close at hand. Repent, and believe the Good News.'*

St Mark's account of the temptation in the wilderness is very short, just two verses. The church has added two later ones and these give us the option of meditating on a second moment in the life of Jesus – the beginning of his public ministry.

We look first at the two central verses (12 and 13) which belong to the original tempting of Jesus in the wilderness.

The Bible tells us first that it was 'the Spirit' who 'drove Jesus into the wilderness'. Jesus was not there because of some minor instruments like the circumstances in which he found himself. Far less was it the work of a spirit that we might label as 'false'; it was 'the true Spirit' who drove Jesus into the wilderness. God himself was in charge of what was happening to Jesus; it was clearly a force which was there to bring him the greatest good he could hope for.

The text also tells us that the Spirit made this move 'immediately', that is right after what went before. What had happened before was God's Spirit coming on Jesus in a movement of renewal. God appeared to him where he stood at the banks of the Jordan, shortly before he moved to take on his work by going to Capernaum and starting his ministry there.

The moment of being tested therefore happened 'immediately' after the moment of purity. It was a realistic movement, a healthy opposition to the coming of the Spirit. It reminded Jesus that his way to the glory of the resurrection was through the cross, in which he would be manifestly one with all the suffering members of humanity.

The expression 'with the wild beasts' is very important. It was truly a terrible situation. The Bible text often refers to God's 'testing' or 'tempting' his son; in this case the 'son' was Jesus himself. God's intention then was that this staying with the wild beasts should be helpful to Jesus as a human being.

Psalm 22:12-13 and 15-16 are important texts in explaining the meaning of 'he remained there for forty days'. They speak of Jesus being purified through a difficult ordeal. They explain the test given to the just man when he feels himself under the influence of evil in all its many forms – like a person under the influence of dogs, lions or oxen.

It was a time of honesty and stability for him therefore; a time for him to be close to God. Satan gave Jesus a good shaking up. It was like God allowing Satan to 'test' Job in the Old Testament (see Job 1 and 2). As 'God tests gold in the furnace' so does he test the just man (note the text of Wisdom 3:6). God was keeping a watchful eye on Jesus, making sure that no harm came to him. It was all for his good.

Deuteronomy 8:2-4 conveys the same meaning when it says, 'He made you feel hunger, he fed you with manna which neither you nor your fathers had known, to make you understand that man does not live on bread alone, but that man lives on everything that comes from the mouth of the Lord. The clothes on your back did not wear out, and your feet were not swollen, all those forty years.' Similarly the book of Nehemiah (9: 21) says, 'Forty years you cared for them in the wilderness; they went short of nothing, their clothes did not wear out, their feet were not swollen.'

These verses are in our minds as we read them in other accounts of the temptation. They appear in the texts of Matthew and Luke; here they are more in our subconscious.

Verses 14 and 15 speak of a moment when God comes into the life of an individual or a community. St Mark notes that at such moments people experience several things.

- A long-awaited moment has arrived. God's truth makes a new apperance. Things we did not think possible now seem reasonable. We thought that things would always be as they were before. Now we see new things as a real possibility for us.

- Spiritual growth seems a real possibility for us. God reveals himself to us in a new way. We had thought that we could feel no different. Now we know that our lives have taken on a new way.

- We feel we can trust this new orientation which God has now given to our lives.

* * *

Lord, we pray today for all those whom your Spirit
has driven out into the wilderness:
- who have been betrayed by a loved one;
- who have lost their job with no hope of getting another;
- who find themselves in prison;
- who have just learnt that they are terminally ill.
The days seem long to them, they feel battered by demons,
surrounded by wild beasts.
Lord, send them your angels to look after them.

Lord, we embark on projects easily and confidently:
- a new relationship;
- a leadership role in our community;
- a new movement, a political party.
But the good feeling does not last.
Your spirit must drive us out into the wilderness
and we must remain there forty long days,
tempted by Satan and surrounded by wild beasts
while angels look after us.
Only then are we fit to commit ourselves.

Lord, during the course of the year
we turn our eyes to many ugly things about ourselves:
- our meanness and envy;
- the hurts we have not forgiven;
- the desire to take revenge.
During this Lent, let your Spirit drive us into the wilderness
and keep us there for forty days,
where we will face up to the demons within us
and the wild beasts tearing at us,
knowing all the time that your angels are looking after us.

Lord, we thank you in the name of all those
for whom this Lent will be a season of grace,
when Jesus will come into their lives.
They will know that the moment they were running away from

has finally come,
a life of holiness will seem within their grasp,
they will turn away from their sin
and give themselves trustingly
to the new vision you have brought them to.

Lord, we thank you for those
who continue to work for reconciliation
where there is hatred and violence:
    - in Israel/Palestine, the land of Jesus;
    - between Iraq and the US;
    - in Sri Lanka;
    - in work places where workers and employers have no trust;
    - where racism divides people.
They are Jesus going into Galilee after John has been arrested, proclaiming
    - that it is a moment not of despair but of grace;
    - that love and harmony are real options;
    - that people can put their trust in the victory of good over evil.

Second Sunday of Lent

Gospel Reading: Mark 9:2-10

²Jesus took with him Peter and James and John and led them up a high mountain where they could be alone by themselves. There in their presence he was transfigured: ³his clothes became dazzling white, whiter than any earthly bleacher could make them. ⁴Elijah appeared to them with Moses; and they were talking with Jesus. ⁵Then Peter spoke to Jesus. 'Rabbi,' he said 'it is wonderful for us to be here; so let us make three tents, one for you, one for Moses and one for Elijah.' ⁶He did not know what to say; they were so frightened. ⁷And a cloud came, covering them in shadow; and there came a voice from the cloud, 'This is my Son, the Beloved. Listen to him.' ⁸Then suddenly, when they looked round, they saw no one with them any more but only Jesus. ⁹As they came down the mountain he warned them to tell no one what they had seen, until after the Son of Man had risen from the dead. ¹⁰They observed the warning faithfully, though among themselves they discussed what 'rising from the dead' could mean.

We often refer to this story as the Transfiguration. In fact, however, Jesus' appearing in glory was merely a new stage in the journey the apostles made with him.

From his first manifestation in the world, Jesus was clearly visible as Saviour of all those in need of help. He appeared so especially to those who felt they were in some sort of need and so wanted to turn to him in their prayer for healing and forgiveness.

The gospels often tell us about this element of Jesus' journey. People were attracted to him for this reason alone, which is also why Jesus withdrew from the crowd and took the decision to live on his own.

Those who went looking for his healing power found it very difficult to find him (Mark 1:40). This was why it was said so frequently that all found it difficult to really recognise him – although they kept coming to him in ever greater numbers.

This incident on the mount of Transfiguration shows us that something radical happened then. Jesus' divinity was now linked to his lowering himself to be with the smallest of all people. He was getting down to the reality of the cross. This was always the truth of Jesus, he always had it within him. He would now be following in the steps of his two great ancestors – Abraham and Moses. He would be leading God's people to salvation by identifying with the least of them.

This would be the path Jesus would now have to follow. This was why it was so important to Peter and the other disciples to take possession of the place and never give it up for somewhere else.

This was also why the Father, in the words 'This is my Son, the Beloved. Listen to him,' showed that this was Jesus at his best and all had to entrust to him their choicest gifts. This was also the reason he made clear to his followers that they would only be able to share this with the others 'after the Son of Man has risen from the dead.'

It is very striking that after Jesus had descended from the holy mountain, he met a devil who, he said quite openly, could only be driven out by prayer. This was the new identity revealed at the Transfiguration.

We reflect on this new identity of Jesus, both for himself and for his chosen disciples. Later on, he began to announce this news to his other people. He had made up his mind that he must go to Jerusalem, die after lengthy persecution by the authorities, and then after his death he would rise again. This was the triumph of his death and resurrection.

- Verse 2: The high mountain is a symbol of the painful journey the apostles must make with Jesus before he can be transfigured in their presence.

- Verses 3 to 6: The glory of Jesus is beyond the capacity of any earthly power, it is from God alone. Note St Mark's comment on why St Peter proposed building three tents: he was desperately afraid of losing the moment.

- Verse 7: The relationship with Jesus is covered by a cloud and yet from within the cloud they experience a renewed commitment to Jesus.

- Verse 8: The apostles are alone with Jesus and they come down the mountain together.

- Verses 9 and 10: It is only when they have seen Jesus die and rise from the dead that the apostles will understand the full significance of the experience.

The dogmas of the Church would be raw flesh without theology – or a
tree without leaves. As devoted feelings clothe the dogma on the one
hand, so does the teaching of theology on the other.
Cardinal Newman

Lord, we thank you for the transfiguration experiences
that you favour us with during this Lent
when for the first time we see Jesus
in his truth as our lowly saviour
    - a Bible passage suddenly becomes deep and enriching for
    us;
    - during a parish mission we feel the power of the message of
    Jesus;
    - we celebrate a liturgy that fills us with consolation;
    - we realise that the following of Jesus has deep implications
    for all of us.
At that moment we experience a glory
that is not from this earth but from you yourself,
and we cry out from the depths of ourselves
that it is wonderful for us to be here.

Lord, we thank you for the long journey we have made
with our spouse, our closest friend.
We remember the day when they first appeared glorious to us,
with a glory we had never thought possible.
We found it wonderful that we should be together,
in fact so wonderful that we were afraid of losing the moment.
We know now that a relationship cannot remain there.
So a dark cloud came over
and covered the relationship with a shadow.
But within the very insecurity of that time
we discovered that this was your beloved
whom we wanted to commit ourselves to forever.
Shortly afterwards, the relationship was stable again
and we came down the mountain together.
But we knew in some vague way
that we would have to live through
many deaths and resurrections
before we could understand the journey we had made.

Lord, we don't take time to know the people we live with:
- we are too busy with our own affairs,
- we judge others by their appearances, how they dress,
what they have achieved.
If only we let them lead us up a high mountain
where we can be alone by ourselves,
they can be transfigured in our presence
and we will see the glory that is within them
and comes from you.

Lord, we ask you to send wise spiritual guides to your church
who will help us grow in our relationship with you:
- who will encourage us to let ourselves be led
up whatever high mountain you call us to;
- who will be part of the transfiguration experience,
conversing with Jesus like Moses and Elijah;
- who will stay with us when the cloud comes
and covers us in shadows;
- and who will warn us
that we must not speak of these things
until we have seen the Son of Man rise from the dead.

Lord, we pray today for those who have committed themselves
to a noble cause;
help them to move freely beyond the first experience
of joy and excitement,
to remain with their commitment
when a cloud comes and covers them in shadow,
for it is from the cloud that they will learn for sure
that it is your work they have given themselves to,
and they can find you in it.

Lord, from time to time you give us beautiful experiences,
moments which bind us to a person or a cause.
But it is only when we have come down from the mountain
and seen that person or cause die and rise from the dead
that we will be able to speak
about what happened on the mountain.

Third Sunday of Lent

Gospel Reading: John 2:13-25

13Just before the Jewish Passover Jesus went up to Jerusalem, 14and in the Temple he found people selling cattle and sheep and pigeons, and the money changers sitting at their counter there. 15Making a whip out of some cord, he drove them all out of the Temple, cattle and sheep as well, scattered the money changers' coins, knocked their tables over 16and said to the pigeon sellers, 'Take all this out of here and stop turning my Father's house into a market.' 17Then his disciples remembered the words of scripture: 'Zeal for your house will devour me.'

18The Jews intervened and said, 'What sign can you show us to justify what you have done?' 19Jesus answered, 'Destroy this sanctuary, and in three days I will raise it up.' 20The Jews replied, 'It has taken forty-six years to build this sanctuary: are you going to raise it up in three days?' 21But he was speaking of the sanctuary that was his body, 22and when Jesus rose from the dead, his disciples remembered that he had said this, and they believed the scripture and the words he had said. 23During his stay in Jerusalem for the Passover many believed in his name when they saw the signs that he gave, 24but Jesus knew them all and did not trust himself to them; 25he never needed evidence about any man; he could tell what a man had in him.

This Sunday we have John's account of the cleansing of the temple. The passage is in two sections:

    - verses 13-17, the cleansing of the temple by Jesus;

    - verses 18-25, a discussion between Jesus and the Jews.

Three questions to ask yourself: what are the temples that people turn into market places today? Why is Jesus cleansing these temples? How is he doing it?

John's approach is different from that of the synoptic gospels. They lay stress on the dishonesty of the vendors – they had come to do business but end up turning the place into 'a den of thieves'. John does not speak of this problem at all. His complaint is not against those who profit from their illegal vending. The fault of the vendors is that they have turned the Father's house into a market, no longer a place of sharing and trans-parency but one where what a person is worth gets primary importance. They forget what the temple was really about; they see nothing beyond what they have set themselves to achieve.

The person who is intent on cleansing these temples is none other than the man Jesus. We cannot afford to see him as some kind of troublemaker or disturber of the peace – we must recognise and celebrate him for who he is. This is often difficult or even impossible for those of us who are intimately involved in this kind of trade.

Today's story tells us that we can identify the person who sets about correcting this fault because he has the original spirit of the founders. This is what St John calls the 'zeal' of Jesus, the inner feeling which makes it difficult for him to accept. We tolerate the profanation of temples very easily; for him it is a situation that he finds totally unacceptable.

Let us look finally at the dialogue between the Jews and Jesus. We see two opposed mentalities. The Jews are concerned with the sanctuary which takes forty-six years to build so that its destruction is a disaster. Jesus is concerned for a different kind of temple – one that can always be rebuilt in three days.

It is only when we have experienced true death and true resurrection that we can understand certain lessons of life. We must now ask ourselves the basic question: how have we ourselves come to this new insight? Has it been for us an experience of death and resurrection?

* * *

Liberty without obedience is confusion, obedience without liberty is slavery. William Penn
Lord, there are so many temples
that people are turning into market places today:
     - children are a sacred trust,
     but we project our own ambitions and our hurts on them;
     - our relationship with our spouse we turn into a battlefield
     where we make sure to occupy the higher ground;
     - we enter into friendships to get advantages for ourselves;
     - the land we see as a source of easy profit;
     - the human body we treat as an object of competitions;
     - a church community becomes a place for prestige and
     power.

We thank you for the times you sent Jesus into those temples;
he made a whip out of some cord and drove us out,
scattering our coins and knocking our counting tables over.
We were angry, hurt and confused,
but looking back we now recognise
that it was zeal for your house that devoured you.

*The only real prayer is one where we are no longer aware that we are
praying.* St Anthony the Great
Lord, there was a time
when we had made our relationship with you
a matter of rewards for good works.
We complained that you let us suffer,
that you left our prayers unanswered,
that others we considered less virtuous than ourselves
were more blessed than we were.
But all the time it was Jesus cleansing your house,
driving away the baggage of the marketplace,
so that we could come to you in humble adoration and trust.

Lord, forgive us that we are no longer indignant
when sacred places are being violated.
We thank you for those whom zeal for your house
has devoured:
    - Martin Luther King overturning the segregation counters
    in the Southern United States;
    - Steve Biko communicating a sense of self worth
    to his fellow South Africans;
    - labour leaders in the Caribbean who brought dignity to
    workers;
    - those who work for peace in a country torn apart
    by long and painful strife.

Lord, we are always fearful
of losing what is secondary to your church
– large numbers, popularity, the patronage of the powerful –
fearful that what has taken forty-six years to build
might be destroyed.
As a result we compromise and tolerate and remain passive.

Remind us, Lord, that the only sanctuary that counts
is the body of Jesus,
his love, his solidarity with the poor and the oppressed;
and once we are truly his body in our society,
we can rebuild in three days
whatever the earthly powers destroy.

Lord, there are so many deep lessons about life
that we learn from our parents and grandparents,
but it is only
after we have passed through resurrection from the dead
that we remember what they taught us
and we believe the words they spoke.

Lord, be with your church in our moments of success,
when many believe in us because they see signs we give
– our schools and other institutions,
– our lively liturgies
– our rallies.
Remind us what people have in them,
so that we may not put our trust in their approval
but only in our fidelity to you.

Fourth Sunday of Lent

Gospel Reading: John 3:14-21

14Jesus said to Nicodemus: 'The Son of Man must be lifted up as Moses lifted up the serpent in the desert, 15so that everyone who believes may have eternal life in him. 16Yes, God loved the world so much that he gave his only Son, so that everyone who believes in him may not be lost but may have eternal life. 17For God sent his Son into the world not to condemn the world, but so that through him the world might be saved. 18No one who believes in him will be condemned; but whoever refuses to believe is condemned already, because he has refused to believe in the name of God's only Son. 19On these grounds is sentence pronounced: that though the light has come into the world men have shown they prefer darkness to the light because their deeds were evil. 20And indeed, everybody who does wrong hates the light and avoids it, for fear his actions should be exposed; 21but the man who lives in the truth comes out into the light so that it may be plainly seen that what he does is done in God.'

You will notice certain themes running through the entire passage. Each of them is expressed in a different metaphor, each has its special emphasis. Some of the themes are well known to us; others are more new. John is like an arranger who works out variations of the basic tune of a well known piece of music.

We read the passage then we do it with this awareness at the back of our minds. We take each section very slowly, giving it our perfect attention.

- Verses 13 to 15 : The theme here is that the Son of Man who will eventually be crucified needs to be lifted up on high so that he can become a source of true life for all his followers. This must happen if he is to have this effect on us. His 'being lifted up' on high makes him stand out from all who look on him. We realise then how much he has to offer his people, especially those of us who are in the desert as Moses and his followers were and as he himself was on the cross at Calvary.

St John adds a variation. He remembers that the serpent who had appeared to the Israelites in the desert in the time of Moses was originally a symbol of death. Our present source of life was originally an object that spoke of death and destruction. A symbol of shame had now become for us a great source of life.

We think of times in our own lives when what was originally for us a mark of death now becomes a sign of life. We think of new life arising out of

- people who when we saw them first reminded us of death;
- the possibility of destruction in this present life which now becomes a source of new life;
- death existing together with the signs of new life.

Death now becomes a source of new life. We stay with the metaphor until it becomes this reality for us.

The passage is also telling us something important about the people who watch the death of Jesus. What had seemed at first only of little consequence, with no special message for God's people, becomes an invitation to new life.

- Verse 16a: God's love for us is expressed practically by his giving us what is most precious to him – his own son whom he loved very specially. He wanted to deliver him from all evil but ended up seeing him sacrificed on the cross. It was therefore a tremendous act of service to us from the great God.

- Verse 16b: The motive for and indeed the actual fruit of God's love is expressed in two possible outcomes for people:

- 'being lost': we must make an effort to understand this concept; being lost includes all the aspects that we know well – not found, left alone by ourselves, without any one that we can turn to;
- 'having eternal life', on the other hand, includes concepts like a gift that does not end with death in any form.

Verse 17 brings back the teaching of the previous verse through the metaphors of condemning and being saved. We need to spend some time with each of the consequences:

- condemning includes concepts like having no hope;
- being saved includes things like being looked after.

Verse 18 brings back the metaphor of being condemned and links it to another conclusion:

- the option of believing in love;
- not believing in God's only Son given for us.

In verse 19 Jesus reflects on how people are condemned; the only valid condemnation is the one which comes from within oneself.

- In verses 20 and 21 the teaching is clarified with an analysis of how we make our choice of darkness or light. We remember times when we made the choice to live from the truth of ourselves, not to rely on what went outside but from what was within. Our deep choices alway come from ourselves, not from outside.

* * *

Many people think that life comes out of celebration when actually celebrations that ever mean anything come out of life itself.
Eugene Kennedy
Lord, we would like to be a source of life
for others without cost to ourselves.
We thank you for true leaders we have met
who knew the law of life as Jesus did,
that we must make ourselves vulnerable,
be open to failure and humiliation,
allowing ourselves to be lifted up
as Moses lifted up the serpent in the desert,
if our followers are to find life in us.

Lord, there was a time when we were afraid of death,
of failing, suffering, being rejected by others.
This fear was a bondage for us.
We thank you for lifting up a Son of Man before us
and inviting us to look honestly at things that frightened us:
we looked on that Son of Man
and how we ourselves tend to live.
We realised then that his death
was truly a source of new life for us.

Lord, we thank you for all those who love
– parents, grandparents, spouses, community leaders –
they love so much that they give what is most precious to them,
their careers, their future security, their own friends,
so that those whom they love
might experience that they can trust
and so not be lost but live.
Lord, we think today of those in our society who are lost:

- addicts to drugs or alcohol;
- those who are eaten up with bitterness and envy;
- those who cannot forgive.

We remember that your will is that they should not be lost;
for them you gave up your only Son.
Forgive us for not mediating your love to them.

Lord, we pray for teachers in schools,
church communities, families.
Remind them that you have sent them into their communities
not to condemn,
but so that through them their charges might be saved.

Lord, there is nothing more terrible in life
than to feel condemned
- to live without purpose;
- to experience failure and rejection whatever happens;
- to know that you will never be admired by others;
and the root of this is not believing that you are loved.
Help us to be the presence of your only Son in the world,
so that people might not go through life feeling condemned.

Lord, we pray for your church,
that we may never give in to the tendency to condemn.
Help us to focus on being true to you
so that others may come to us not out of fear of being condemned
but out of the truth that is in themselves.

Lord, we thank you for the journey to grace
that many of us are making during this Lent.
For many years you were calling us,
inviting us to look honestly on our addictions, our vanity, our envy.
We hated the light, avoided it
for fear that the truth about ourselves should be exposed.
During these days we were brought to look at ourselves
and come out into the light,
feeling inner peace because we knew that what we were doing
we were doing in you.

Fifth Sunday of Lent

Gospel Reading: John 12:20-33

²⁰*Among those who went up to worship at the festival were some Greeks.* ²¹*These approached Philip, who came from Bethsaida in Galilee, and put this request to him, 'Sir, we would like to see Jesus.'* ²²*Philip went to tell Andrew, and Andrew and Philip together went to tell Jesus.* ²³*Jesus replied to them: 'Now the hour has come for the Son of Man to be glorified.* ²⁴*I tell you, most solemnly, unless a wheat grain falls on the ground and dies, it remains only a single grain; but if it dies, it yields a rich harvest.* ²⁵*Anyone who loves his life loses it; anyone who hates his life in this world will keep it for the eternal life.* ²⁶*If a man serves me, he must follow me, wherever I am, my servant will be there too. If anyone serves me, my Father will honour him.* ²⁷*Now my soul is troubled. What shall I say: Father save me from this hour? But it was for this very reason that I have come to this hour.* ²⁸*Father, glorify your name!' A voice came from heaven, 'I have glorified it, and I will glorify it again.'* ²⁹*People standing by, who heard this, said it was a clap of thunder; others said, 'It was an angel speaking to him.'* ³⁰*Jesus answered, 'It was not for my sake that this voice came, but for yours.* ³¹*Now sentence is being passed on this world; now the prince of this world is to be overthrown.* ³²*And when I am lifted up from the earth, I shall draw all men to myself.'* ³³*By these words he indicated the kind of death he would die.*

Verses 20 to 22 show us some Greeks 'wanting to see Jesus'. It is interesting that they made their way to Jesus through a disciple who had a Greek name – Andrew who was from Bethsaida and had come with Jesus all the way from Galilee.

This quickly became one of the main principles of evangelisation – people must be approached by those like them. The principle was followed in the Acts of the Apostles and the letters of St Paul. St Paul himself was an exception in that he was a Jew, but his name Paul fitted more specially the gospel of the Greeks.

Verse 23 shows us that Jesus is fully conscious that at this stage of his life 'his hour has come'. He knows he is in a crisis moment. This is something that happens from time to time in the life of every person. It usually happens to us just once or twice; it is a time when we feel at the bottom of the pile.

Anything can happen to us; we have all gone through this and must measure our responses by what we know was in the mind of Jesus as he went through it.

Verse 24 is a very brief parable. We learn first to feel the pain of 'it falls on the ground'. We can well imagine what this involves. The seed has fallen on the ground and it is just there. It waits to see if it will lie there unused and helpless; here and now it will be open to every eventuality.

Then we enter into the second moment of 'it dies'. The 'dying' reminds us that we are actually in a position of being closed to new life. We are not sure whether we will lie there or whether this death will lead to new life.

This 'hour' has two possible outcomes:

- We can remain only a single grain, safe in ourselves but also isolated with no possibility of bringing out further harvest. This may well describe how we are at this particular time.

- We can yield a rich harvest. We are then sure of bringing forth fruit in others. We allow our passing (dead though it be to us) to bring new life to others. Their life will be more full because of what we have done for them.

Verse 25 is the same teaching but the contrast is now between
- clinging to the present and losing what one has;
- on the contrary, risking the present with the effect of saving the future.

Identify with both possibilities. One is tragic, the other glorious.

Verse 26 makes the teaching personal. 'If a man serves me, he must follow me, wherever I am, my servant will be there too.' Jesus himself has made this journey of faith. He allowed himself to fall on the ground in uncertainty and then to die. He was totally unsure of what would happen afterward, whether he would bring life to others or not, but he went ahead and accepted it.

'If anyone serves me, my Father will honour him'. Jesus broadens the picture. His 'father' here includes all those who give this person the honour he or she deserve.

As a follow up, verse 27 invites us to accompany Jesus on his journey. This is John's account of what the synoptic gospels relate as Jesus' well known 'agony in the garden'. His first petition is that the Father would change his mind: 'Father save me from this hour; my soul is sorrowful even unto death.' This then becomes the second petition, 'Nevertheless let it be as you, not I would have it.' It finally ends with 'Let your will be done'.

From Jesus' words, we can then gauge the movement from Jesus' first petition, 'save me from this hour,' to the more glorious one of 'Father, glorify your name.' This is the first petition of the Our Father and in biblical language means the same as the second and third petitions - 'your kingdom come' and 'your will be done'.

In verses 28 to 30 Jesus says, quite simply, that the voice from heaven, 'I have glorified it and will glorify it again' arose not for the sake of Jesus himself but for the sake of the onlookers – 'It was not for my sake but for yours.' The onlookers will then be able to see for themselves that everything that happened to Jesus came from their own experience of suffering.

Verses 31 and 32 express the attitude of Jesus as he faces his hour, 'Now sentence has been passed on this world and the prince of this world is to be overthrown.' In Jesus' own self-effacing he shows no self-pity and no bitterness. He is sad but totally confident that God's work will be done through him, 'When I am lifted from the earth I shall draw all people to myself.'

* * *

To win one new person of tomorrow for the faith is more important for us than to keep the faith of two people of yesterday. Karl Rahner

Lord, we remember today all those who know
that the hour has come for them:
    - couples about to commit themselves to each other for life;
    - people, secure in their jobs, who know you are calling them
    to move into some new field;
    - parents who must now let go of their children;
    - friends who have decided to break off a relationship
    which is harmful to them;
    - families facing a drop in their standard of living.
Help them to feel Jesus making the journey with them.
Remind them of his pain and how he had to tell himself
that unless the grain of wheat falls on the ground and dies
it remains only a single grain,
but if it dies it yields a rich harvest.

Lord, we thank you that the church in many countries
has taken the risk of falling on the ground and dying:
    - has lost the support of the powerful and the wealthy
    by embracing the cause of the poor;
    - has preached ideals of chastity in societies
    that are permissive;
    - has allowed little people to follow their own pace and to
    make mistakes.
And now it is yielding a rich harvest.

Walking in the truth of who I am. St Teresa of Avila
Lord, as we look back on our lives we remember how
we did not take the risks we should have taken
and so have remained a single grain
instead of yielding a rich harvest.
Help us to live with our mistakes, to give up our regrets,
letting them fall on the ground and die,
trusting that there is another kind of harvest that we can yield.

Lord, the first priority of the wealthy nations of the world today
is to preserve their wealth.
We thank you for the prophetic voices
that have been speaking out,
reminding these nations of the message of Jesus,
that if they remain turned in on their worldly possessions
they will lose them all,
whereas if they take the risk of sharing with others
they will experience peace and security for the future.

Lord, we who are in positions of authority over others
– parents, teachers, priests, community leaders –
we like to prescribe things for others,
handing on abstract teachings on right and wrong.
Remind us that we can only share our own journeys,
inviting others to follow us so that where we are,
they may one day be too,
and leaving it up to you to honour them.

Lord, we think today of those whose souls are troubled
as they meet their hour:
    - activists facing imprisonment or even death;

    - priests and religious
    suddenly confronted with the implications of their vows;
    - church leaders as they face up to the frustrations
    of acting democratically.
We feel for them as in their confusion they ask you,
'What shall I say? Father save me from this hour.'
Give them the faith to see that it was for this very reason
that they have come to this hour,
and to invite you to glorify your name.

Palm Sunday

Gospel Reading: Mark 15:21-41

21*The soldiers led Jesus out to crucify him. They enlisted a passer-by, Simon of Cyrene, father of Alexander and Rufus, who was coming in from the country, to carry his cross.* 22*They brought Jesus to the place called Golgotha, which means the place of the skull.* 23*They offered him wine mixed with myrrh, but he refused it.* 24*Then they crucified him, and shared out his clothing, casting lots to decide what each should get.* 25*It was the third hour when they crucified him.* 26*The inscription giving the charge against him read: 'The King of the Jews'.* 27*And they crucified two robbers with him, one on his right and one on his left.* 29*The passers-by jeered at him: they shook their heads and said, 'Aha! So you would destroy the Temple and rebuild it in three days!* 30*Then save yourself: come down from the cross!'* 31*The chief priests and the scribes mocked him among themselves in the same way: 'He saved others,' they said 'he cannot save himself.* 32*Let the Christ, the king of Israel, come down from the cross now, for us to see it and believe.' Even those who were crucified with him taunted him.*

33*When the sixth hour came there was darkness over the whole land until the ninth hour.* 34*And at the ninth hour Jesus cried out in a loud voice, 'Eloi, Eloi, lama sabachtani?' which means, 'My God, my God, why have you deserted me?'* 35*When some of those who stood by heard this, they said, 'Listen, he is calling on Elijah.'* 36*Someone ran and soaked a sponge in vinegar and, putting it on a reed, gave it him to drink saying, 'Wait and see if Elijah will come to take him down.'* 37*But Jesus gave a loud cry and breathed his last.*

38*And the veil of the Temple was torn in two from top to bottom.* 39*The centurion, who was standing in front of him, had seen how he had died, and he said, 'In truth this man was a son of God.'* 40*There were some women watching from a distance. Among them were Mary of Magdala, Mary who was the mother of James the younger and Joset, and Salome.* 41*These used to follow him and look after him when he was in Galilee. And there were many other women there who had come up to Jerusalem with him.*

The gospel reading for Palm Sunday is the entire story of the passion according to St Mark. We suggest that you focus on the last part, and divide it into several sections for meditation. Each section describes an incident in these last hours of Jesus' earthly life; all of them are important for our meditation today.

Verse 21. Contrary to John's account, according to which Jesus 'carries his own cross', the three synoptic gospels speak of a person who was asked to carry it for him. His name here is given as Simon of Cyrene. The evangelist notes that two of his sons eventually became well known members of the Roman community. Christians have always seen in Simon a symbol of our universal vocation to share in the sufferings of Jesus.

Verse 22. All the gospels note the name of the place where Jesus was crucified. This one gives the meaning as 'the place of the skull'. It was a symbolic name as the place, though seemingly attached to death, was destined to become the source of new life in our world.

Verses 23-41. Mark's account of the actual crucifixion is extremely simple – almost as if the reality was too painful to dwell on. We can however note some of the details:

- verse 23: they offered him some wine which he refused; this was surely a powerful symbol that he did not want to be saved from this, his final moment of suffering;

- verse 24: they shared out his clothing; what we have here is clearly a reference to two extracts from the psalms – Psalm 15:9-10, and Psalm 21:15. Jesus is portrayed to us as a reminder that in our present lives we meet plenty of opposition. We can however bring salvation to all and be saved by our present action;

- verse 25: they crucified him at around the third hour; this was significant since in fact it was the time when people were traditionally purified from all their sins;

- verse 26: the inscription with the charge of being the King of the Jews is of course helpful to all – the great King of the Jews was also king of us all. It is very interesting that with this lofty title he was crucified with two thieves.

Verses 29-31. (Note that there is no verse 28 – we are not sure why.) For the gospel writers, the mocking of Jesus was more significant than the physical pain of the crucifixion.

The charge that he 'saved others but could not save himself' is of course perfectly true, but not in the sense that his accusers meant it.

Verse 32. St Mark, like St Matthew, makes no reference to one of the robbers being converted. Both robbers reject Jesus since he made no move to deny their own condemnation. This was of course very significant for the gospel writer so that he could affirm the power of Jesus' death.

In verse 33 a deep darkness came over the whole land, 'from the sixth to the ninth hour'. This was clearly a sign of the great darkness which came over the hearts of all human beings at this time – a darkness which leaves us all very unfocused.

Verses 34-35. It will be useful to read Psalm 22 (21 in the Psalter) so that we can get the deep significance of the cry of Jesus, 'Eloi, Eloi, lama sabachtani – my God, my God, why have you deserted me?' It was really a moment of total desertion, such as only God's faithful followers have experienced. Hebrews 5:7 will also help your meditation here.

Verse 36. The cry to see if 'Elijah will come to take him down' was very important. It reminds us (once more) that Jesus did not want to renounce his chosen way of suffering alongside us.

In verses 37-38 the death of Jesus is told in a very dignified way. There are no extra details to distract us in any way.

Secular and sacred used to be portrayed as totally separate realities. Now the death of Jesus in the secular world has abolished the gap between them.

Verse 39. The act of faith of the centurion is a climax of the whole gospel of Mark. This was clearly intended by the writer. We have been led to expect it right through the gospel ever since Jesus 'proclaimed the Good News from God: the Time has come and the kingdom of God is close at hand. Repent and believe the Good News'.

Verses 40-41 introduce the faithful women. According to Mark, only women remained faithful to Jesus even to the end of his brief but very scarred life. Some of these women were in fact at the tomb on Easter Sunday morning.

* * *

Lord, we thank you for those precious moments
when you allowed us to experience
that we played a significant part in your work of grace:
  - we were there when a holy person was dying, and said the
    final prayers;

- a national crisis arose, we were in the right place
and did our duty to the country;
- members of our community shared their sorrows with us;
- we were at prayer and suddenly felt our solidarity
with the suffering of the world.
It was a fleeting moment but the memory remains.
It must have been like that for Simon of Cyrene
when he happened to be passing by,
coming in from the country,
and they enlisted him to carry the cross of Jesus.
Thank you, Lord.

Lord, you often make a place of death the source of new life:
- we were abandoned by our friends,
but learned how deep our inner resources were;
- a parent died and the family came together as never before.
You teach us that you always bring life,
and this is why your Son Jesus was not afraid
when they brought him to a place called Golgotha,
which means the place of the skull.

Lord, we thank you for the members of our church
who are not afraid to be associated
with those whom society labels disreputable:
- those who work with AIDS patients;
- movements like St Vincent de Paul and the Legion of Mary;
- worker-priests.
Often they are criticised and mocked,
but we see in them Jesus crucified with two robbers,
one on his right and the other on his left.
It can be rightly said of them
that their only interest is in saving others,
and that, like Jesus,
they are not unduly concerned with saving themselves.

'It was essential that Jesus should become completely like his brothers so that he could be a compassionate and trustworthy high priest of God's religion.' Hebrews 2:17
Lord, people sometimes think
that those of us who are leaders in the church
must always be calm and composed.
We thank you for teaching us
that when you yourself seem to be silent
we can cry in a loud voice,
'My God, my God, why have you deserted me?'

'To destroy human power nothing more is required than to be indiffer-ent to its threats and to prefer other goods to those which it promises.'
R. H. Tawney
Lord, how true it is that success and popularity
are not really important in life.
The only important thing is that some unbelieving centurion,
seeing how we live and die, could say,
'In truth, this was a son of God.'

Lord, when great people remain faithful unto death,
showing no anger or resentment to their enemies,
but on the contrary continuing to love and forgive,
it shows us how false are the barriers we set up
to separate people into bad and good;
the veils we have erected in your temple
are torn in two from top to bottom.

Lord, we thank you for faithful followers of Jesus,
those who, like the women in the gospel,
look after him in Galilee where it is safe,
and then come up to Jerusalem with him,
even though it is dangerous,
and are there watching with him as he hangs on the cross.

Easter Vigil

Gospel Reading: Mark 16:1-7

*When the Sabbath was over, Mary of Magdala, Mary the mother of James, and Salome, brought spices with which to go and anoint him. *And very early in the morning on the first day of the week they went to the tomb, just as the sun was rising. *They had been saying to one another, 'Who will roll away the stone for us from the entrance to the tomb?' *But when they looked they could see that the stone – which was very big – had already been rolled back. *On entering the tomb they saw a young man in a white robe seated on the right hand side, and they were struck with amazement. *But he said to them, 'There is no need for alarm. You are looking for Jesus of Nazareth, who was crucified: he has risen, he is not here. See, here is the place where they laid him. *But you must go and tell his disciples and Peter, "He is going before you to Galilee; it is there you will see him, just as he told you".'*

The gospels all tell us that Jesus rose from the dead. They give us, however, two different accounts of this central moment of his life.

- In St Mark 9:19, St Luke (gospel and Acts of the Apostles), and St John, the apparitions of Jesus after his resurrection take place in Jerusalem. This was the place where he had recently been crucified and put to death.

- In St Matthew and in this section of St Mark, Jesus is said to return to Galilee after his death. It is there that the later apparitions take place.

Each of the two accounts has its own greatness and richness. In our meditation then, we should concentrate on the text before us; for the time being we ignore the other accounts, even though we may be more familiar with them.

St Mark tells his story from the perspective of the women who went to the tomb. We naturally follow them and interpret the story from their point of view. This also happens to be ours at certain moments in our lives.

We can also read it from another point of view – from the perspective of the disciples who, in contrast to the women, remained indoors. They happened to be there at this time and they received the good news about the risen Jesus from the women who spoke from their experience.

Verses 1 and 2. The women in the story are all three symbols of people who know how to go out and watch faithfully over someone who has died. The text tells us that they 'brought spices with which to anoint him'; they did not, therefore, expect any resurrection from the dead. This is important for us as very often we too have no indication that we can expect a dead person to start a new life. We do not expect them to give rise to a fresh beginning.

The text gives us three expressions symbolising new life: 'very early in the morning', 'on the first day of the week, they went to the tomb', 'and the sun was rising'. All three remind us that the day of great darkness mentioned in St Mark's gospel did not last 'forever'. The events on this morning, very early the next day, brought a new dawn. It was truly a time of new light.

Verses 3 and 4. The stone in front of the tomb is symbolic. It symbolises the many obstacles which we know can lie between us here and now and the working out of the new story of grace.

We think of examples:

- persons who hold us back because they do not want us to go forward with some kind of newness;

- objects which we know will stand in our way unless we take active steps to get rid of them and move to a new kind of relationship;

- God himself is often experienced as someone who distracts us from giving ourselves fully to others. We think for example of people we feel naturally attached to – a spouse, children, friends, fellow-workers, people who share in our political platform. We react to them as if our being close to God means that we should love them less.

Verses 5 and 6. The words of the young man in the white robe express the heart of the mystery of the empty tomb. With him, therefore, we enter into the dramatic contrast between the two attitudes of the women:

- a fear of things or objects that we know still stand in the way of our future progress;

- the reality of the risen Jesus; he is now totally free of what limits us to the here and now.

Verse 7. This text gives us the striking commission given to the women. It tells us to remember that we need to go back to the place where we started our great adventure. After the loss of some glorious person, we need to return to that place. When we go back to our first search, we will truly understand the significance of the seemingly dead Jesus who has risen again.

* * * *

Lord, we thank you for faithful people:
   - friends who stay with us when we let them down;
   - members of our parish who persevere in the community in times of discord;
   - those in our movement who are not discouraged
   by corruption and betrayal within it;
   - people in the Middle East
   who continue to work for peace.
While most of us looked on past hopes as dead and gone,
they, like the women at the tomb of Jesus,
continued to mourn for what they had lost.
So they were there very early in the morning,
when a new day had dawned
and the sun had started rising again.
They were able to announce to us who had lost hope
the good news that it was the first day of a new beginning.

Lord, we remember a time when we were in some bondage:
   - we were in the grip of some addiction;
   - our family life was in deep crisis;
   - unemployment had us totally discouraged.
Now, looking back, we remember how we worried
about something that turned out to be no problem at all:
   - what our friends would say;
   - how one particular child would react;
   - whether our health would stand up to work.
We were the women on Easter morning asking themselves
who would roll away the great stone
from the entrance to the tomb,
when the moment of grace had already come
and the stone was quite irrelevant to their situation.
Thank you, Lord.

'Walk the dark ways of faith and you will attain the vision of God.'
St Augustine
Lord, forgive us for continuing to focus on the past:
- we harp on wrongs done to us by parents or teachers;
- we regret mistakes we made, opportunities we missed;
- we want to prove we are better than others;
- we try to rebuild relationships that have ended;
- we resent getting old or sickly.
Send us someone like the young man in the white robe
who spoke to the women at the tomb of Jesus
to tell us that crucifixion is not the end,
we must not look for Jesus in a tomb,
because he has risen, he is not there.
Your will is that we go back to Galilee to resume our lives
because he is going before us there
and it is there that we will see him, just as he told us.

'All nations have opportunities which they may grasp if only they can summon up the courage and the will.'
Sir Arthur Lewis, West Indian economist
Lord, there are nations today that are trapped
in an endless cycle of racial, ethnic or religious conflict
– the Middle East, the Basque Country, Sudan.
We thank you for the women of these nations who,
like Mary of Magdala, Mary the mother of Jesus, and Salome,
have seen with their own eyes
that life cannot be contained in a tomb,
and have gone to tell their leaders
that they must move forward to a new place
where they will find life, just as you told them.

Lord, sometimes the good news of resurrection from the dead
is so overpowering that all we can do is to run away,
frightened out of our wits.
Even though we have a wonderful message to transmit,
for a long time we can say nothing to a soul.

Easter Sunday

Gospel reading: John 20:1-10

¹It was very early on the first day of the week, and still dark, when Mary of Magdala came to the tomb. She saw that the stone had been moved away from the tomb ²and came running to Simon Peter and the other disciple, the one Jesus loved. 'They have taken the Lord out of the tomb,' she said, 'and we don't know where they have put him.' ³So Peter set out with the other disciple to go to the tomb. ⁴They ran together, but the other disciple, running faster than Peter, reached the tomb first; ⁵he bent down and saw the linen cloths lying on the ground, but did not go in. ⁶Simon Peter who was following now came up, went right into the tomb, saw the linen cloths on the ground, ⁷and also the cloth that had been over his head; this was not with the linen cloths but rolled up in a place by itself. ⁸Then the other disciple who had reached the tomb first also went in; he saw and he believed. ⁹Till this moment they had failed to understand the teaching of scripture, that he must rise from the dead. ¹⁰The disciples then went home again.

John's account of the resurrection is in two stages:

- verses 1-2 are about Mary of Magdala's experience;

- verses 3-10 tell us about the experience of the two disciples.

In verses 1 and 2 you might like to focus on the symbolism of it being 'still dark' and yet a 'first day' of a new time. The large stone symbolises all the forces, human and other, that keep God's grace in the bondage of the tomb.

Your experience will help you interpret how Mary responded. Did she run in confusion? Or in fear?

The story of Peter and the disciple whom Jesus loved can be read from various points of view. You can take them together as experiencing the resurrection, focusing on the details, especially the cloths lying on the ground, useless now since Jesus was alive, but also on the fact that until they saw the empty tomb they did not believe the teaching of the scriptures.

St John makes a point of contrasting the two apostles. If you would like to meditate on this aspect of the story, see Peter as symbol of the church leader, while 'the other disciple' is the one who, while having no position of authority, is specially loved by Jesus and, perhaps as a result, is first in faith.

Lord, we thank you for moments of grace.
We had been in a situation of death
    - a relationship that meant a lot to us seemed dead;
    - an addiction held us in its grip;
    - our country was locked in civil strife.
Then the day came that would turn out to be
the first of a new era.
We were mourning as usual,
like Mary of Magdala
making a routine visit to the tomb of Jesus,
but saw that the stone had been moved away from the tomb.
Naturally, we looked for some simple explanation:
'They have taken the Lord our of the tomb
and we don't know where they have put him,'
but it wasn't anything like that,
it was what the scriptures teach us,
that your work must always rise again.

'They can kill a bishop, but they cannot kill the church which is the
people.' Archbishop Romero, some days before he was martyred
Lord, we thank you for people of faith.
They believe the teaching of the scriptures
that your work may lie in the tomb for some days
but it must rise again.

'When the underprivileged unite and struggle for justice, is that not a
sign of the presence and action of God in our time?'
Musumi Kanyaro, Committee of Women in Church and Society,
Lutheran World Federation
Lord, as we look around the world today
we see what Peter and the disciple whom Jesus loved saw
as they entered his tomb.
Cloths are lying on the ground
that we can recognise for what they are
attitudes of passivity that look like fine linen
but in fact kept your chosen ones in the tomb.
Whereas you have once more fulfilled
what you taught us in all the scriptures
and we had not really believed until this moment:

that you will always raise up your chosen ones
when the world imprisons them in a tomb.

Lord, we pray today for those who were baptised last night:
today they have enthusiasm, for them you are alive and present;
but there will certainly come a time
when they will experience you absent,
when prayer will be like Mary of Magdala
going in the gloom of early morning
to visit the tomb of Jesus.
In fact, they will be like people
who mourn for a spouse or a child
without even having the comfort of the dead body to look at.
This is the way they will have to pass
because until they have had experiences like this
they will not really believe
the teaching of the scriptures
that your grace cannot be overpowered by evil
and that your presence within us must always, like Jesus,
rise again from the tomb.

Lord, we like to feel that we have you within our grasp:
    - that our prayers are always answered;
    - that we are living in a way that is pleasing to you;
    - that the times, gestures and words of our prayers are just
    right.
Teach us that we must be prepared to lose that security
and experience being abandoned, until we live in trust only
and see all those things that we considered important
like the cloths in the empty tomb of Jesus
fine linen cloths, but they were keeping him in the tomb.
Now we see them on the ground
and also the cloth that had been over his head
not with the linen cloths but rolled up in a place by itself.

Second Sunday of Easter

Gospel Reading: John 20:19-31

19In the evening of the same day, the first day of the week, the doors were closed in the room where the disciples were, for fear of the Jews. Jesus came and stood among them. He said to them, 'Peace be with you,' 20and showed them his hands and his side. The disciples were filled with joy when they saw the Lord, 21and he said to them again, 'Peace be with you. As the Father sent me, so am I sending you.' 22After saying this he breathed on them and said, 'Receive the Holy Spirit. 23For those whose sins you forgive, they are forgiven; for those whose sins you retain, they are retained.' 24Thomas, called the Twin, who was one of the Twelve, was not with them when Jesus came. 25When the disciples said, 'We have seen the Lord,' he answered, 'Unless I see the holes that the nails made in his hands and can put my finger into the holes they made, and unless I can put my hand into his side, I refuse to believe.' 26Eight days later the disciples were in the house again and Thomas was with them. The doors were closed, but Jesus came in and stood among them. 'Peace be with you' he said. 27Then he spoke to Thomas, 'Put your finger here; look, here are my hands. Give me your hand; put it into my side. Doubt no longer but believe.' 28Thomas replied, 'My Lord and my God!' 29Jesus said to him: 'You believe because you can see me. Happy are those who have not seen and yet believe.' 30There were many other signs that Jesus worked and the disciples saw, but they are not recorded in this book. 31These are recorded so that you may believe that Jesus is the Christ, the Son of God, and believing this you may have life through his name.

Today's gospel reading, like all of St John's gospel, is an interweaving of several themes. It is not possible to follow up all the themes together; we must focus on one at a time, going deeply into it and allowing it to reveal some deep truth about Jesus, about ourselves and about life.

Here I invite you to focus on the apostle Thomas; this is in accord with the Catholic church's liturgical tradition for the Second Sunday of Easter. Therefore, although the reading includes two of Jesus' resurrection appearances – both of them deeply moving – we stay with the second, the dialogue between Jesus and Thomas, and let the earlier appearance provide the context. We are free to identify either with Thomas or with Jesus, but not with both at the same time.

We need to be clear on how we understand Thomas. The popular interpretation puts him in a bad light, as 'doubting Thomas'. This, however, is not the movement of the text, which culminates in Thomas' admirable act of faith, the most explicit in the New Testament – 'My Lord and my God!'

We are more in accord with the spirit of the text, therefore, when we look at Thomas as a model of faith. He was right to insist that before he could believe in Jesus' resurrection he must see the holes the nails made in his hands, put his finger into the holes and his hand into the great wound made by the centurion's lance.

Thomas teaches us the important lesson that we must not separate the resurrection from the cross, since we are called to be followers of Jesus. He also teaches us the truth of the church and of our individual spiritual growth. We cannot live the life of grace, the 'risen life', authentically unless we bear in our bodies the wounds of the cross. This means being conscious that we develop the capacity to love and to be loved only by dying to ourselves. Our wounds are also a constant reminder of our frailty, and that it is God's grace that raises us up to new life.

St Paul's epistles show that the first Christians needed the corrective of Thomas' faith. They tended to relate with the risen Jesus without reference to his crucifixion. They forgot that they were called to be 'followers of Jesus crucified', choosing to die with him so that they could rise with him (see especially 1 Corinthians 1).

We Christians fall into the same error today when our lives and our teachings proclaim an abstract 'disembodied' Jesus, dispenser of graces and teacher of morality – we forget the historical person who was put to death for proclaiming the kingdom of God.

Thomas professes the true faith of the church. We too must insist that the Jesus we follow is the true Jesus, the one whose risen body bears the wounds of Calvary.

Jesus is the model leader and spiritual guide. He is pleased to give Thomas the assurance he is looking for, and then challenges him to look forward to the day when he will believe without see-

ing – always in the Jesus who passes through death to resurrection.

The blessedness of believing without seeing came from the
experience of the early church. Jesus is not moralising, but inviting Thomas – and us – to celebrate great people of faith, in our
local communities and worldwide, who take up their cross with
confidence in the resurrection.

As always in our meditation we must not limit ourselves to
personal relationships. We celebrate the resurrection faith lived
by communities, nations and cultures.

* * *

*'You who remain ever faithful even when we are unfaithful, forgive our
sins and grant that we may bear true witness to you before all men and
women.'* Pope John Paul II, Service of Forgiveness, March 2000
Lord, we thank you for the moments of grace
of this Lenten season,
when – as individuals and as a church community –
we walked in the footsteps of Jesus
by passing from death to new life.
We thank you in particular for the great day
when our church publicly asked forgiveness
from other religions and cultures.
We thank you for Pope John Paul
who, like Jesus with St Thomas,
invited us to see the holes
that the nails of arrogance and self-righteousness
had made in the body of Christ,
and to put our fingers into the holes,
to put our hands into the huge wound
which the lust for power has made in his side,
so that we could recognize how,
just as you raised Jesus from the dead,
you do not allow his Body, the church, to remain in the tomb,
but always raise her up to new life.

Lord, we thank you for the times when reconciliation
emerged triumphantly from the tomb of conflict:

- the spirit of dialogue between our church and Jews, Muslims, Hindus, and African traditional religions;
- the European Union created by former enemies;
- the Good Friday agreement in Northern Ireland;
- the peace process in the Middle East.

Lord, we thank you for the experience of the military in Iraq.
We pray that they will hear your voice calling on them all
to remember those who have been hurt,
who still have holes that the nails made in their hands
and can put their finger into the holes they made,
and unless they can put their hands into their side,
they will refuse to believe.
Do not let us forget the terrible legacy of hatred and resentment
which had to be overcome;
invite us to put our fingers into the holes made by nails,
our hands into the great wounds made by lances,
so that we can recognise with awe and wonder
the spark of your divine life that is within us all.
Remind us too of those who worked for peace
during the long years of conflict
when it seemed that they were working in vain.
How blessed were they who did not see
and yet continued to believe
in your power to bring new life into the world.

'Whoever sees anything of God, sees nothing of God.' Meister Eckhart
Lord, lead us to the blessedness of not seeing and believing.

'Go for broke, always try to do too much, dispense with safety nets, aim for the stars.' Salman Rushdie
Lord, we thank you for friends, leaders and spiritual guides
who challenge us as Jesus challenged Thomas.
When we commit ourselves to a cause
because we have tested its reality,
they invite us to experience
the blessedness of believing without seeing.

'Beware of the seduction of leaving the poor to think about them.'
Jean Vanier
Lord, forgive us for wanting to help
those in need without sharing their pain,
we look for their resurrection but do not want to see their
wounds:

- young people have been deeply hurt and we serve them
with pious exhortations;
- we become impatient with those who continue to mourn
the death of a spouse or a child;
- we think we can restore a broken relationship by merely
saying we are sorry;
- we propose reconciliation between warring factions without acknowledging past wrongs;
- we pray for peace in the world and do not agonise over its
terrible injustices.

We thank you for people like Thomas
who will not let us get away with easy solutions;
they insist that we must see the holes that nails have made
in the hands of victims,
put our fingers into the holes and our hands into wounds
that lances have made in their sides,
and only then believe that they have within them
the capacity to rise to new life.

*'We admitted to God, to ourselves, and to another human being,
the exact nature of our wrongs.'*
Step 5 in the 12 Step Method of Alcoholics Anonymous
Lord, when we are converted from an addiction
to alcohol, drugs, power or sex,
we are so anxious to make a new start
that we try to forget the hurt
which was at the root of our problem

- the loneliness of our childhood
- the sense of racial inferiority
- our disability
- the fear of failure.

We thank you for sending us friends who insist
that we must face the reality of the past.

We pray that like Jesus welcoming Thomas,
we will invite them to put their fingers
into the holes the nails have made
and their hands into our sides,
so that they can walk with us in our new life.

Third Sunday of Easter

Gospel Reading: Luke 24:35-48

35*The disciples told their story of what had happened on the road and how they had recognised Jesus at the breaking of bread.* 36*They were still talking about all this when he himself stood among them and said to them, 'Peace be with you!'* 37*In a state of alarm and fright, they thought they were seeing a ghost.* 38*But he said, 'Why are you so agitated, and why are these doubts rising in your hearts?* 39*Look at my hands and feet; yes, it is I indeed. Touch me and see for yourselves; a ghost has no flesh and bones as you can see I have.'* 40*And as he said this he showed them his hands and feet.* 41*Their joy was so great that they still could not believe it, and they stood there dumbfounded; so he said to them, 'Have you anything here to eat?'* 42*And they offered him a piece of grilled fish,* 43*which he took and ate before their eyes.* 44*Then he told them, 'This is what I meant when I said, while I was still with you, that everything written about me in the Law of Moses, in the Prophets and in the Psalms, has to be fulfilled.'* 45*He then opened their minds to understand the scriptures,* 46*and he said to them, 'So you see how it is written that the Christ would suffer and on the third day rise from the dead,* 47*and that, in his name, repentance for the forgiveness of sins would be preached to all the nations, beginning from Jerusalem.* 48*You are witnesses to this.'*

On this Sunday we are still meditating on the resurrection of Jesus. As always, the secret of good meditation on this feast is to remember our own experiences of death and resurrection.

Verse 35 is the conclusion of a previous incident. The two disciples had met Jesus when they were on the road to Emmaus. They had had a long and fruitful meeting with him but only came to recognise him at the breaking of the bread – a clear reference to the Holy Eucharist celebrated by the communities of Christians.

Verses 36 to 43: Jesus interrupts the conversation of the disciples by appearing to them. He greets them with his customary words , 'Peace be with you', telling them that they can be at peace with themselves, with one another and with God. They are in a state of 'alarm and fright' but he speaks to them with patience and compassion.

Verses 44 and 45 tell the story of how the disciples grew gradually into Jesus' message of wisdom. He had been telling them things all along. It was only when he had died, however, and had risen that their minds were finally opened so that they could see for themselves that everything written about him was true. The Law of Moses, the Prophets and the Psalms had all been truly fulfilled in him.

Verses 46 to 48 give us the content of the lesson they have learned. He had 'opened their minds to understand the scriptures'. Now he tells them how they are to go out and preach it.

The first fact they must announce is that the Christ would suffer and then on the third day rise from the dead. This is the central act of Jesus our Saviour. Everything else about him is summed up in that one fact of history. All his long and many works beforehand now take their reality from this. They have their reason and their fulfillment in this alone. We can see the implications of this from his many miracles and teachings.

His message is clear. It is one of repentance for the forgiveness of all sins. We must learn that, like him, we too must first die to what we consider closest to us and then rise again with a new life that we can share with all. This message is to be preached not merely to Jews and the people of Jerusalem but to all the nations of the world.

They are the witnesses to the wider world of this new fact of history – Jesus risen from the dead tells us how we too will be able to experience the presence of God. We will see him not merely in himself but also in all his works and promises.

* * *

Lord, we remember with gratitude our resurrection experiences:
- one of our children was at death's door but got well and healthy again;
- failure left us down-hearted, our self-confidence destroyed; gradually we got back our enthusiasm
and felt able to take on new challenges;
- we hurt someone dear to us and thought we could never be friends again,
but we were forgiven and it was as if nothing had ever come between us;
- we spent years in bondage to drink or drugs;

we thought we could never get out of it;
then someone restored us to healthy living.
We remember now the wonderful moment when we knew
that life had come back.
We thought at first we were seeing a ghost,
we were agitated and felt doubts rising in our hearts.
Hesitantly we were able to touch and see for ourselves.
Our joy was so great we still could not believe
and stood there dumbfounded.
Then we learnt that everything told us in the Law of Moses,
the Psalms and the Prophets was to be fulfilled in him.

Lord, we pray today for all who have been involved in the work
of the military in different parts of the world:
    - in Iraq as local and foreign workers for peace and reconciliation
    - in Israel and Palestine as searchers for a new life
    for all inhabitants
    - in the Basque Country bringing about a new society in
    which all would be welcome
    - in Sri Lanka, working for a better society for all.
We pray that all may see you and recognise in their suffering
the frustration of death
so that they like you will be the only ones
who can bring peace to their countries and to the wider world.

Lord, as teachers we sometimes meet children
who have been deeply hurt.
We get impatient with them, want them to trust us right away.
Help us to be like Jesus and walk step by step with them,
inviting them to touch and see for themselves,
assuring them that a ghost has no flesh and bones
as they can see we have,
showing them our own wounds,
and taking their food to eat before their eyes.

Lord, it takes us a long time to learn the deep lessons of life:
    - that at one time or another we have to give ourselves
    completely;
    - that we are responsible for our own destiny;
    - that love grows to maturity out of many reconciliations;

- that there can never be lasting peace without justice.
Our parents told us, while they were still with us,
but we resisted them.
We thank you that after a great crisis
their words came back to us,
as real as if they were standing before us,
and our minds were opened.
We saw that every page of the Bible
was teaching us this all the time,
every psalm, every sacred book said it,
but only now could we tell it to the nations
because it was written not merely in books, but in our hearts,
and we were witnesses to it.

Lord, we pray for those who dream of a better society
and who are discouraged by their failures
or the failures of good people.
Send them some Jesus person to stand among them and say,
'Peace be with you!'
and show them his own wounded hands and feet,
showing them from his own experience
that everything in the Law of Moses,
the Prophets and the Psalms, has to be fulfilled
so that their minds can be opened and they can see
how it is written into the laws of life
that all great projects must die
and only on the third day rise from the dead.

Lord, as parents, leaders, guides
we think we can hand down prescriptions to others
with no reference to their own experience.
As a result, we call others to repent
but do not communicate forgiveness,
or we offer a false forgiveness without repentance.
But we are witnesses that those who preach to the nations
must always start from Jerusalem,
the place where they abandoned their Lord
and experienced that he rose from the dead
and returned to stand among them.

Fourth Sunday of Easter

Gospel Reading: John 10:11-18

11Jesus said 'I am the good shepherd: the good shepherd is one who lays down his life for his sheep. 12The hired man, since he is not the shepherd and the sheep do not belong to him, abandons the sheep and runs away as soon as he sees a wolf coming, and then the wolf attacks and scatters the sheep; 13this is because he is only a hired man and has no concern for the sheep. 14I am the good shepherd; I know my own and my own know me, 15just as the Father knows me and I know the Father; and I lay down my life for my sheep. 16And there are other sheep I have that are not of this fold, and these I have to lead as well. They too will listen to my voice, and there will be only one flock, and one shepherd. 17The Father loves me, because I lay down my life in order to take it up again. 18No one takes it from me; I lay it down of my own free will, and as it is in my power to lay it down, so it is in my power to take it up again; and this is the command I have been given by my Father.'

It is an ancient custom in our Catholic Church that this Fourth Sunday of Easter time is given to a reflection on chapter 10 of St John's gospel, with its theme of Jesus as the Good Shepherd. In each of the three years, on this Sunday we spend time on just one section of the chapter, reflecting on it.

In more recent years, it has also become customary that on this Sunday we remember specially our church's need for more people who will give themselves to the task of shepherding God's people. They do so by joining the ministry of the entire church. On this Sunday then, we pray for more and better vocations to the priesthood.

This year's passage goes from verse 11 to verse 18.

Verses 11-13: the passage starts off by establishing a striking contrast between two people: the good shepherd, and the hireling.

Good shepherds are noted because they are willing to lay down their lives for their sheep. Everyone in the world will feel touched by this fact of history which we can all see and appreciate – even though in our culture we may have in fact no shepherds to point to. The sheep belong to them, and they really care for them. Whatever happens to the sheep also touches them.

There were and still are others, however, who look after their sheep not as their own but simply as 'hirelings'. They are in charge of the sheep but they don't have a feel for them; they have never given anything of themselves to them.

As soon as they see a wolf coming, they run away. They know the sheep do not belong to them, are not really theirs, and so they abandon them. The wolf attacks and scatters the sheep, sending them off in different directions. Now they will look for other green spots wherever they can find them. The places they look to will include some which are not true pastures at all; they may provide new opportunities, but will not be truly nourishing.

The so-called hirelings included many in the audience at the time. We think of people like the scribes, the Pharisees, the chief priests and the elders. They took on the role of rulers of the people because they needed to have authority over them. They wanted the popularity and the wellbeing it brought them.

We can think of similar examples in our time. We remember people who say they will look after the sheep
- only because no one else is doing it;
- because it panders to their sense of their well-being;
- because no one else is really interested.
We will certainly find that somewhere in our lives we have a combination of the two themes. We are all part of the good shepherd and part of the hireling. Lord, teach us how to keep the two parts in our own hearts – and to accept that we have both within each of us.

In verses 13 and 14 the theme is developed further. The good shepherd knows well that the Father knows and loves all his sheep. This is a tricky question. It gives the impression that it is not merely a question of a shepherd liking his sheep. This would be to misunderstand the passage. The shepherd loves the sheep, but he is also very aware that his love for them did not originate with himself. He has received it from the heavenly Father in whose hands he lies.

This is the deep reason why we lay down our lives to protect all our sheep. We know we will be persecuted by others for standing by our promises to accept this as part of our eternal destiny. This is what God wants for us. We acknowledge this and try our best to live up to it.

Verses 15-16: There are other sheep who we know do not belong to us here and now but we are still attached to them. They are not part of our own community, but we know that the Father knows and loves them all. The Father recognises too that they will have to become one. Soon they will all be together, living with peace under one Shepherd. As Christians we know too that we will be one of those who are called to be among them as their shepherds.

Verses 17-18: What the Father loves about the Good Shepherd is stated more clearly. He loves him because he lays down his life and will soon take it up again. This is a particular aspect of the passage which we can give some stress to. No one takes our life from us. We lay it down of our own free will. As it is in our power to lay it down and take it up again, this is what we do with the various temptations God sends us in our lives. We know how to accept them and do something important about them.

This is not something we have thought out for ourselves. It is a great and glorious commandment which we have received from our Father who continues to dwell in heaven.

* * *

'With this people, it costs nothing to be a good shepherd.'
Archbishop Romero
Father, we thank you for calling us
to be shepherds of your flock.
Like all good shepherds
we are willing to lay down our lives for the sheep.
We are not like hirelings, who look after your sheep
because of the importance they have received from them.
Since the sheep do not belong to them,
they abandon them and run away
as soon as they see a wolf coming.
Then the wolf attacks the sheep and scatters them.
This is because they are only hired men
and have no concern for the sheep.

'A man ought not to consider his chance of living or dying. He ought only to consider on any given occasion whether he is doing right or wrong.' Socrates

Lord, we thank you for loving your sheep
with your personal love
and then handing them over to us.
Because we know you,
we can lay down our lives for your sheep,
knowing that we will beg for new life for them.

'We think we are fleeing from God, but in fact we are running into his arms.' Meister Eckhart

Lord, there are many sheep you have who are not of our fold,
but you want us to lead them as well.
We thank you for having given them to us
so that very soon there will be just one shepherd.

'Prayer is not given to us to change the world. It is meant to change us so that we can change the world.' Sr Joan Chittister

Lord, we thank you for loving us
because we have power to lay down our lives
in order to take them up again.
No one takes our lives from us.
We lay them down of our own free will
and it is in our power to take them up again.
This is the great and glorious command we have received
from our Father who is in heaven.

Lord, we thank you for those sons of ours
who will give themselves to the service of your people
as their good shepherds.

Fifth Sunday of Easter

Gospel reading: John 15:1-8

¹*Jesus said to his disciples: 'I am the true vine, and my Father is the vinedresser. ²Every branch in me that bears no fruit he cuts away, and every branch that does bear fruit he prunes to make it bear even more.* ³*You are pruned already, by means of the word that I have spoken to you. ⁴Make your home in me, as I make mine in you. As a branch cannot bear fruit all by itself, but must remain part of the vine, neither can you unless you remain in me. ⁵I am the vine you are the branches. Whoever remains in me, with me in him, bears fruit in plenty; for cut off from me you can do nothing. ⁶Anyone who does not remain in me is like a branch that has been thrown away – he withers; these branches are collected and thrown on the fire, and they are burnt. ⁷If you remain in me and my words remain in you, you may ask what you will and you shall get it. ⁸It is to the glory of my Father that you should bear much fruit, and then you will be my disciples.'*

Each year, on the fifth and sixth Sundays of Easter, the gospel readings are taken from the long discourse which, according to St John, Jesus gave to his apostles on the night before his passion. This is contained in chapters 13 to 17 of the gospel. This Sunday's extract gives us the parable of the vine and as always it has different perspectives which we need to go into.

The passage starts with the words, 'Jesus said these words to the disciples.' This little introductory phrase reminds us of an important point: Jesus' words were never spoken at some indeterminate time; they were said by him at a particular moment. At this time, for example, the apostles were present with him; they seemed to be looking ahead to the coming passion and anticipating the part they were to play in it.

In fact we know now that they were not ready for it. He was giving them a warning about what was going to happen. He was also telling them of what lay in the future for them once the passion and death of Jesus was over.

Verse 1. The Father is the vine dresser. The parable is telling us first that Jesus is the true vine and his Father who dwells in the heavens is the vine dresser. We need to spend some time just meditating on this simple but very deep passage. Jesus is the humble servant of Christians, suffering so that we can all be safe. The Father meanwhile is a general overseer; he is situated way above our heads, in heaven. This is telling us something very important about Jesus' mission in the world. It is reminding us of how he saw himself and of his deep relationship with his Father in heaven.

Verses 2 and 3. Christians then are branches of the 'true vine'. When a branch bears no fruit, the reason is clear – it is not linked to the vine; the Father then simply cuts it away and lets it lie there so that it dies without producing any more fruit. If on the other hand, a branch does bear some fruit, the heavenly Father is also very busy. He prunes it so that it can bear even more.

Verse 3. The interpretation then changes. It asks the question, 'What is the pruning instrument?' The answer is simply that it is the actual words of the great Jesus – 'It is by means of the word I have spoken to you.' Jesus' words then are not mere words, they are pruning instruments; they can change our behaviour and can make important differences happen in how we deal with one another.

Jesus then makes a further distinction. 'Make your home with me as I make mine in you.' For ordinary people, 'being in the vine' merely means making a choice, then letting it influence how we deal with others.

In Jesus however, it is rather a matter of accepting that we are in him. We can then allow ourselves to move from that link and so touch the reality of the people we meet.

Verses 4 and 5. The parable takes a new turn. Though linked to the old we get a new development. No branch of the vine can bear fruit all by itself, it must remain part of the vine. The branches too cannot bear fruit unless they remain linked with him, and are settled with him. We think of people in our time who bear fruit but these are the results of selfishness and of self-righteousness. They do not come from making themselves available to Jesus, the source of all selflessness in the world.

'Cut off from me then, you can do nothing'. We think of people who bear fruit but are not tied to Jesus. Jesus of course stands for all who are truly life-giving to people. Their present religious affiliation is no obstacle to bearing this wonderful fruit.

Verse 6. Those who do not remain in him are like branches

which have been thrown away. They wither and eventually die. These branches are collected and then thrown into the fire. They are useless until they can be totally burnt away and so disposed of.

Verse 7. This is what happens when a branch remains attached to the vine and bears fruit from it: 'You will ask for what you will and you will get it.' The person who lives in Christ has a special relationship with the Father in heaven, a relationship based on intimacy with Jesus.

Verse 8. This is what being a disciple is all about – 'It is to the glory of God that you should bear much fruit.' There is a relationship of great love between Jesus' disciples and the Father. It is based entirely on the intimacy between them. Remember of course that this intimacy is not a matter of receiving a Christian upbringing.

* * *

'The purpose of the Master is to help you see the uselessness of hanging on.' Zen saying
Lord, we remember times of great crisis in our lives:
    - a friendship of long standing breaking up;
    - we lost our job;
    - we or someone dear to us, was seriously ill;
    - our country went through a time of great unrest.
We felt totally lost, as if you had cut us off
and we were a dead branch lying on the ground next to the tree.
But that wasn't it.
What had happened was that we had stopped bearing fruit
and you were being a good vine dresser,
pruning away dead branches
and letting us get in touch with you at a deeper level,
so that your love would flow through us
and we could bear fruit again.

'The resurrection is like the first eruption of a volcano, which shows that it is the interior of a world, where God's fire is already burning.'
Karl Rahner
Lord, our civilisation has lost its energy:
we have become complacent about our accomplishments

and the fruit we have borne;
we no longer have the creativity to face new challenges.
We pray that your church may speak the words of Jesus today,
pruning away the dead branches of greed,
individualism, the desire to dominate,
so that humanity may bear fruit more abundant than before.

Lord, as teachers, parents, leaders,
we sometimes have to correct others.
Give us the wisdom that we need
to be good vine dressers after your image,
that we may not be afraid to prune what is stopping life,
and yet not so harsh
that those we correct may feel cut off from us
and unable to bear fruit again.

Lord, we remember at this time
those who are involved in conflicts.
We pray that like Jesus himself
they may work for the true salvation of all the world.

'In giving us his love, God has given us his Holy Spirit, so that we can love him with the love wherewith he loves himself.' Meister Eckhart
Lord, we thank you for the wonder of friendship.
We remember those who have become loyal friends to us.
They accept us as we are, just as we accept them.
We are part of their lives,
so that our joys and sorrows affect them as theirs affect us.
Wherever we go we are still together
because we have become part of each other.
Truly they have made their home in us,
and we our home in them.
Lord, this is how you want to relate with us,
and us to relate with you.
Lord, people who work for a new kind of society
often think they can achieve it on their own,
following their own pace
with no regard for the feelings of others.
As a church we have been guilty of this too,

and so have those of us who have authority in the church.
Remind us, Lord, that we are branches of a vine
– the community, the nation, humanity, nature –
and a branch cannot bear fruit if it is cut off.
We may prosper for a while
by dint of our own energy and enthusiasm,
but sooner or later, like many others before us,
we wither, are collected, thrown on the fire and burnt.

'We don't own the truth, and I need the truth of others.'
Bishop Pierre Claverie
Lord, people speak about becoming your disciples
as trying to be perfect
and achieving great things,
so that only the strong willed can get there.
But it isn't like that at all.
It is a matter of learning to remain in your love,
letting the stories of Jesus enter into the story of our lives,
so that we live permanently in him and present to you.

Gradually, we stop worrying about what we want
and we find that whatever we ask for we are getting.
As for good works, they are like fruit
which appears on the branches of a tree when the season comes
we don't have to bother about them at all,
because they are the work of your glory.
That is how we become your disciples.
Thank you, Lord.

Sixth Sunday of Easter

Gospel Reading: John 15:9-17

9Jesus said to his disciples: 'As the Father has loved me, so I have loved you. Remain in my love. 10If you keep my commandments you will remain in my love, just as I have kept my Father's commandments and remain in his love. 11I have told you this so that my own joy may be in you and your joy be complete. 12This is my commandment: love one another, as I have loved you. 13A man can have no greater love than to lay down his life for his friends. 14You are my friends, if you do what I command you. 15I shall not call you servants any more, because a servant does not know his master's business: I call you friends, because I have made known to you everything I have learnt from my Father. 16You did not choose me, no, I chose you; and I commissioned you to go out and to bear fruit, fruit that will last; and then the Father will give you anything you ask him in my name. 17What I command you is to love one another.'

Today's passage follows directly on last Sunday's. The metaphors, however, are not as dramatic. We must therefore make an effort to use our imagination in reading and eventually in interpreting them.

Verse 9 provides us with the key to the whole passage. We must therefore give it all our attention. The rest of the passage will then illustrate some aspect of it.

This passage tells us that we come to others with a love which we ourselves have experienced from others. This is telling us two important things.

- The first is that we love others from something we feel in ourselves. There are people outside ourselves whom we love. It isn't something we do because we have been ordered to do; we just feel it and then act accordingly.

- On the other hand, the love we feel for others has come from somewhere else. It was placed within us by those who loved us first. When we love therefore, we are re-enacting something we have inherited from others. It did not come only from us.

We need to spend some time meditating on these two facts. Once we get them right, we will be able to decide how to prolong our desire to love – the love we have within us and which we have to practise on the others we meet in the course of our lives.

The term 'love' is over-used, both in our sacred language and in our secular language. The love we speak about therefore tends to remain abstract. In interpreting a passage like this one then, we must link it to a personal memory. We have to remember some act of love which touched us very deeply.

We remember something a person said to us or allowed to happen to us. They would be saying something like: I am suffering this for you now and I am doing it so that you too can be of service to others when your turn comes. When the person told us this, it made a very deep impression on us. Ever afterwards we would always return to it and remember what it meant to us. We know that we can now suffer for others because this other person suffered with us. They were helping us to lift others and because of that, we now know what we must go through so that others will feel safe with us. We think of that as we bring up our children and all those whom the Lord has entrusted to our care.

Through this memory, we know that when we are deeply loved we do not have to be enslaved to those who loved us. We know we can trust them. It will naturally be someone who was or eventually became very important for us. Perhaps one of our parents, an uncle or aunt, a brother or sister. It could also be someone who later became a deep friend. We remember too other people who loved us sincerely in our lives – a teacher, a friend, someone we met on our life journey.

We can also apply the passage to our relationship with the wider world. In all the great trouble spots of the world there are always people who spend a lot of their time working for peace between warring factions. This has happened in areas like Palestine, Iraq, the Basque Countries. They don't make the news headlines but they are really there and as we read this passage we are with them within our hearts.

Jesus does a very interesting thing then. He says, 'As the Father has loved me, so I have loved you.' This is telling us that we give ourselves to others in the same way that others have given themselves to us. This is very true, isn't it? Once we love others we find that we can share with them the truth of who we really are.

Verse 10 takes us a little further. It invites us to move in a new direction, as Jesus makes the connection between 'keeping commandments' and 'remaining in his love'. This is telling us something important about 'commandments'. In this passage they do not refer to a series of obligations. They are rather a general commandment to accept what the other person is doing for us. Keeping his Father's commandments means simply that Jesus can remain calm within the awareness of his Father's love.

Verse 11 brings in the theme of joy. This is a new development again. All love produces joy. It is like an unnamed corollary of giving one's life to others. If our love doesn't produce joy, it can't be right. We have to add something to it which we may have neglected.

Verse 12 starts by repeating the connection that was made earlier, 'This is my commandment, love one another as I have loved you.' The Christian commandment to love is based on Jesus' love for us. We love not merely from ourselves but because the love of Christ has taken charge of us.

Verses 13-15. Jesus then goes on to make the connection between love and the relationship between friends. He goes to the heart of what being a friend is all about. It means seeing another in the light of our experience.

'A servant does not know his master's business, but I have made known to you everything I learnt from my Father.' Let us spend some time with these imposing words. We take what we can from them and then let them take charge of us.

Verse 16a stays with friendship and goes back to the theme of bearing fruit which we saw last Sunday. It stresses first the choice of the person who wants to make us his friends – 'You did not choose me, no I chose you'. This is so important. We often act as if we are the ones responsible for loving others. We do not really chose the person we decide to love. It is God who chooses us to reach out to them. We must be aware of this fact and respond accordingly.

Then Jesus gives an important lesson. 'I commissioned you' means first that he has sent us out and that we are to go out and bring forth results. The results are simply 'to bear fruit', to show the world what our love has accomplished. Then he adds another important corollary, 'the kind of fruit that I know will last'. It must not be a fruit that no one can understand or accept. It must be the kind that we know will last.

Verse 16b. Then Jesus makes a very important point. 'The Father will give you anything you ask him in my name.' The Father in heaven will therefore give honour to all those who bear the name of Jesus, written in their hearts.

Verse 17 is the climax, striking in its simplicity. When all is said and done, what really counts in life is the principle of love. Once we know how to love, we will have kept all the Lord's commandments.

* * *

'Spiritual poverty clings to nothing and nothing clings to it.'
Meister Eckhart

Lord, forgive us for being so busy
when we come into your presence.
We have to tell you all our needs
in case you might forget some of them.
We make many resolutions in case you don't think well of us.
We are anxious to get some teaching from you
that will keep us faithful to your will.
We thank you for the times when you invited us
just to be quiet and remain in your love,
your permanent unconditional love,
the kind you had from your Father.

Lord, we have made the commandments
into cold, objective obligations
and many of them, at that.
We thank you that they are gestures of love
    - the tender embrace between husband and wife before leav-
    ing for work,
    - the words of wisdom that a great leader speaks to his inti-
    mate followers on his deathbed,
    - the wave of friends at the airport.
They are all gestures that we treasure
because they tell us that we are loved
and set us free to give ourselves to others.
Lord, when we look at our lives we discover a history of love.
We were loved when we were small,

as Jesus was loved by Joseph and Mary.
And that love freed us;
it was a starting point from which we could trust others
and give ourselves to them.
And now our children, those whom we have loved in our turn,
have grown up and become loving people too.
Lord, that history of love is your presence in the world.

'Be as uninteresting as a glass of cold, clear uninteresting water.'
Aidan Kavanagh
Lord, we thank you for our friends.
We remember when we knew them first.
We admired them so much that we just wanted to please them,
not really to understand them – just like servants.
Then gradually we became friends,
as we learnt to trust each other,
to let ourselves be known so that we could share
what was most intimate to us,
the kind of things only you taught us,
and there was no such thing as 'this is my business'.
The interesting thing is that we have come close to you too.

*'Baby, will you remember me when you wake on Ash Wednesday
morning? You know how Ash Wednesday is always a different story.'*
David Rudder
Lord, the ideal for great people today
seems to be that they give orders and demand obedience.
We have those who know and then the rest who know nothing.
We thank you for Jesus and those who follow his style,
who look on their followers as friends
and make known to them their dreams for themselves
and for the world.
Only they can bring about true community.

Lord, we thank you for the joy of married love,
when you don't have to prove yourself or try to be different
but can just relax in someone's love.
Truly that is a joy that is complete.

'Be men and women of the world but not worldly men and women.'
Jose Maria Escriva
Lord, we sometimes act as if our plans for society are our own
and we must destroy all who oppose us.
But the hopes we have for the church,
for our country, for the world,
are your gift to us, the passion we feel is your doing.
We are your servants sent to carry out your commission,
and our achievements are the fruit you cause to emerge.
So even if we die before we achieve what we set out to do,
and even if our successes are short-lived,
the fruit we bear will endure because they come from you.

'If you love God, the pain does not go away, but you live more fully.'
Michael Hollings
Lord, we thank you for those precious moments
when we know that your command to love,
though very simple,
was all that we needed.
It summed up the law of life,
the secret of peace and prosperity,
and the only hope for the world.

Feast of the Ascension

Gospel Reading: Mark 16:14a, 15-20

14a*Jesus showed himself to the Eleven* 15*and said to them, 'Go out to the whole world; proclaim the Good News to all creation.* 16*He who believes and is baptised will be saved; he who does not believe will be condemned.* 17*These are the signs that will be associated with believers: in my name they will cast out devils; they will have the gift of tongues;* 18*they will pick up snakes in their hands, and be unharmed should they drink poison; they will lay their hands on the sick, who will recover.'* 19*And so the Lord Jesus, after he had spoken to them, was taken up into heaven: there at the right hand of God he took his place,* 20*while they, going out, preached everywhere, the Lord working with them and confirming the word by the signs that accompanied it.*

At the beginning of today's passage we are reminded that these words were once spoken by Jesus himself to some disciples who were facing a difficult time. They felt very disorganised and lost; here now was Jesus standing before them and giving them a way to go forward. He continues to do this for us today through different 'messengers' whom God sends to us. We must be aware of them and thank God for them.

Jesus makes a first crucial statement to his followers: they are to 'go out into the whole world and proclaim the Good News to all creation'. We think today of many parts of creation where the gospel of Jesus has not yet been preached.

We think of signs in the modern world which we can associate with true believers:

- 'In my name they will cast out devils.' Many people in our modern world think that no one cares for them, not even God. True believers, however, speak in words which convey that gifts like true selflessness can bring help for all.

- 'They will have the gift of tongues.' There are people in the world today who cannot speak in new languages; they use words that cannot touch unyielding hearts. True believers however will be able to communicate their message of love to all they meet, no matter what their original circumstances were.

- There are people who can act out their role as evangelisers, even in what seems to the rest of us as very difficult circum-

stances. They venture into difficult worlds. They work in difficult surroundings, among prostitutes, drug addicts and other
outcasts of society. They can 'pick up snakes in their hands and
be untouched by them'. We can say about them that, 'they will
remain unharmed even when they drink deadly poison.'

- Finally, Jesus tells us that 'true believers' can 'lay their
hands on the sick who will recover.' There are people who can
lay their hands on those who are sick and see them recover before
their very eyes. It is truly a wonderful experience of God's salvation and 'true believers' can feel it happening.

The passage concludes with a beautiful saying about the
Lord Jesus. It is said of him that 'he was taken up to heaven' and
that 'at the right hand of God, he took his place.' We who believe
can now think of the Lord Jesus sitting at the right hand of God.
We are in this world surrounded by all our difficulties and yet
we feel great trust in the Lord.

'They, going out, preached everywhere' and the 'Lord is
working with them and confirming the word by the signs that
accompanied it.' As believers, we know well that the Lord is
with us. He is confirming what we say by the signs he has sent to
accompany us, and the great miracles he achieves through us.

* * *

*'In the church's history, missionary drive has always been a sign of vi-
tality, just as its lessening is a sign of a crisis of faith.'*
John Paul II, *Encyclical Redemptoris Missio*, 1991
Lord, there comes a time in life when we know
that what we believe in is good news for the whole of creation.
We feel like the apostles when they met Jesus
after his resurrection.
It is strange, but the conviction always seems to come
after we have experienced a setback –
some of our members may have deserted us
as Judas deserted Jesus.
Yet we know we must go out to the whole world.
Our cause is with you,
as safe as Jesus taken up to heaven
and taking his place at your right hand,
so that we can go out, preaching everywhere,
our words confirmed by the signs which accompany them.

Lord, there are certain signs that are the mark of true believers.
Demons have been causing havoc in our community
and no one has been able to confront them –
a person of faith will cast them out in one moment.
Believers can express an old message in a totally new way,
so that people who have been listening to that message for years
will suddenly become convinced.
The rest of us are afraid of going to some places
for fear we might be corrupted:
believers do it and remain totally unharmed.
They can enter into discussion with enemies of the faith
and remain calm and loving.
They go to someone whom the community has written off
as a hopeless case
and at the touch of their hands
this person returns to normal living.
Lord, we thank you for believers.

*'Anyone who loves his life loses it; anyone who hates his life in this
world will keep it for the eternal life.'* John 12:25
Lord, it is clearly a law of life
that we must eventually commit ourselves
– to marriage,
– to a noble cause,
– to the following of Jesus.
We must take the risk.
If we hold back, afraid of this baptism,
we are condemned to lives of mediocrity.
To go forward in faith is the only way to be saved.

*On the day that the children of Israel crossed the Red Sea so miracu-
lously, God was surrounded by angels who sang and danced. They noticed that God was crying. 'Are you not glad?' they asked. 'How can I
rejoice?' God asked, 'My children are also drowning.'* Jewish legend
quoted by Rabbi Hugo Gryn at a vigil for the Gulf War, London 1991
Lord, forgive us for setting limits to your love.
Remind us that the good news you revealed to us
is to be proclaimed to all creation.

Lord, so often as a church we give people the idea
that following Jesus can be done
with minor adjustments to their lifestyle.
Help us to teach plainly, like Jesus,
that being disciples means
taking enormous risks of being drowned,
but unless we are baptised in him, he cannot save us.

*'This is the end of the Chinese people's adolescence, and their initiation
into political maturity. They are no longer waiting to be liberated; they
are now ready to pay the price to liberate themselves.'*
Liu Binyan, dissident Chinese journalist
Lord, we thank you for people and cultures
who have been through crucifixion experiences
and have emerged with their faith and their courage intact.
We pray that like the apostles at the ascension of Jesus
they may now go out into the whole world
and announce with confidence the good news
that the human spirit cannot be enclosed in a tomb
and will always rise again.

Liturgical Notes for Pentecost

Knowing the background to the liturgical celebration of Pentecost is important to help us understand the feast correctly. People often say to me that they are unhappy with the way Pentecost is celebrated in the liturgy; they find it comes and goes too quickly. Easter gets plenty of importance, having its own 'octave', so that the celebration continues for eight days; Ascension is celebrated until Pentecost, but Pentecost itself is over in one day, and then we are back in Ordinary Time. Churches are beautifully decorated in red – but only for one day.

There is a simple reason why Pentecost lasts one day only: in the church's liturgy, Easter is one fifty-day celebration, and Pentecost marks its close. This was one of the changes brought about by the liturgical reforms of the Second Vatican Council (1962-1965). Before that, Pentecost – known as Whit Sunday – was celebrated as a major feast, with its own vigil and octave.

Restoring the importance of the liturgical seasons was one of the major conciliar reforms. The *Decree on the Liturgy* states (107 and 108): 'the liturgical year is to be revised so that the traditional customs and discipline of the sacred seasons shall be preserved and restored.' It added, 'Their specifric character is to be retained so that they duly nourish the piety of the faithful as they celebrate the mysteries of the Christian redemption,' and again, 'The minds of the faithful should be directed primarily towards the feasts of the Lord whereby the mysteries of salvation are celebrated throughout the years' so that 'the entire cycle of the mysteries of salvation may be suitably recalled.'

The seasons remind us that being followers of Jesus means more than obeying his commandments; it means being in union with him, in the words of Clyde Harvey's wonderful hymn, 'being the body of the Lord, having his spirit coursing through our souls.'

Each season celebrates a particular moment in the life of Jesus; we refer to these as 'mysteries' because he continues to live them in us today. We don't merely 'remember' the seasons, we 'celebrate' them, recognising similar stages in our own lives.

As the Vatican Council stated, 'They are in some way present at all times; the faithful lay hold of them and are filled with saving grace.'

There are five seasons, and they are arranged chronologically to correspond to the stages of Jesus' life:

- during Advent he is in Mary's womb;
- at Christmas he is a baby and then a little child;
- during Lent he is a powerful adult, preaching repentance and new life;
- in the Sacred Triduum he is powerless, passing through death to resurrection.
- Easter is the fifth and final season; it celebrates the last stage in Jesus' life when he did three things:
  • he rose from the dead,
  • ascended into heaven,
  • sent the Holy Spirit on his followers.

These are three different historical events but also three aspects of the one 'mystery' of Jesus' triumph over death.

  • The resurrection reminds us that his tomb was empty, death had no power over him.

  • The ascension that he was no longer limited to one place and time but was at the right hand of the Father and at the same time 'with' his followers as they went out into the whole world 'making disciples of all nations'.

  • The sending of the Spirit that he was now really present within them – the 'short time' had passed and they could 'see him' again (cf John 16:17).

The sequence of the different aspects of the Easter event varies in the New Testament accounts. St Luke's gospel (which we read on the feast of the Ascension in Year B) tells us that Jesus ascended on Easter Sunday, and in the gospel readings for the feast of Pentecost St John relates that Jesus breathed the Spirit on the disciples on 'the evening of the same day' – Easter Sunday. It is also significant that, according to the lectionary, we read the story of the coming of the Holy Spirit in the first reading of Easter Monday, and that of Jesus' promise to send the Spirit on the Sundays and weekdays of the fifth and sixth weeks of Easter time.

The liturgy, then, far from downplaying the sending of the

Holy Spirit, highlights it. But it also gives us some important pointers on how we are to understand this event. I will just mention three.

1. People sometimes refer to Pentecost as 'the feast of the Holy Spirit', but that is not a good expression. It is a feast of Jesus, the 'mystery' of his sending the Holy Spirit on his followers, the moment when he became present to them in a new way – by being with them.

2. We too come to a stage in our lives as parents, teachers, church ministers and spiritual guides, when we have to let go of those God has entrusted to our care and let them live their own lives. Like Jesus, we must 'breathe on them', so that they may be guided inwardly by the values we taught them. Like Jesus too we can do that only if we have first given our lives for them – which will include being crucified.

3. The coming of the Holy Spirit is an event in our lives as it was for Jesus' disciples. It is the moment when we realise that following Jesus is not a matter of keeping commandments but of having him live within us. The experience is always the culmination of a journey – we first have to look wonderingly at an empty tomb; to see the risen Jesus and then to have him vanish from our sight; to wait a long time in Jerusalem, trusting that the Lord's promise will be fulfilled.

Pentecost

Gospel Reading: John 20:19-23

¹⁹*In the evening of that same day, the first day of the week, the doors were closed in the room where the disciples were, for fear of the Jews. Jesus came and stood among them. He said to them, 'Peace be with you', ²⁰and showed them his hands and his side. The disciples were filled with joy when they saw the Lord, ²¹and he said to them again, 'Peace be with you. As the Father sent me, so am I sending you.' ²²After saying this he breathed on them and said, 'Receive the Holy Spirit. ²³For those whose sins you forgive, they are forgiven; for those whose sins you retain, they are retained.'*

In John's version, the sending of the disciples involves several stages; each one has its own special lessons for us.

The first stage is the meeting with the disciples in the room. We read this part of the story in conjunction with the story of Jesus' meeting with St Thomas, which occurs later. The disciples are afraid; they have closed themselves off from the rest of the world. The events of the previous week had climaxed in Jesus' crucifixion, and they now fear for their own lives. Jesus enters and stands before them, he appears to them with no previous warning, in contrast to what happens in the other gospels. He stays with them and his word challenges them.

The words 'Peace be with you' give us an important message. In a true sense, the disciples do not need to have any further sending of the Holy Spirit. They can feel his presence among them. They can now relate in peace, with themselves, with one another and with their God.

Jesus then invites them to look at his hands and his side, at the signs that he had truly risen from the dead. This important lesson would become clearer after he appeared to Thomas. Further references to the resurrection would have to wait; now they had to appreciate fully that his wounds on the cross were real and had a purpose. Those who are today in difficulty can now know that they too are agents of the world's salvation.

In the second part of the story Jesus tells his disciples the wonderful news that they were sent by the Father. This is really the deep meaning of the sending of the Holy Spirit. All disciples must feel within their hearts the wonderful message that they too have been sent as Jesus was sent. The Father sent him into the world so that he could truly die for it. Jesus in his turn has sent his followers into the world. They must be for others what he had been for them. People could now live in union with him no matter what difficulties they were facing. Their suffering can bring the world closer to God. They must feel within themselves that by their personal sufferings they can help others experience the good news, and lift up humanity to a higher place with God.

The third event which symbolised the coming of the Holy Spirit is the deepest of all. The story is in two phases.

- Jesus breathes on the apostles. He had experienced a reality within himself that he wanted to communicate to the disciples. He wanted to teach them that they too can feel within themselves the power of being loved by God, a power that had always been his. He wanted them to experience this, to feel it within themselves. Being loved by God, they must be able to share it with one another. They must feel so close to God that no matter what suffering they might undergo, they would always bring greater glory to God and to one another.

- Jesus' word now explains his gesture. The disciples must receive the Holy Spirit so that, like Jesus, they may have the inner feeling that they are moved by a deep force from within themselves. They too must be able to lift up the rest of the world by giving themselves.

Finally, by the sending of the Holy Spirit, the disciples are given the power to forgive one another's sins or to retain them. This is truly a powerful saying. It tells us very powerfully how we are to relate to one another. We can forgive one another's sins, but we can also do the opposite and retain them. It tells us what we are called to in this world. This is a wonderful gift and we thank God for it.

The lessons in this passage have great meaning for us because all of us come to a similar stage in our lives sooner or later. As parents, teachers, church ministers or spiritual guides we come to a point where we have to let go of those God has entrusted to our care. We must let them live their own lives. Like Jesus, we too must tell them that they are sent, that we can 'breathe on them'. They will have to be guided from within by the values we have taught them. Like him too we can do that only if we have first given our lives for them – and this will naturally include being crucified.

What happened to the apostles in their personal lives happens to us also in our public lives. As public servants or employers, we too must hand on to others what we have learnt from others in our own lives. We do it as leaders of businesses or communities, and of course most especially as leaders of our church communities. To all who relate with us we can say as Jesus said, 'The Spirit that I have within me I must hand over to you, so that you too can enjoy it.'

* * *

'Walk the dark ways of faith and you will attain the vision of God.'
St Augustine
Lord, we thank you for this Easter season
which we have now completed.
We thank you for the times
when we have to stand hopefully before an empty tomb,
times when we see you and live with you
and then have you vanish from our sight
and have to wait for you in Jerusalem
for what seems an interminable time,
until eventually your promised Spirit
comes on us and we can live again.

'The literal meaning of scripture is the field, while the deeper and more profound spiritual reading is the treasure hidden in the field.'
Origen
Lord, we thank you for the times
when we have remained hidden from others.
We too were afraid that the terrible deeds
that were done to Jesus might be done to us.
Then you walked through our closed doors and,
with no advance warning, you came to stand among us.
You did not condemn us.
You merely assured us that we can live in peace.
You made us feel secure – within ourselves,
with one another, and with you, our only God.

Lord, we thank you for the times
when we felt we were really thirsting
to go to others as you sent us to them.
We too can tell others the good news
that they can rise from the dead and find new life in you.

Lord, we thank you for the times that we can say to one another
what Jesus said to his disciples.
We too have felt within us that feeling of being close to God.
We would like to share this feeling
with all those you have given to us.
Help us by word and gesture to make this a reality.

'Understanding can follow where experience leads.' St Bernard
Lord, we thank you that
just as you have felt his inner spirit within you,
you eventually became able to breathe on us.
We could then feel your presence within us.
We knew then that you were at work among us.

*'The gravest sin committed against our country is to have classified the
struggle of the Guatemalan people as the work of communists.'*
Rigoberta Menchu
Lord, remind us that we who have been blessed
by the sending of the Holy Spirit do not belong to the world.
We therefore have the ability to forgive
the real sins of your people,
but we can also retain those which need to be retained
and not forgiven.

The Feast of the Trinity

Gospel Reading: Matthew 28:16-20

¹⁶*The eleven disciples set out for Galilee, to the mountain where Jesus had arranged to meet them. ¹⁷When they saw him they fell down before him, though some hesitated. ¹⁸Jesus came up and spoke to them. He said, 'All authority in heaven and on earth has been given to me. ¹⁹Go, therefore, make disciples of all the nations; baptise them in the name of the Father and of the Son and of the Holy Spirit, ²⁰and teach them to observe all the commands I gave you. And know that I am with you always; yes, to the end of time.'*

This Sunday the liturgy invites us to celebrate the feast of the Trinity. In our church we tend to look at the Trinity as a doctrine. It is something we are meant to hold and believe; we learn about it with our minds and with our reason. But we add the *proviso* that we cannot understand it. 'Understanding' is viewed as the important thing; if we can't understand it we are not making much progress with it.

This is not, however, the best way to approach the doctrine of the Trinity. What we need to do is to retrace the journey made by the church. We enter into the spirituality of Jesus through the practice of *lectio divina*. Gradually we find that we experience the Trinity as a 'mystery'. This is the liturgical sense of the word. It is something we celebrate because we know it makes us better human beings, as we follow ever more closely in the footsteps of Jesus.

If we base ourselves on the gospel texts we come to the Trinity as something we experience. Our model is Jesus himself: the Trinity for him was what he lived, it explains how he experienced himself, how he related with his Father and with the Spirit, with others and with the earth itself. The church, reflecting on his experience, was later – and only gradually – able to formulate the church doctrine of the Trinity. The gospel reading for this Year B is an excellent starting point for this journey.

Jesus saw that authority in the world was something that was 'given' to him. It was a 'gift' he had received from the Father. It was given to him by someone in heaven, his Father who dwells in heaven. It was not a truth that he was able to discover for himself, nor one that he came to experience from his own decisions. It was always something he had 'received.'

As Son he was able to exercise this gift. He had the authority to do this. He practised the reality of the Trinity with personal power. He exercised this authority for himself and from his own observation. Having received it from outside himself, he put it into practice in the way he related with people.

Jesus therefore did not have to hold on to his authority. He took the decisions for himself, or it was decided for him in the name of the Father. In either case, he practised it by handing over his authority to the care of his disciples. Since the authority was something 'given' to him, he was able to give it over with no personal regrets.

Jesus lived his 'Trinitarian spirituality' especially from the time he felt able to depart from the world. He had always been humble in how he handled his authority; now he could be totally confident in handing on to others everything he had accomplished. This was why he could say with full freedom that he could hand everything over to the Holy Spirit.

'All authority is given to me,' he told his disciples once he had decided to leave his mission in their hands. They could 'go therefore' wherever they wanted, trusting that wherever they went, he would be alongside them, adding to what they believed in whatever he wanted for them to achieve.

We too, then, must be conscious of our authority as 'given'. It is never possessed by us. We too can exercise it confidently and humbly and then willingly pass it on to others when the time comes. Evil qualities like jealousy or possessiveness or a fear of letting go are symptoms that the Trinity is not real for us. It means that we take authority as ours and not as 'given'.

The things we can feel free to hand on to others include all forms of authority, especially that of our faith in Jesus. We must therefore take 'baptising in the name of the Father, of the Son and of the Holy Spirit' in a very wide sense. It does not merely refer to our church baptism; it includes the entire work of the church, the process of inviting people to experience authority as Jesus did.

We take the time to celebrate the many people who have shared this 'baptism' with us. We pray that they too will have the grace to approach 'all nations' with this wide and tolerant 'Trinitarian Spirit.'

* * *

Lord, we thank you for the various ways
in which you reveal your presence to us:
there are times when we experience you as Father
through teachers, community leaders,
members of our family, spiritual guides
to whom you have given authority in heaven and on earth,
so that we feel empowered spiritually
and can assume responsibility in our workplaces
and in public life.
At other times we experience you as Son,
through the great people you send us as companions.
They do not talk down to us.
When we fail in some great enterprise and have to start again,
like the eleven disciples setting out disconsolately
to return to Galilee,
they come up and speak to us as fellow pilgrims
who have themselves been defeated,
so that they can tell us now to go out confidently
and share our wisdom with all the nations.
At other times again, you are deep within us, like our breath,
so discreet that we do not even advert to your presence;
but you are the source of life and energy, always with us,
so that even when we feel lost and discouraged we can say,
yes, you will be there till the end of that time.
Thank you for our being baptised
in the name of the Father, of the Son and of the Holy Spirit.

Lord, people in authority often cling to those in their charge.
We tend to do it as parents, teachers,
ministers in the church, political leaders.
Help us to be more like Jesus
when he met the apostles in Galilee,
free enough to know
that our work is not limited to the here and now,
that if we have helped others in any way we can tell them to go,

because wherever they are we will be with them.
When we understand this,
we are truly baptised in the name of the Trinity.

*'If there is any lover of God living on this earth who is continually kept
from falling, I do not know about it, for it was not shown to me. But
this was shown, that in falling and in rising we are always preciously
kept in the same love.'* Julian of Norwich
Lord, we pray for those
who are feeling discouraged at this moment
because they have committed some sin
that has them feeling ashamed.
Remind them that you are with them always,
yes, even to the end of this time.

Lord, we pray for all of us who are called to exercise leadership
in public life, in your church,
in our homes and neighbourhoods, on the world stage.
Help us to imitate Jesus; to be conscious, like he was,
that all authority in heaven and on earth is given to us for a time,
after which we commission those we have worked with
to go out into the world.
We are not afraid to move on because we trust
that whatever values they have learned from us
are like commands we have given them
which they will observe and will hand on in their turn,
so that we will be with them always, yes, to the end of time.

*'Unity is taught by Moses; the prophets proclaim duality; in the
gospels we meet the Trinity.'* St Epiphanus
Lord, you have created our human family
in your image and likeness,
baptised us in the name of the Blessed Trinity.
As individuals and as cultures you have made us all different
so that each of us has been given a unique share
in your universal authority in heaven and on earth.
We exercise this authority, not as a personal possession,
but as a gift we have received from someone else in the family
and then shared with others,

so that even though we are here for a few short years
and then move on,
wherever in the world your great command of love is observed
we are all present and will continue to be until the end of time.

The Body and Blood of Christ

Gospel Reading: Mark 14:12-16, 22-26

12*On the first day of the Unleavened Bread, when the Passover lamb was sacrificed, his disciples said to Jesus, 'Where do you want us to go and make the preparations for you to eat the passover?'* 13*So he sent two of his disciples, saying to them, 'Go into the city and you will meet a man carrying a pitcher of water. Follow him,* 14*and say to the owner of the house which he enters, 'The Master says: Where is my dining room in which I can eat the passover with my disciples?'* 15*He will show you a large upper room furnished with couches, all prepared. Make the preparations for us there.'* 16*The disciples set out and went to the city and found everything as he had told them, and prepared the Passover.* 22*And as they were eating he took some bread, and when he had said the blessing he broke it and gave it to them. 'Take it,' he said 'this is my body.'* 23*Then he took a cup, and when he had returned thanks, he gave it to them, and all drank from it,* 24*and he said to them, 'This is my blood, the blood of the covenant, which is to be poured out for many.* 25*I tell you solemnly, I shall not drink any more wine until the day I drink the new wine in the kingdom of God.'* 26*After psalms had been sung, they left for the Mount of Olives.*

We can approach this passage from two perspectives. On the one hand, it can help us celebrate the gift of the Holy Eucharist as told in St Mark; on the other, we can let the special way St Mark tells the story of the Last Supper help us reflect on the symbolism of the sacrament.

Verses 12 to 16 tell the story of how Jesus prepared for the feast. The apostles asked him , 'Where do you want us to make the preparations for you to eat the passover?' Jesus' answer gives us a context which will help us understand how the Last Supper fits into our own lives.

The Supper was part of a passover meal; it was not something that happened by chance. It took place in the context of the great feast. This feast has given Jesus' Last Supper a special place in our Christian lives. We must be aware of this.

These verses also give us an insight into Jesus' way of operating. He had friends everywhere, even in places like Jerusalem. He could rely on them. Indeed he depended on them to provide all that was needed to celebrate the great feast of the passover. St Mark is stressing here a version of the Last Supper which is in continuation with the account presented by the Book of Exodus. We can therefore apply some of the points made there to our celebration of the Eucharist.

In verses 22 to 24 we meditate on St Mark's account of the events, and we avoid focusing on the other accounts, or allowing them to influence our meditation. The author notes that Jesus took the bread 'while they were eating'. This reminds us that in its original form the Eucharist had a place in people's ordinary lives.

After saying the blessing, Jesus broke the bread, then said 'take it' and added, 'this is my body'. We need to reflect on this, the body of Christ which we receive in the Eucharist is his real body. It is the one we venerate in our daily lives, the one we relate with in our normal aspirations and desires, the one we meet in all our difficulties.

In the following verse we see that Jesus had already 'returned thanks' when he said the next words. After they had drunk the wine, he told them, 'this is my blood'. Here again, we have a definite statement - this is blood of Christ. Everything we believe about his blood we can now say of the Eucharist. We relate to it as we would normally do for his blood, remembering all our instincts about what blood is intended for.

Jesus adds that this blood is that 'of his covenant' and we must take some time to meditate on this. The blood of the covenant was what united people with their God and made them one.

It is said that the blood 'is to be poured out for many'. This has made a deep impression on our Christian life. It refers first of all to the many people who will be touched by the Eucharist – Christians of every denomination who feel that their God cares for them wherever they are. It also includes all of humanity; all human beings will be affected by this teaching in some way or other. It will make them more conscious that God is close to them, that he follows them in every mood and in every atmosphere.

We must look at verse 25 very specially. It is unique to St Mark. We must ask ourselves, starting from our own experi-

ence, why did Jesus say these words. They are clearly there to
make the link between what happened at the Last Supper and
what happens in heaven. This is an aspect of the Eucharist
which we tend to neglect. Here we are invited to remember it.

Feel the drama of verse 26. Jesus clearly wanted to link the
events of the supper with what happened afterwards. He took
the decision to go out in the company of his disciples. He would
do this resolutely, with two goals in mind. The first was to confront the reality of God who was asking him to sacrifice his life
on the mountain. The second was to confront Judas and his
newly accepted adversaries from the Roman Empire. He would
now meet them on the Mount of Olives.

Both these things are powerful reminders to us that we need
to link what happens at the Eucharist with the reality of our lives
later on. They will have many applications for the centuries of
the Eucharist which followed. They should always be there to
protect us against false interpretations.

* * *

Lord, on this great feast we thank you for the times
when we gather as disciples to celebrate your Passover,
and you are present with us,
saying 'Take and eat, this is my body,'
then saying 'This is my blood, the blood of the covenant,
which is poured out for many.'

'No one takes my life from me; I lay it down of my own free will,
and as it is in my power to lay it down, so it is in my power to take it up
again.' John 10:18
Lord, when things are going wrong for us, we panic,
we act as if we are no longer in control.
We thank you for people like Jesus.
Even as he entered Jerusalem,
knowing that there he faced the hostility of many
and that they were determined to put him to death,
he remained in control of his destiny.
He knew that he had friends in that hostile city
and could plan the celebration of the Passover.
Lord, a time comes in life when we have to give ourselves

as spouses, parents, church ministers, public servants.
We have to say to those we serve, 'Here, take it, this is my body';
we have to say, 'Here, this is my blood,
the sign of the covenant between us;
I am pouring it out for you and through you for many others.'

Lord, you always seem to send us friends
who stand by us in difficult times.
We quarrel among ourselves,
they let us down from time to time,
but the meals we share in times of crisis
seal a sacred covenant between us,
so that we can leave together for our Mount of Olives.

'There will have to be an incubation of the Christian mystery in the originality of your people, so that in the future its native voice, clearer and more sure, may join in harmony with the various voices of the universal church.' Pope Paul VI to the Bishops of Africa in Uganda, 1969
Lord, your will continues to be
that every community of disciples
should eat the body and drink the blood
of your incarnate Word,
so that they may experience the Covenant in a new way,
never again to be content with the old,
as they drink the new wine of your kingdom.

Do you really wish to pay homage to Christ's Body? Then do not neglect him when he is naked. At the same time that you honour him here with hangings made of silk, do not ignore him outside when he perishes from cold and in nakedness. For the one who said, 'This is my body' also said 'When I was hungry, you gave me nothing to eat.'
John Chrysostom
Lord, remind us always that when Jesus tells us
'Take it, this is my body'
he is also speaking of the poor
whom we meet on our life's journey,
and when he says,
'This is my blood which is to be poured out for many,'
he is also speaking of those who suffer innocently today.

'If humankind on this planet has a future, then theology and religious institutions have to collaborate in promoting communities of prayer, understanding and redemptive praxis.' Matthew Lamb, theologian

Lord, we pray that church communities today
may live again the experience of the Last Supper,
becoming communities
where members give their body and blood
in the service of one another and of all men and women,
where they dream of the day
when they will drink new wine in your kingdom,
and where, having sung their psalms,
they will go out together to confront the world.

Celebrating Ordinary Time

This coming Sunday, after Lent and Easter, the liturgy returns to Ordinary Time, which began in January. Ordinary Time was restored as a distinctive period of the liturgical year by the Second Vatican Council; it was one of the Council's most important reforms, and it can help us grow spiritually.

The name itself is significant; Ordinary Time means 'the time of the order', reminding us that in the early centuries before the emergence of Lent, Christmas and the other Seasons, the church's liturgy followed its own 'order' which did not correspond to national festivals. Having no political power, the Christians of that time had no choice – they could not impose their festivals on the rest of society.

Ordinary Time is a living reminder therefore that the church existed – and even flourished – at a time when it was ignored by civil society. This is still the situation today in many parts of the world: where it is a minority group (as in much of Asia); where members are not allowed to practice their faith in public (as was the case in Socialist countries); or where society pursues different interests, as in the Western world during Advent ('Christmas shopping season'), Christmas ('party time' or even 'beginning of the Carnival season') and Easter ('school holidays'). We accept our minority status calmly and confidently, as our ancestors in the faith did; during Ordinary Time, we remain faithful to our 'liturgical order' as a source of the energy we need to preserve our Christian values.

In the post-Vatican II liturgy the lectionary of Ordinary Time follows the ancient tradition called 'continuous reading *(lectio continua)*, that is to say that one particular book of the Bible is read from beginning to end, according to the order in which it was written. Passages are not chosen according to themes (as happens during the 'Seasons'). We receive them as they occur in the Bible text and welcome them as God's word for us, just as we welcome people and events when they come our way without our having chosen them.

Continuous reading teaches us the important lesson that the Bible is one unified book – the Word Made Flesh in a wide variety of circumstances, each of which brought its own unique perspective and added its own insight into the Word. The original Word became clearer as time went on. We read the Bible 'historically' therefore, aware of the particular circumstances in which the Word was Made Flesh, and the stage of its evolution. In our Catholic understanding of the Bible, the process continues. The biblical text remains sacred but each historical era – including our own – throws new light on it and is in turn illuminated by it.

During Ordinary Time continuous reading is done on both weekdays and Sundays. The two weekday readings are often taken from different books, independently of each other. On Sundays the arrangement is different. Of the three readings

- the gospel texts are a continuous reading of one of the synoptics;
- the first reading is taken from the Old Testament and is chosen to correspond to the gospel reading;
- the second reading is a continuous reading of one of St Paul's epistles.

The continuous reading of the gospels focuses on one section of the life of Jesus.

- His public ministry, starting after the temptations and ending before the passion, death and resurrection. It invites us to experience Jesus as a human being who carried out his life work within historical circumstances. This is part of the human condition and he accepted it fully. Continuous reading corrects the common tendency of experiencing Jesus as a disembodied 'voice' speaking to us 'from heaven' or some indeterminate place.

- The Jesus of the gospels – at least as experienced in continuous reading – 'the kingdom of God'. This is a biblical expression meaning God's plan for the world – the world as it would be if God were in charge. It is spelt out in some detail in various Old Testament texts as a world of harmony and abundance for all.

- Jesus could not dictate how this goal would be lived out in practice. Like us, he had to adapt to circumstances he could not control. At times he was in control (e.g. in Galilee), at other times (e.g. on the cross) he had to accept circumstances which others imposed on him.

The Jesus we meet in continuous reading is therefore a living lesson that we too are called by God to live 'historically'.

- Like Jesus we are God's sons and daughters, made in God's image and likeness, endowed with freedom. We choose to set goals for ourselves and we are responsible for being faithful to them.

- Like him too we are limited creatures. We too must live out our goals within historical circumstances which we can influence but only to some extent. We grow spiritually by 'living with' them. We combine idealism and realism and seek the wisdom to know the difference, according to the well-known 'Serenity Prayer'.

The continuous reading of the Sundays of Ordinary Time focuses on the synoptic gospels. There are slight differences in the way each gospel tells the story of Jesus' public ministry, but one thing they have in common – their 'one optic' – is that they divide it into three historical stages.

1. He started in Galilee. It was a triumphant period, great crowds followed him and hung on his words, but there were already rumblings of opposition, originating from the leaders in Jerusalem.

2. At a certain point of the Galilean ministry, Jesus decided it was time for him to go to Jerusalem and confront the religious leaders. He journeyed there, on foot naturally, but continued his teaching, the difference being that he focused more on his disciples than on the crowds.

3. Jesus arrived in Jerusalem and ministered there, in an atmosphere of heightened opposition and impending crisis.

We start the Sundays of Ordinary Time in early January, and interrupt them for Lent. Several Sundays are replaced by feasts such as the Trinity and Corpus Christi.

Second Sunday in Ordinary Time

Gospel Reading: John 1:35-42

35As John stood with two of his disciples, 36Jesus passed, and John stared hard at him and said, 'Look, there is the lamb of God.' 37Hearing this, the two disciples followed Jesus. 38Jesus turned round, saw them following and said, 'What do you want?' They answered, 'Rabbi,' – which means Teacher – 'Where do you live?' 39'Come and see' he replied; so they went and saw where he lived, and stayed with him the rest of that day. It was about the tenth hour. 40One of these two who became followers of Jesus after hearing what John had said was Andrew, the brother of Simon Peter. 41Early next morning, Andrew met his brother and said to him, 'We have found the Messiah' – which means the Christ – 42and he took Simon to Jesus. Jesus looked hard at him and said, 'You are Simon son of John; you are to be called Cephas' – meaning Rock.

On this Sunday, every year, there is an extract from St John's gospel, taken from the beginning of the public ministry of Jesus, which serves as a preliminary to the continuous reading which will begin on the following Sunday.

In this passage we have St John's account of the calling of the first disciples. It differs markedly from the account given in the synoptic gospels, and has its own richness and depth.

The passage is in three sections:

Verses 35-36: The testimony of John the Baptist: admire the marvellous humility of the precursor, model for all those involved in giving guidance to others. You might also like to spend some time reflecting on the famous title of Jesus, Lamb of God.

Verses 38-39: The encounter between the disciples and Jesus is simple and down-to-earth, but also very deep. Let it remind you of meetings that have affected you or people you know.

Verses 40-42: To understand the power of the story, you must be aware of the significance of names in the Bible. A person's name indicates the nature of the person, who the person is deep down. In giving Peter a new name, therefore, Jesus invites him to rise to new possibilities. It is important that Jesus had to 'look hard at him' before he could discover what this new name should be.

Lord, we thank you for people who guided us
but did not try to possess us:
parents, teachers, spiritual guides, friends.
For a time we stood with them.
Very simply, like John the Baptist,
they said to us, 'Look, there is the one you should follow,'
and hearing this we followed that person.

Lord, there are many people
who want to do great things for you,
to excel in mighty deeds that will win them glory.
But from time to time someone comes into our lives
and just by looking at them we can say,
'Look, there is a lamb of God,'
someone who is willing to do the humble things,
to be patient and to endure.
That is Jesus passing by.

*'It is time to realise that neither socialism nor good-neighbourism nor
respect can be produced by bayonets, tanks or blood.'*
Edward Shevardnadze
Lord, we pray for leaders.
So often they think they can win our allegiance
with threats or great promises and propaganda.
Sometimes even church leaders think like that.
Teach them that to win people's trust is a deep process.
They cannot force it on us.
We must start following them ourselves
and only then should they ask 'What do you want?'
They will always find that what we want to know
is how they are in the truth and honesty of their homes.
They must come straight with us, invite us to come and see,
and then be willing to have us stay with them.
Only after that will we be able to say,
'Yes, we have found our Leader.'

'Often I go off in dreams about living and being with the poor; what the poor need, however, is not my dreams but my concrete presence.'
Jean Vanier

Lord, we are like Jesus only when we turn to those following us
and invite them to come and see where we live
and then let them stay with us the rest of the day.

Lord, forgive us for allowing all transactions
to become occasions for making money,
even such deeply human encounters as healing a sick person.,
counselling those in distress,
or protecting the rights of the oppressed.
These meetings should be like what happens
between Jesus and his first disciples –
human beings going to visit a leader
and spending a day with him
and then saying to their friends,
'We have found someone who can save us.'

Lord, like many other societies around the world,
we have a tendency to categorise people.
We characterise whole groups as lazy,
or incompetent, or dishonest
because they belong to a particular ethnic group;
or because they attend a certain kind of school;
or because they live in a particular part of the city.
Send us people like Jesus who will look deeply at others,
dispelling all prejudices,
and will say to them: 'Society has called you by one name;
from now on you shall be known as free and creative people.'

Third Sunday in Ordinary Time

Gospel Reading: Mark 1:14-20

14*After John had been arrested, Jesus went into Galilee. There he proclaimed the Good News from God.* 15*'The time has come,' he said, 'and the kingdom of God is close at hand. Repent, and believe the Good News.'* 16*As he was walking along by the Sea of Galilee he saw Simon and his brother Andrew casting a net in the lake – for they were fishermen.* 17*And Jesus said to them, 'Follow me and I will make you fishers of men.'* 18*And at once they left their nets and followed him.* 19*Going on a little further, he saw James son of Zebedee and his brother John; they too were in their boat, mending their nets. He called them at once* 20*and, leaving their father Zebedee in the boat with the men he employed, they went after him.*

On this Sunday, we begin the continuous reading of St Mark's gospel, which will be interrupted during Lent and Easter but will eventually take us to the arrival of Jesus in Jerusalem in November of this year.

The journey begins in Galilee, the northernmost province of Palestine. This is where Jesus lays the foundation for his work of salvation. You might like to stay with this context of the passage – the humble beginnings (even in relationship with the rest of Palestine, Galilee is on the periphery) of what was to become a mighty work which has still not been completed.

The passage is in two sections:
- verses 14-15: a summary of the preaching of Jesus;
- verses 16-20: the call of the first disciples.

The first section is short, but every word is precious. Stay with the context of 'after John had been arrested,' remembering the enormous impact that the Baptist had made on the whole country, and gauging from that the traumatic effect of his arrest. Yet, what seemed to be the end of a movement was the beginning of something new.

Take 'the kingdom of heaven' in a down-to-earth way, as an expression meaning the kind of society which would correspond to what God wants. 'Is at hand' means that it is within our grasp.

The second section may seem artificial at a first reading, but it is the classical story of the moment of grace, sudden and yet totally natural in the sense that it seems to happen so easily, like a ripe fruit falls in our hand.

The two calls are clearly meant to be similar – St Mark is telling us that this is how a call always works out.

* * *

Lord, we thank you for the changes
that have taken place in Eastern Europe.
They happened so suddenly and unexpectedly –
yet it is always how moments of grace happen.
Like when John the Baptist was arrested
and it seemed that the movement of religious renewal
in the country had been blocked,
but that was the occasion for Jesus to go into Galilee
and proclaim the Good News from God.
So it was in those European countries.
People just knew that a new era was at hand,
they must change their ways of thinking and acting,
and trust that something great and wonderful
was in store for them. Thank you, Lord.

'Some would consider our hopes utopian. It may be that these persons are not realistic enough, and that they have not perceived the dynamism of a world which desires to live more fraternally.'
Pope Paul VI, *Populorum Progressio*
Lord, the role of the church
is to preach the good news of God to the world,
and the good news is that
the kingdom of heaven is within our reach,
if only we repent and believe that it is possible.
Lord, we pray for all the preachers of the gospel,
especially those who give homilies at Sunday services.
Teach them not to be abstract in their preaching,
but to proclaim the Good News of God as Jesus did –
as new possibilities which are at hand.
They must of course preach repentance –
but not as an imposition from outside;
rather, as good news within ourselves,
good news which we can trust.

*'To destroy human power nothing more is required than to be indiffer-
ent to its threats and to prefer other goods to those which it promises.
Nothing less, however, is required also.'* R. H. Tawney

Lord, your Son Jesus knew how to break the power of evil.
When John was arrested,
he went into Galilee and preached the good news
that the kingdom of heaven was at hand.

Lord, in the modern world
we are accustomed to calculate things
before coming to decisions.
We have feasibility studies, computer printouts and charts.
Eventually we think
that personal relationships can be planned too,
like choosing a marriage partner or a friend,
picking those we want to work with us on a project.
But we cannot plan those decisions.
These things work by a kind of instinct,
like Jesus walking along the Sea of Galilee
and seeing two fishermen casting a net in the lake
and then saying to them, 'Follow me'
and they left their nets and followed him.

Lord, when we want to start some work,
we like to start with the spectacular.
Teach us the way of Jesus, that when the time for action comes
we should go to the periphery of life
and choose a few companions,
letting the kingdom grow from there.

Fourth Sunday in Ordinary Time

Gospel Reading: Mark 1:21-28

21In the city of Capernaum, on a sabbath, Jesus went to the synagogue and began to teach. 22And his teaching made a great impression on them, because, unlike the scribes, he taught them with authority. 23In their synagogue just then there was a man possessed by an unclean spirit, and it shouted, 24'What do you want with us, Jesus of Nazareth? Have you come to destroy us? I know who you are, the Holy One of God.' 25But Jesus rebuked him, saying, 'Be silent and come out of him! 26And the unclean spirit, convulsing him and crying with a loud voice, came out of him. 27They were all amazed, and they kept on asking one another, 'What is this? A new teaching – with authority! He commands even the unclean spirits, and they obey him.' 28At once his fame began to spread throughout the surrounging region of Galilee.

As we go on with our continuous reading of St Mark's gospel, we find Jesus in Galilee where he starts his public ministry. This passage is in three parts:

- verses 21-22: a summary of the teaching of Jesus in the synagogue;
- verses 23-27: an example of his ministry of driving out unclean spirits;
- verse 28: the effect of Jesus' ministry.

In the first section, the emphasis is on the contrast between Jesus and the scribes. Here the scribes are symbolical of those who are content to record the teachings of others; Jesus speaks with personal authority.

In verse 28 St Mark evokes, as he often does in his gospel, the spread of Jesus' reputation. Ask yourself how the passage is being fulfilled today, of the church or of any great movement.

* * *

Lord, when we look back on our lives
we realise that most of those
who gave us moral teachings spoke platitudes.
They were scribes recording what others had said.
But we thank you that from time to time

you sent us someone like Jesus
who spoke from their own experience,
and shared honestly what they were feeling;
these made a deep impression on us,
because unlike scribes they spoke with authority.

*'When the church concerns herself with the development of peoples, she
cannot be accused of going outside her own specific field of competence,
and still less outside the mandate received from the Lord.'* Pope John
Paul II, *Sollicitudo Rei Socialis*
Lord, when the church confines herself
to going to the synagogue and teaching,
concerning herself with what is internal to her, many are happy
they rejoice that she is making a deep impression on them.
But your will is that we should go further
and cast out the demons of our society –
racism, class conflicts,
discrimination against the disadvantaged.
When the church does this there are convulsions and loud cries.
We thank you that in many countries
the church has persevered in following Jesus,
and people have been astonished and questioned themselves,
and her reputation has spread
as one who gives orders to unclean spirits and they obey her.

Lord, we remember a time
when we were held in bondage by an inner force:
   - we could not forgive;
   - we did not want to commit ourselves because we were
   afraid of failure;
   - ambition was clouding our vision of the truth.
Then someone began to speak, challenging us to face the truth
   - one of our children, a friend, a bible passage.
We got angry, denied it vehemently, wept, complained to another.
Like the man in the gospel,
we went into convulsions and cried aloud.
We realise now that it was because we knew
that the Holy One of God was with us,
he had come to do away with our sin.

Eventually, after a long struggle,
we recognised the demon for what it was,
and it went out of us.
Thank you, Lord.

*'I can only reach that depth in my neighbour that I can reach in my
own spirit.'* Mathew Kelly, Cistercian monk
Lord, our teaching will be new and will have authority behind it
only if we have accepted its authority within our own selves.

*'Once brought into the light of mutual love, demons lose their power
and quietly leave us.'* Henry Nowen
Lord, we thank you
for the times when we have been able to share deeply
with a friend
and something that was holding back
our spiritual growth left us.
We knew that Jesus of Nazareth was with us.

Lord, prayer is a moment when we pass
from experiencing the teaching of Jesus as something vague
to knowing that it has authority behind it,
it gives orders even to unclean spirits and they obey it.

Lord, a movement will spread
only if it moves from teaching in a closed room
to casting out the unclean spirits which are oppressing society.

Fifth Sunday in Ordinary Time

Gospel Reading: Mark 1:29-39

²⁹On leaving the synagogue, Jesus went with James and John straight to the house of Simon and Andrew. ³⁰Now Simon's mother-in-law had gone to bed with fever, and they told him about her straight-away. ³¹He went to her, took her by the hand and helped her up. And the fever left her and she began to wait on them.

³²That evening, after sunset, they brought to him all who were sick and those who were possessed by devils. ³³The whole town came crowding round the door, ³⁴and he cured many who were suffering from diseases of one kind or another; he also cast out many devils, but he would not allow them to speak, because they knew who he was.

³⁵In the morning, long before dawn, he got up and left the house, and went off to a lonely place and prayed there. ³⁶Simon and his companions set out in search of him, ³⁷and when they found him they said, 'Everybody is looking for you.' ³⁸He answered, 'Let us go elsewhere, to the neighbouring towns, so that I can preach there too, because that is why I came.' 39 And he went all through Galilee, preaching in their synagogues and casting out devils.

Today's gospel passage is in three sections:
- verses 29-31: Jesus heals Peter's mother-in-law;
- verses 32-34: a general statement on Jesus' ministry of healing;
- verses 35-39: Jesus chooses to expand his ministry to neighbouring towns.

We can take one section at a time, on its own; or we can try to discern a movement flowing through the entire passage – this is the approach I propose. The passage then reveals a new dimension of Jesus' ministry, the general outlines of which are drawn in these first Sundays of Ordinary time.

On the Third Sunday, Jesus announced the overall goal of his ministry – the kingdom of God. The Fourth Sunday (Mark 1:21-28) showed that his ministry is a ministry of casting out unclean spirits with authority. On this Fifth Sunday, we get the further insight that Jesus will always be restless, he will never 'have somewhere where he can lay his head.' He will always be on the lookout for new areas where his gospel needs to be preached.

This has also been the mark of Jesus' followers. In every age and culture, the church has had its 'missionaries', men and women of generous spirit, happy and successful where they were, who realised that the gospel was not being preached among cultures, ethnic groups or social classes which were neglected by society and by the church. They stepped out courageously and moved into these 'neighbouring country towns' so that the gospel of God's love could be 'preached there too'.

Paul and Barnabas were the first. They left the prosperous community of Antioch to bring the good news to the Greek cities of Asia Minor. One thousand years later, St Francis of Assisi turned his back on his noble and wealthy family and lived as a brother among the poorest people of his area. In our time, Mother Teresa, comfortable and successful in a well established religious order, decided to move out and found a new community entirely dedicated to the dying on the streets of Calcutta.

In the secular world too, all great people come to the time when they must step out into an area their movement has neglected up to now. Nelson Mandela, for example, decided at some point in his life that he would work for reconciliation with his oppressors. People have given up successful careers in law, medicine, finance, education or management to work for the advancement of neglected communities.

It happens to all of us, at one time or another, that we find the courage to break new ground, to be reconciled with someone who had hurt our family, to move into some field where our services are needed. This passage celebrates such moments of grace – in the life of Jesus and in our lives.

In recent years, our church has often made similar moves in many countries. It has given up its prestige and influence, risked loosing the patronage of the wealthy and the powerful, and stood at the side of the oppressed, 'preaching there too'.

It would be good to spend some time with the expression 'because that is why I came'. Like so many phrases in the Bible, it is brief and seemingly simple, but it can transform our consciousness radically. When the church neglects the marginalised it is always because it has forgotten the reason 'why it came'.

The gospel passage reminds us that we will not take bold new decisions unless we are inwardly free, as Jesus was. It also teaches us the secret of his inner freedom – his regular, deep, personal prayer, the fact that he would 'leave the house and go off to a lonely place to pray there' – another haunting little phrase.

* * *

Lord, answering your call is often difficult.
Sometimes we are discouraged by our failures,
but at other times it is success that prevents us.
Like Jesus, we must go against those who admire us
and the work we are doing.
They want us to continue where we are,
they remind us of the good we do for people,
as friends, teachers, doctors, nurses or counsellors,
how we take them by the hand and help them,
so that the fever leaves them and they can wait on us.
They point out the people bringing to us all who are sick,
and those who are possessed by devils,
so that it feels as if the whole town is there
crowding round the door or our house.
We ourselves are pained to leave the many who are suffering
from diseases of one kind or another,
or who need devils to be cast out.
Teach us to follow the example of Jesus;
remind us that if we want to do your will
we must learn to get up in the morning, long before dawn,
and leave our house to go off to a lonely place and pray there,
so that when others come in search of us saying,
'Everybody is looking for you,'
like Jesus, we will be free enough to choose
what we know is right for us.
We will go to neighbouring regions where no one else has gone,
relate to those we have been keeping at arm's length,
so that we can bring the good news of your love there too,
remembering that this is why we have come into the world.

Lord, forgive us, your church, that we have become complacent,
that we are content to congratulate ourselves
at whole towns crowding round our doors.

We pray that we will never lose the missionary spirit of Jesus,
so that, just as he went through all Galilee,
the church too will go through all areas of society
and all cultures,
preaching your love wherever people are gathered,
and casting out every kind of evil spirit.

Sixth Sunday in Ordinary time

Gospel Reading: Mark 1:40-45

40A leper came to Jesus and pleaded on his knees: 'If you want to,' he said, 'you can cure me.' 41Feeling sorry for him, Jesus stretched out his hand and touched him. 'Of course I want to!' he said. 'Be cured!' 42And the leprosy left him at once and he was cured. 43Jesus immediately sent him away and sternly ordered him, 44'Mind you say nothing to anyone, but go and show yourself to the priest, and make the offering for your healing prescribed by Moses as evidence of your recovery.' 45The man went away, but then started talking about it freely and telling the story everywhere, so that Jesus could no longer go openly into any town, but had to stay outside in places where nobody lived. Even so, people from all around would come to him.

Today's passage is in three sections:
- verses 40-41: Jesus heals a leper;
- verses 42-45a: Jesus protects his identity;
- verse 45b: the people still come to him.

As with last week's passage, we are free to focus on one section alone or to see the three sections as a unit, one moving into the other.

1. The healing of lepers is a feature of Jesus' ministry – appropriately, since leprosy is a powerful symbol of the alienation which he came to free humanity from. In meditating on this passage, we are free to identify the particular form of leprosy we have experienced. We will then become freer to decide for ourselves who we want to identify with:
- the leper, the one who has been healed from uncleanness;
- Jesus, the one who brings the marginalised into the community.

The story is told imaginatively and every detail can touch us:
- the helplessness of the leper, 'pleading on his knees';
- the pathetic 'if you want to' – the leper dares not put too much hope even in the one he knows can cure him;
- the immediate healing once he is touched.

Then there is the greatness of Jesus
- entering into the pain of the man ('feeling sorry for him,' as

the Jerusalem Bible translation has it, does not convey the compassion for the man that Jesus feels in his heart);

- Jesus 'stretching out' his hand, indicating that he must reach far out from where he is at present in order to meet the leper where he is;

- once the man has been touched the healing is immediate.

2. This section introduces the theme of what scholars have termed 'the messianic secret' – Jesus' vain attempt to conceal his identity until the time is ripe. This messianic secret is related in all three synoptic gospels, but it is stressed most strongly in St Mark. Scholars have done extensive research to determine what was Jesus' motive for insisting on the messianic secret. In *lectio divina,* however, our approach is to start from our human experience. We ask ourselves questions like:

- what in our experience corresponds to the messianic secret?

- what does our experience teach us about why Jesus insisted on the messianic secret?

- how does the concept of the messianic secret help us to understand ourselves and the way we must live out our vocation in the world?

This approach from experience reveals that all of us human beings have to work out for ourselves what is our God-given mission in the world, what we have to offer others that no one can do in our name. Like Jesus, we will find that we must struggle to preserve our 'messianic secret'. We do not allow others to define our mission to them.

Our passage, if taken as a unit, brings out that those whom we have helped and who admire us are among the 'others' we must resist. Our success with them can be an obstacle to our remaining faithful to our personal vision. They remind us that we have touched them but we learn from gospel passages like this one that it was a painful struggle for Jesus, as it is for us.

3. Leaders who speak from their inner truth are very precious. Nowadays many leaders are content to make conventional statements – 'this is what I am about'. What St Mark says of Jesus will be true of all those to whom we relate – we may be unpopular to them; it will seem very hard for them to reach us. These things don't matter, however, – 'even so, people from all around will come to us.'

This must also be what attracts people to the church. It is not our business to make ourselves attractive. All the church's efforts must be devoted to being true to its vision. Often in history, the church has gone along with the values of the world. There were times when we accepted slavery, supported the imperialist ideology of the colonial powers, allowed ourselves to be protected by the armies of states.

We thank God that in many parts of the world, in recent centuries, the church has learned to keep its distance from these popular sayings – like Jesus we must learn to 'stay outside where nobody lives.'

* * *

'People are made people through other people.' African proverb
Lord, we remember a time when we felt unclean:
    - we were ashamed of our sexuality;
    - we did something which made us want to hide ourselves;
    - we let down our fellow workers or our team;
    - we deceived someone who trusted us;
    - we betrayed the ideals of a social movement we belonged to.
Like the lepers in Jesus' day,
    - we felt isolated, unclean, with no sense of self-worth;
    - we didn't want to mix with friends or family.
Then one day we felt able to come to someone
who we felt could bring us healing:
one of our parents, a friend or neighbour,
a priest or other member of our church community.
We remember how we felt at that moment,
pleading on our knees, not literally perhaps,
but our body language showed
how nervous and insecure we were – like the leper –
hopeful and yet so unsure of ourselves
that even though we trusted the person,
something within us still whispered, 'If you want to ...'
We thank you for the compassion of that Jesus person,
laughing off our doubts and saying, 'Of course I want to!'
stretching out a hand across the wide expanse
which separated us,
so that we felt touched and held.

There was no more to say then,
the warmth in that touch said, 'Be cured!'
and at once we were cured of our feelings of uncleanness,
and we felt able to show ourselves to the community.

Lord, we think today of societies torn apart by ancient feuds,
so that the different communities look on each other as lepers:
- dissenters and those who accept the status quo in the
United States and other prosperous countries
-Israelis and Arabs in the Holy Land
- Tamils and Sinhalese in Sri Lanka
- warring factions in the Republic of the Congo.
We thank you for sending them people like Jesus
who recognise in those of the opposing side
human beings who beneath their hostility
are really pleading to be accepted
and to belong to the wider community.
Like Jesus with the leper,
they assure these others
that they want to work together with them,
they are anxious to stretch out their hands
across the centuries of violence and deeply entrenched barriers.
They touch them, and it seems that in an instant
resentment, suspicion, inability to forgive
and to trust are overcome.

*'To have convincing authority we must share the journeys of people,
enter their fears, be touched by their disappointments, their questions,
their failures, their doubts.'*
Timothy Radcliffe, former Master General of the Dominicans
Lord, as a church
in the various communities that make up our state,
we want to care for those who are neglected by the majority
- those who are divorced and remarried;
- members of the gay community;
- those who belong to a lower class than ourselves;
- members of a different culture or sub-culture.

Forgive us for wanting to care for them
while standing aloof and feeling superior,
so that we become angry when people are suspicious of us
and wonder whether we really want to cure them.
We pray that our church may have Jesus' generosity of spirit
which will allow us to understand
how leprosy breeds suspicion,
so that we will brush away their doubts
and stretch our hands as far as we need to,
until we can touch their pain
and they will feel part of our community.

Lord, it is a long and painful struggle
to remain true to ourselves,
and we thank you that your Son Jesus
underwent that struggle with us.
On the cross he remained faithful
while the chief priests and elders taunted him,
at other times too, he had to keep his distance
from those who admired him,
talked freely about his great deeds
and told his story everywhere.
We pray that we may be stern like him
in being faithful to our personal goals,
like him refuse to go openly into any town
and spend long periods in places where nobody lives.
Even so, people from all around will come to us,
and we will then be able to relate with them
from the truth of ourselves.

'When you become important, it is easy to fall from a true prophet into a false one.' Jean Vanier
Lord, forgive us, your church,
for the times when we have allowed ourselves
to be defined by those whom we have helped:
   - the graduates of our schools;
   - those who have been cured at our hospitals;
   - the conquistadors and colonial governors with whom we
   collaborated.

Forgive us for feeling proud
when they started talking about us freely
and telling the story everywhere.
We thank you that in many countries of the world,
your church took the decision to follow in the footsteps of Jesus
and reach out to those whom society treats as lepers,
even though this meant becoming isolated,
no longer going openly into any town,
staying outside where nobody lived.
A strange thing happened –
even so, people from all around kept coming to her!

Seventh Sunday in Ordinary Time

Gospel Reading: Mark 2:1-12

¹*When Jesus returned to Capernaum some time later, word went round that he was back;* ²*and so many people collected that there was no room left, even in front of the door. He was preaching the word to them* ³*when some people came bringing him a paralytic carried by four men,* ⁴*but as the crowd made it impossible to get the man to him, they stripped the roof over the place where Jesus was; and when they had made an opening, they lowered the stretcher on which the paralytic lay.* ⁵*Seeing their faith, Jesus said to the paralytic, 'My child, your sins are forgiven.'* ⁶*Now some scribes were sitting there, and they thought to themselves,* ⁷*'How can this man talk like this? He is blaspheming. Who can forgive sins but God?'* ⁸*Jesus, inwardly aware that this was what they were thinking, said to them, 'Why do you have these thoughts in your hearts?* ⁹*Which of these is easier: to say to the paralytic, 'Your sins are forgiven' or to say, 'Get up, pick up your stretcher and walk'?* ¹⁰*But to prove to you that the Son of Man has authority on earth to forgive sins,' –* ¹¹*he said to the paralytic – 'I order you: get up, pick up your stretcher, and go off home.'* ¹²*And the man got up, picked up his stretcher at once and walked out in front of everyone, so that they were all astounded and praised God saying, 'We have never seen anything like this.'*

Today's passage is complex. Scholars have analysed it and shown that the passage is an interweaving of several stories, each with its own theme.

We can see three themes running through it:

a) the healing of the paralytic;

b) the forgiveness of sins;

c) the controversy with the scribes.

We can remain with one theme, or meditate on them as a unit, each theme flowing into the next.

The following division can be helpful in identifying the different strands in the passage:

a) verses 1-2 : the setting;

b) verses 3-4 : the paralytic makes his appearance;

c) verses 5-11: dialogue:

d) verse 12 : the result.

The healing of the paralytic is a tremendous story with many lessons about how we are called to respond to the vagaries of our daily lives.

As in all the healing stories, we are free to focus either on the one who was healed, or on Jesus the healer. If we are identifying with the paralytic, we make the journey with him in three stages, at each stage allowing the imaginative language to bring back memories which touch us. We can also identify with Jesus, the healer.

We are 'carried on a stretcher by friends', people of faith who 'lower us from the roof' to the presence of the healer. In last week's story, the leper symbolised the experience of feeling unclean, unworthy to associate with the community we belong to. The paralysed man symbolises a different experience, when we feel helpless, we cannot 'walk on our own', take charge of our lives, make decisions, take initiatives, respond creatively to the challenges of life. As a result of Jesus' ministry, we are able 'to stand up in front of the crowd' and to 'go off home'.

We celebrate the wonderful moment when we are healed from our paralysis – we 'get up, pick up our stretcher' and 'walk out in front of everyone', so that 'they are all astounded.'

We start from the experience of 'paralysis' resulting from failure of one kind or another. Jesus healed a variety of ailments and it is good to make a distinction between the different ailments, allowing each one to symbolise a particular form of human suffering. We think of various ailments such as suffering from some form of sickness; feeling that we don't have enough confidence to speak out for ourselves; feeling that we have failed in some aspect of our lives and therefore cannot affirm our independence.

We celebrate parents, teachers, counsellors, friends, whose tender compassion ('my child') has empowered us when we felt paralysed.

The issue of Jesus and the scribes is in two parts:

(a) verses 6 and 7

(b) Jesus responds, verses 8 to 10.

Here again the story is told in stages. Jesus discerns the root cause of the paralysis – sins have not been forgiven. How often our paralysis is due to the fact that we haven't experienced ourselves as forgiven – by ourselves, by those we love – those our modern language calls 'significant others', or then by God.

Few people have the wisdom to discern the root problem which keeps us paralysed. Once we hear those wonderful healing words, 'My child, your sins are forgiven,' 'at once' we are healed of the paralysis. We can identify with the amazement of the crowd as they see the healing power of forgiveness.

As often happens in the gospels, the teaching is in the form of a controversy. Jesus and the scribes represent two possible ways of dealing with the situation. We have followed both ways at different times; often they are two tendencies struggling for power within ourselves.

We can interpret 'Son of Man' in two senses.

a) He is one person, the Messiah, Jesus, and by extension his Body, the church. The passage then celebrates the church's ministry of forgiving sins, through the sacraments, counselling, spiritual direction, or (as has happened from time to time in recent years) by being an agent of reconciliation between warring factions in a community. Jesus asserts his power against the scribes who are sceptical about it.

b) It has a collective sense – weak human beings. The scribes then are ourselves when we doubt the power of individuals or communities to break down barriers and forgive. The response of Jesus is our personal response – we know we can do it.

Verse 10 is difficult to interpret. It is first of all a sign that the different themes mentioned above have not been neatly meshed. It is not necessary to know the exact meaning of the verse; getting the general movement of thought is sufficient.

* * *

'Always try to do too much, dispense with safety nets, aim for the stars.' Salman Rushdie

Lord, we remember a time when we felt paralysed
and had to be carried on a stretcher:
- we had failed in an enterprise we had set our hearts on;
- we were let down by someone we trusted;
- we had committed a sin we never thought we would fall into;
- our prayer life had become dry.

We thank you for loyal friends
who, like the four men
who stripped the roof over the place where Jesus was,
went to considerable trouble
to bring us before the one who could heal us.
They made an appointment for us,
insisted on getting us in ahead of others,
fitted us into a crowded schedule.
We thank you for the Jesus they brought us to,
who understood that we had allowed our sins to paralyse us
    - the foolish decisions we had taken;
    - our arrogance;
    - the secret addictions we had not attended to.
We heard ourselves being called 'beloved child',
we were told that our sins were forgiven,
that we must pull ourselves together and make a new start.
The words had an instant effect –
we got up, picked up our stretcher
and walked out in front of everyone,
so that they were all astounded
and praised you, saying 'We have never seen anything like this.'

Lord, we thank you for the ministry of forgiveness
exercised by the ministers of your church,
    - through the sacrament of reconciliation,
    - counselling sessions in presbyteries;
    - mediation in social conflicts.
We celebrate the countless paralytics
– individuals, couples, communities -
who were brought by friends to hear the healing words,
'My child, your sins are forgiven,'
and then picked themselves up
and walked out in front of everyone.
They thought to themselves
that no one on earth had the authority
to tell them that their sins were forgiven;
now they are astounded and praise you, saying
'We have never seen anything like this.'

'Able to approach the future as a friend without a wardrobe of excuses.'
W. H. Auden
Lord, we thank you for the times
when you send people to confound the scepticism
which prevents us from seeing the potential
within ourselves and our communities.
So often, like the scribes in the time of Jesus,
we remain locked in the past,
thinking that only some miraculous intervention
can raise us up from our paralysis,
and that we would be blaspheming
if we were to say that our sins can be forgiven.
Then you send us someone like Jesus
who is inwardly aware of how we are thinking
and has the moral authority to order us
to 'get up, pick up your stretcher and go off home.'

'Hope for a great sea-change
On the far side of revenge.' Seamus Heaney
Lord, we pray today for societies that are paralysed
because warring factions cannot forgive the sins of the past:
    - Black and White in the US
    - Arabs and Israelis
    - Tamils and Sinhalese in Sri Lanka.
There are sceptics sitting among them,
like the scribes in the time of Jesus,
doubting in their hearts
that you have given your human sons and daughters
the authority on earth to forgive sins.
Send them leaders like Jesus who are inwardly aware
that many have these thoughts in their hearts,
but see the faith of those who are looking for a new future
and pronounce the words
that all the ancient sins have been forgiven,
command the former enemies
to throw away the symbols of their past paralysis,
and go off to make their country a home for all,
so that all will be astounded and say,
'We never thought we would see anything like this.'

Eighth Sunday in Ordinary Time

Gospel Reading: Mark 2:18-22

18*One day when John's disciples and the Pharisees were fasting, some people came and said to Jesus, 'Why is it that John's disciples and the disciples of the Pharisees fast, but your disciples do not?'* 19*Jesus replied, 'Surely the bridegroom's attendants would never think of fasting while the bridegroom is still with them? As long as they have the bridegroom with them, they could not think of fasting.* 20*But the time will come for the bridegroom to be taken away from them, and then, on that day, they will fast.* 21*No one sews a piece of unshrunken cloth on an old cloak; if he does, the patch pulls away from it, the new from the old, and the tear gets worse.* 22*And nobody puts new wine into old wineskins; if he does, the wine will burst the skins, and the wine is lost and the skins too. No! New wine, fresh skins!'*

Today's passage teaches us an important lesson about our relationship with God – it must be rooted in experience, the joy of knowing that we are loved unconditionally. Without this experience, religion becomes joyless, and fussy, even cruel – a matter of keeping laws. This is true not only of religion but of all our deep relationships with other people or with a cause to which we have given our lives. The story of Jesus is a living lesson of this truth, and nowhere more clearly than in today's passage – this is why it is found in all the synoptics.

A lot of the above thoughts come home to us as we think about the situation in the world today. We have our own threats of war, and of unimpeded authority. These exist not merely in Iraq but also in the former Yugoslavia, in the Basque Countries, Israel/Palestine, in the former republic of the Congo, in Sudan, in Sri Lanka and India/Pakistan.

The passage is in two sections:

- verses 18-20: a controversy between Jesus' disciples on the one hand and the Pharisees and John's disciples on the other;

- verses 21-22: two parables taken from everyday events.

The first controversy has two protagonists whom we can recognise from experience.

1. Jesus is the wise and compassionate leader. He is able to keep the balance between

- experience, the time of celebration, a wedding feast (a celebration of love) when the attendants 'have the bridegroom with them';
- rules and discipline (fasting), appropriate for the time when 'the bridegroom is taken away.'

He is also the kind of leader who knows he can trust his followers to find out for themselves when 'the time of fasting' has come.

We remember times when people in bondage tried to fit our free spirits into their narrow categories. We have all done this,

- as parents, denying to our children opportunities that we ourselves enjoyed;
- as leaders of communities (including religious communities);
- as teachers, spiritual guides, friends.

2. John's disciples and the Pharisees. In Mark's version, by the way, it is not merely the Pharisees themselves who complain but 'some people' who share their narrow-mindedness. Their religion knows nothing of experience, they only know about discipline. As a result, they are narrow-minded, resentful and bitter.

We can see these complainers as people who have become stuck in their ways. We can see them as people who have stayed with positions which we ourselves have long abandoned.

It is better, however, to see them as representing a stage we all go through. The passage then traces our spiritual journey to maturity. We start off in bondage, making discipline an end in itself; we become resentful of those who are having a good time. One day, Jesus calls us to freedom; we learn how to enjoy our relationship with God, fully aware that another time will come later on when 'the bridegroom will be taken away'. The journey is ongoing. We constantly fall back into the bondage stage and God must always be sending us Jesus to call us back to freedom. We must feel some compassion for the complainers; we have been there, and there is still something of them in us.

Verses 21 and 22 can be read on their own or as an application of the teaching in the previous verses. They refer to two everyday incidents: patching a cloak, and putting new wine into new wineskins.

Here again, the two metaphors are both in story form and we

must enter into their movement, feeling the pain of those who do not follow the story and, on the other hand, the joy of those who do. Our church as a whole has had to make this journey. We have been part of that journey ourselves. We too want to put on a new patch and graft it onto the old, have tried to patch a cloak by adding some old cloth or to put new wine into old wineskins. Leaders of social movements commit this fault too when they lose the enthusiasm of their first conversion; they become self-important, suspicious and authoritarian towards those they are in charge of. We feel the pain and hurt of 'both new and old being spoilt'. The narrow-minded suffer from what is said to them and so do the free spirits who are now being held back.

* * *

'All I have written is as straw compared to what I have seen.'
St Thomas Aquinas
Lord, we thank you for moments of grace
    - when, in prayer, your presence is very real, almost tangible;
    - when we and our spouse or a friend feel at one with each other;
    - when we experience harmony in the workplace or at home;
    - when everything comes together in our team;
    - when a project on which we have worked hard eventually starts working;
    - when our party gains a resounding victory at the polls.
At such times, we do the right thing spontaneously
without anybody telling us what to do,
without having to make an effort, without needing rules.
It is like being at a wedding feast,
with bride and groom going around to all the guests,
the music playing and everyone having a good time
being free and spontaneous.
We thank you for wise people like Jesus
– parents, priests and religious, friends, employers
    - who encourage us to enjoy these good times,
    - who don't spoil things by reminding us that the euphoria will not last.
They know and we know

that a time will come when the feast will be over,
bride and groom will take off for their home
and we will have to get back to rules and discipline.

'When you don't know what to do, have a party.'
Jim Wallis, Christian campaigner for non-violence in the US
Lord, you often send us free-spirited people,
in our church communities, neighbourhoods,
and within our families.
They ignore the rules but seem very happy and fulfilled
and attract many people,
while we who have kept rules don't enjoy ourselves as they do.
We are resentful, like John's disciples, the Pharisees
and those who accompanied them
when they complained to Jesus about his disciples not fasting.
Send us wise and compassionate teachers like Jesus
who will help us to understand
that we have forgotten the purpose of rules,
and will invite us to celebrate
the beautiful relationships we have
and remember the times when life was
like a great wedding feast.

'We are so busy doing things for God that we don't have any time for God.' Michael Hollings
Lord, you know how easy it is for us to get our priorities wrong,
in our families, church communities,
neighbourhoods, schools, workplaces:
  - we focus so much on good order that people don't feel at
    home with us;
  - work becomes an end in itself rather than a way to achieve
    wellbeing;
  - spontaneity is stifled by rules.
Send us Jesus who will show us that the most effective way
of ensuring the right balance is to have moments of feasting,
and when these are finished, then we will have our rules.

'Some men look at the world as it is and ask, 'Why?' Others dream of
worlds that have never been thought of and ask, 'Why not?''
George Bernard Shaw

Lord, there are always those among us
who do things differently,
work out new solutions, dream new dreams,
put forward possibilities that we never thought of.
Forgive us that as a church, as parents, or teachers,
we try to fit them into our categories
> - like unshrunken cloth on an old cloak which pulls away
> the new from the old, so that the tear gets worse;
> - or like new wine into old wineskins which bursts the skins
> and the wine is lost and the skins too.

Send us wise teachers like Jesus who will remind us
that a cloak must be patched with new cloth
and new wine is for new wineskins.

Lord, forgive us that like the Pharisees and John's disciples
we have allowed your joyful world to become a sad place
where only those who work hard and produce are honoured,
and everybody must conform to the norms and be respectable,
with little room for spontaneity.
Social movements we embraced with enthusiasm
in time have been corrupted by ambition, anger and violence.
The glorious message of Jesus
we have turned into a joyless list of do's and don'ts.
In our church we have become suspicious of one another
and of the world,
and especially of those we see enjoying themselves.
Forgive us especially for bringing up young people into our ways,
projecting our fears onto them,
patching a cloak with old cloth and putting into old wineskins
this sparkling new wine you have given us.
We pray that our church will be a place of freedom and festivity,
a great wedding feast,
where fasting is a temporary exercise that keeps us awake
as we await the joyful return of the bridegroom.

Ninth Sunday in Ordinary Time

Gospel Reading: Mark 2:23-3:1-6

23One Sabbath day Jesus happened to be taking a walk through the cornfields, and his disciples began to pick ears of corn as they went along. 24And the Pharisees said to him, 'Look, why are they doing something on the Sabbath day that is forbidden?' 25And he replied, 'Did you never read what David did in his time of need when he and his followers were hungry – 26how he went into the house of God when Abiathar was high priest, and ate the loaves of offering which only the priests are allowed to eat, and how he also gave some to the men with him?' 27And he said to them, 'The Sabbath was made for man, not man for the Sabbath; 28so the Son of Man is master even of the Sabbath.'
1He went again into a synagogue, and there was a man there who had a withered hand. 2And they were watching him to see if he would cure him on the Sabbath day, hoping for something to use against him. 3He said to the man with the withered hand, 'Stand up out in the middle!' 4Then he said to them, 'Is it against the law on the Sabbath day to do good, or to do evil; to save life, or to kill?' But they said nothing. 5Then, grieved to find them so obstinate, he looked angrily round at them and said to the man, 'Stretch out your hand.' He stretched it out and his hand was better. 6The Pharisees went out and at once began to plot with the Herodians against him, discussing how to destroy him.

This reading is a teaching on the sabbath – one of the crucial issues faced by Jesus in his ministry, and one that is still crucial today. To see the relevance of the passage, we need to understand the sabbath as a symbol – like fasting in last Sunday's passage. In Jesus' time, the sabbath symbolised the complex network of laws which governed the Jewish religion. In our day it symbolises the many 'laws' that tyrannise us – the market, fashion, success, popularity, respectability, social roles, and so forth. Laws can also be a bondage in our church when we allow them to become inflexible.

Laws can become tyrannical in two ways. They can be more important than relationships – this is the problem addressed in last Sunday's passage. This Sunday the focus is different – a law which serves the interests of the rich and powerful and works against the poor. The passage teaches this lesson through two stories.

Many people have difficulties with this passage because in it we are told that Jesus 'looked angrily at them'. There are two issues involved here: a) the method, and b) the content of this particular passage.

Let us look at method first. As always, we come back to the basic point – what kind of teaching is the Bible? It is not an abstract text book, teaching through logical, precise definitions which can be 'defended' against objections. It is a collection of sacred stories which we are invited to enter into. By doing so we discover the truth – about ourselves, about life, about God.

Naturally, we don't enter into a Bible story passively. We come to it with our questions and our reservations. These are the starting point of a friendly dialogue with the text, a dialogue we engage in trustingly – trusting both ourselves and the text. As in all true dialogue, we trust that eventually our reservations will be dealt with, and the text will 'stretch' us.

This is particularly important when reading the stories of Jesus, because he is the revelation of the one true God and challenges us to turn away from our false gods.

We take Jesus then as the text presents him to us. We don't reject the evidence of the gospels, saying 'Jesus could not have done this because he is perfect and perfect people don't do this.' This was the response of the religious authorities at Jesus' time, 'This man could not be from God.' We start from the opposite point: Jesus did this, and therefore perfect people (sons and daughters of God) do this. We dialogue with the text until we find that we can say from the truth of ourselves, 'I now see why he did that,' 'What I thought was wrong was really right'. This is the conversion moment, the change of consciousness, the transformation we seek in our practice of *lectio divina*. This conversion is not violent: 'My reservations were justified, but I have grown.'

Let us now look at the passage we have before us. The argument against this text goes: Jesus could not have been angry with the Pharisees, because people who are perfect do not get angry with those who disagree with them. We start from the opposite point, remembering people whom we admire very deeply (sons and daughters of God) who 'looked angrily around' at those who disagreed with them, deeply 'grieved at their hardness of heart'.

We think of the great saints of our time – Nelson Mandela, Gandhi – and of our own personal saints. They too felt indignation at what they saw 'around them'. There is a tendency in spirituality today to make the calm, detached and passionless person the ideal. In the process we often end up losing any sense of indignation, saying instead, 'On the one hand ... and on the other hand; we have to understand where they are coming from ...; they are very nice people when you get to know them ...; we also have our faults...' And we end up doing nothing. This is not the biblical ideal.

The passage tells us that what the world needs is more people who are passionately angry about its injustices. The issue then becomes how to integrate anger so that it becomes a positive influence for us and for the world.

The first thing we need to clarify is what makes us angry. Most of us were brought up to think that God is made angry by sexual sins first and foremost, then by missing Mass or defecting to other religions or churches. According to the gospels, however, those kinds of things did not interest Jesus very much. What made him angry – and should make us angry today – is that people with withered hands are not even noticed, while leaders argue with great passion about laws. He is angry that there are many with withered hands in our church communities, unnoticed by leaders and theologians who are arguing about liturgical rules, about whether people of other religions are saved, about natural law, and so forth.

In recent years we have had the spectacle of eminent theologians and cardinals of the church spending months discussing whether we can say that the church has sinned. They have not noticed that women, black people, gay people, third world cultures are agonising over having to forgive the church for the wrongs done to them. We forget about the law of the market or of economic growth, or the stability of the world's economic systems. I think that Jesus is 'looking around at them' very angrily indeed – and so too should we!

The second question we must ask is whether our anger is destructive or constructive. Jesus' anger does not paralyse him. He remains focused on the man, saying to him, 'Stretch out your hand' which we can interpret as 'Let's talk about the things that can embarass and paralyse you.' His anger makes him more alert to the person's needs.

With the Pharisees, his anger is mixed with 'grief'. He does not hate them; he feels a great sadness at how far they have fallen.

Let us now turn to the two stories in the gospel reading.

Verses 23 to 28 portray the disciples of Jesus as simple, unsophisticated, disingenuous – they are hungry so they pick ears of corn. The Pharisees, on the other hand, are well educated and articulate and use their learning to interpret the law in their own favour. Jesus is a protector of the poor. As a theologian, he interprets the Bible in their favour, 'He pulls down princes from their thrones and exalts the lowly' (Luke 1:52).

The wonderful saying, 'The Sabbath is for man, not man for the Sabbath', can be translated as 'The Sabbath – like all human laws – is for the poor, not the poor for the Sabbath.' This is a crucial lesson for the 'laws' that govern economics today, at both national and international levels. Jesus is the model of those who 'proclaim' to the world today that the interests of the poor are primary. He calls us as church to do likewise.

Chapter 3, verses 1 to 6, teach the same lesson through another story. Here the Pharisees are so concerned for the law that they don't notice the person with a withered hand, he is not important to them.

Once again, Jesus is the champion of the poor. For him, these persons' interests are primary, he makes them 'stand out in the middle'. Jesus is no academic observer. He is passionately committed to the poor, 'grieved and angry' he moves to action – 'Stretch out your hand.'

Applying this story to the situation in the world today, the man with the withered hand symbolises the millions of people who are 'withering away' in poverty and despair. Their 'hands' made by God to create and to embrace are idle. They remain unnoticed while the so-called experts, the consultants and advisers, the Pharisees of today, are 'watching to see' if anyone dares to challenge their understanding of what is really important.

Jesus lives in the great church leaders of our time who are indignant at this lack of concern on the part of the world's rulers. They are 'grieved to find them so obstinate' and 'look angrily around at them'.

Lord, we thank you for sending us Jesus people
to lead us on the journey to freedom:
friends, parents, grandparents,
priests or religious, spiritual guides,
fellow workers, employees.
We remember the laws that held us in bondage:
    -the rules laid down for us by our first teachers at school,
    - what is 'respectable' and what is 'just not done',
    - the severe commandments of God the taskmaster,
    - our own determination to be perfect.
We remained silent, concealing our hurts,
like the man with the withered hand.
Jesus came to us in the form of one who defends us,
explained the scriptures for us, showed us how,
like David when he went into your house,
ate the loaves of offering and gave some to his men.
You have always been sympathetic to those in need;
and how the Sabbath is for people, not people for the Sabbath.
Jesus invited us to stand out in the middle
without shame or guilt.
We understood then that we could be spontaneous,
do what we feel like as we go along,
like the disciples picking ears of corn,
and ignore haughty people who try to make us feel guilty
as if we are doing something that is forbidden.

Lord, forgive us that like the Pharisees in the time of Jesus
we in our church today interpret your law
in a way that penalises the poor:
    - those who can speak well, and have friends and relatives in
    the clergy, get marriage annulments more easily;
    - we excuse the sins of the wealthy and are harsh on those of
    the poor;
    - our language is uncompromising when we speak about gay
    people.
We ignore the people with withered hands
suffering in silence at the back of our communities
while we quarrel about issues that do not concern them:
    – whether our liturgical translations are close to the Latin;

- should the priest say Mass facing the people;
- are we applying strictly the doctrines of the catechism.
Send us theologians like Jesus who will interpret the scriptures
as Jesus interpreted them for the Pharisees
when he showed them that your law
always favours those in need,
and that the Sabbath is for the poor, not the poor for the Sabbath.
We pray that in our church
the people with withered hands will always stand out
in the middle of our discussions
and that we will invite them to stretch out their hands
so that we can feel their pain, and so they can be healed.

*'Every perspective on economic life that is human, moral and Christian
must be shaped by three questions: What does the economy do for people? What does it do to people? How do people participate in it?'*
US bishops, pastoral letter on Economic Justice for All
Lord, your people instituted the sabbath
so that they could experience that they were equal in your sight,
but the Pharisees used it to exclude those who needed most
to be reassured that they were your chosen ones.
Today again you have inspired the human family
to create trade institutions to ensure that
the goods of the earth can circulate freely
and that all the members of your human family
may enjoy the prosperity you will for us.
Forgive us that in our modern world
the market has become as sacred as the sabbath was for the Jews;
our Pharisees too get very upset
if anyone disrespects the market,
even in ways as small as picking ears of corn along the roadside.
Meanwhile they don't notice the millions whose creative hands
have withered away from neglect and despair.
We pray that we as a church will not remain passive
but will feel the indignation of Jesus,
grieve at the obstinacy of our contemporaries,
look angrily around at what is happening,
and proclaim with Jesus
that the market is for people, not people for the market.

Tenth Sunday in Ordinary Time

Gospel Reading: Mark 3:20-35

20*Jesus went home again, and once more such a crowd collected that they could not even have a meal.* 21*When his relatives heard of this, they set out to take charge of him, convinced he was out of his mind.* 22*The scribes who had come down from Jerusalem were saying, 'Beelzebul is in him,' and, 'It is through the prince of devils that he casts devils out.'* 23*So he called them to him and spoke to them in parables, 'How can Satan cast out Satan?'* 24*If a kingdom is divided against itself, that kingdom cannot last.* 25*And if a household is divided against itself, that household can never stand.* 26*Now if Satan has rebelled against himself and is divided, he cannot stand either – it is the end of him.* 27*But no one can make his way into a strong man's house and burgle his property unless he has tied up the strong man first. Only then can he burgle his house.* 28*I tell you solemnly, all men's sins will be forgiven, and all their blasphemies;* 29*but let anyone blaspheme against the Holy Spirit and he will never have forgiveness; he is guilty of an eternal sin.'* 30*This was because they were saying, 'An unclean spirit is in him.'*

31*His mother and brothers now arrived and, standing outside, sent in a message asking for him.* 32*A crowd was sitting round him at the time the message was passed to him, 'Your mother and brothers and sisters are outside asking for you.'* 33*He replied, 'Who are my mother and my brothers?'* 34*And looking round at those sitting in a circle about him, he said, 'Here are my mother and my brothers.* 35*Anyone who does the will of God, that person is my brother and sister and mother.'*

We can divide this passage into three sections:

Verses 20 and 21: the attitude of Jesus' relatives. They are typical of people who because of their status think they take charge of Jesus but in fact do not understand him at all.

Verses 22 to 30: confrontation between Jesus and the Scribes. In verse 22 the Scribes are just as presumptuous and just as wrong-headed as the relatives. In verses 23 to 25 Jesus responds to the Scribes with the kind of commonsense that comes from simple and single-minded people. In verses 26 and 27 we read a dramatic parable, evoking the harsh struggle between good and evil and how goodness must conquer evil at its very roots. Verses 28 to 30 are different. Do not approach them rationally,

but on the feeling level. Experience the discouragement of Jesus
as he confronts people who use religious language to excuse evil.

Verses 31 to 35: a second story of Jesus and his relatives. A
dramatic meeting between Jesus and his relatives; they are totally
out of his sphere and he has understood this and accepted it.

* * *

Lord, we thank you for
the great followers of Jesus we have known:
– Mother Teresa and Archbishop Romero;
– people we have known personally in our own countries,
who have taken great risks
and found themselves surrounded by the needy
while wise and powerful people
were convinced that they were out of their minds
and wanted to take charge of them.
This always happens when Jesus comes into the world.

Lord, we pray for your church, that we may always be humble.
Do not let us become like the relatives of Jesus,
presuming that because we are practising Catholics
we know what is your mind,
or like the Scribes coming down from Jerusalem,
thinking that knowledge of our faith
enables us to judge who is doing the work of the devil.

Lord, one of the terrible sins in our day
is that when people work for justice
we label them communists and atheists;
causes close to your heart,
such as putting the poor first, terrify us.
What hope is there for us then?
When people do wrong knowing it is wrong
they can always hear your word and turn back to you.
But when we enlist you in the service of false values
and look on the work of your Holy Spirit as evil,
how can we hear your call to repentance
and ask your forgiveness?

Lord, as members of your church
we do many things to help those in need.
But through the Pope and the bishops
you call us to go further and work for a new kind of society
'where the poor Lazarus can sit down
at the same table with the rich.'
Remind us that no one can make his way
into the strong man's house and burgle his property
unless he has tied up the strong man first,
and that therefore we must let your powerful word
enter into the hearts of us all
to subdue the demons of self-centredness and greed
which are at the root of the world's problems.

Lord, we pray for parents.
Many do not walk with their children on their spiritual journeys,
or enter into their deepest aspirations
so that a day comes when they have to stand outside
and send messages asking for them,
and then realise with great sadness that these children of theirs
have new brothers and sisters and mothers
in those who share their sacred values.

Lord, we thank you for those
who have stepped out of their cultures,
their age-groups, or their social class in the service of others.
There will be times when they hear within themselves
the call of mother and brothers outside asking for them.
May they at such moments look around like Jesus
at the many people sitting in a circle around them,
and recognise that they have found
mothers and brothers and sisters
in those who do your will.

Eleventh Sunday in Ordinary Time

Gospel Reading: Mark 4:26-34

26Jesus said to his disciples: 'This is what the kingdom of God is like. A man throws seed on the land. 27Night and day, while he sleeps, when he is awake, the seed is sprouting and growing; how, he does not know. 28Of its own accord the land produces first the shoot, then the ear, then the full grain in the ear. 29And when the crop is ready, he loses no time: he starts to reap because the harvest has come.'

30He also said: 'What can we say the kingdom of God is like? What parable can we find for it? 31It is like a mustard seed which at the time of its sowing in the soil is the smallest of all the seeds on earth; 32yet once it is sown it grows into the biggest shrub of them all and puts out big branches so that the birds of the air can shelter in its shade.' 33Using many parables like these, he spoke the word to them, so far as they were capable of understanding it. 34He would not speak to them except in parables, but he explained everything to his disciples when they were alone.

We see Jesus in this passage searching for the right metaphors to illustrate the concept of the kingdom of God, and we are reminded that today we need to find new images to illustrate our own vision of God's kingdom.

Verses 26b to 30. A farmer has sown a tiny seed; he now watches and waits for it to bear fruit. Jesus makes a comparison between the small and negligible start and the extraordinary results. The farmer is in no hurry, he simply waits and lets things happen. Whatever happens will take its own time and he must certainly not try to hurry it. He does not try to find out how this happens, but allows things to develop as they will. When the time is ripe the farmer knows that he must get to work.

Stay with the slow movement, the first signs of the crop before it is harvest time. Experience the contrast in the last verse when the time comes and everything seems so easy and natural.

We think of parents who worked hard for their children and then one day they saw that it was time to move on and let them go. We remember leaders who gave their all to their jobs and then one day knew that the time had come to let others take over. We think of church pastors who gave themselves to their work and must now allow others to take their place.

Verses 30 to 32. In this parable Jesus makes a distinction between the small beginning and the final flowering. 'At the time of the sowing it is the smallest of all the shrubs of the earth.' We remember small acts that we know about and that have led to great results. Acts of love and kindness and loyalty that were done without thinking about what would happen in later years. Looking back, we now see that a great tree grew out of it with plenty of space for people from other classes and tribes to benefit from it. We think also of the many cultures that have found their home in the Bible.

In your meditation you can start from the time of sowing the little seed, a time of enormous potential; or you can start from the time of full growth and remember the small beginnings.

Verses 33 and 34. You might ask yourself why a great teacher would decide not to speak except in parables.

* * *

Lord we thank you for the times
that a Bible passage touched us deeply.
When we first read it we knew it was a beautiful word;
so we just received it like a seed sown on the land.
Then we carried on with our daily lives knowing that somehow
the words of the passage were there within us
weaving in and out of our experience.
Gradually we began to catch glimpses of its meaning.
Then, quite unexpectedly, it all came together
and we knew that the passage was ours
and all we had to do was enjoy it and give you thanks.

Lord, in our modern world there are many things we can do
just by pressing a button or turning a switch;
eventually we come to think we can move people like that too.
Remind us that helping others to grow
is something totally different.
It is rather like throwing a seed on the land;
night and day we sleep, we are awake,
the seed is sprouting and growing, how we do not know.
We see some results and we think that the crop is ready
but we have to wait a little longer.

Only when the harvest has come can we start to reap.
Lord, we pray for those who work the land,
that they may reverence it and trust its rhythms
remembering that the land has many secrets they do not know,
that it must do things of its own accord,
and only when the crop is ready must they start to reap.

Lord, it is not easy
to keep the vision of Jesus alive in the world today.
The things we preach may sometimes seem irrelevant or trivial:
love your enemies, put the poor first in your calculations,
practise modesty.
Yet we know that we must keep preaching these things
because if that tiny seed continues to be sown
one day it will become the biggest shrub in the whole world,
it will put out big branches and the birds of all the air
will shelter in its shade.

Lord, our leaders like to stand over us
and hand down instructions.
But you are not like that.
You speak your word in parables, in Bible passages,
in things that happen to us, in people.
We cannot get to the bottom of them,
but you give us time
because you only teach
as far as we are capable of understanding.
Then when the time comes
we understand the parable so clearly,
with so much joy;
it is as if you had taken us aside as your own special pupils
and explained everything to us.
Lord, help us to relate to others as you relate to us.

Twelfth Sunday in Ordinary Time

Gospel Reading: Mark 4:35-41

35With the coming of evening that same day, Jesus said to them, 'Let us cross over to the other side.' 36And leaving the crowd behind, they took him, just as he was, in the boat; and there were other boats with him. 37Then it began to blow a gale and the waves were breaking into the boat so that it was almost swamped. 38But he was in the stern, his head on the cushion, asleep. 39They woke him and said to him, 'Master, do you not care? We are going down!' And he woke up and rebuked the wind and said to the sea, 'Quiet now! Be calm!' And the wind dropped, and all was calm again. 40Then he said to them, 'Why are you so frightened? How is it that you have no faith?' 41They were filled with awe and said to one another, 'Who can this be? Even the wind and the sea obey him.'

Unlike the passages of the last two weeks, this Sunday's passage is, in one sense, a single story and we must read it as a whole. But in another sense, it tells two stories – one of Jesus and one of the apostles. Each has its movement that we can enter into, and there is a striking contrast between the attitudes shown in each.

As you meditate, observe how you are situating yourself in relation to the passage: which of the two stories are you identifying with, the one of Jesus or the one of the apostles? Is it your personal story or the story of someone who has touched your life? Does Jesus remind you of some person or of God himself? Is this something that is happening now or something that has happened in the past?

Answering these questions will help you enter into the story.

* * *

Lord, humanity finds itself in a bad way:
- recurrent famines in parts of Africa and surplus food in Europe;
- an unending spiral of violence in the Middle East;
- no way out of poverty and unemployment in every country;
- the constant threat of nuclear disaster and terrorism.

The waves are breaking into our boat
so that it is almost swamped
and we have the impression that we are going down.

All this time the values of Jesus are there within our reach
– compassion, trust, love of enemies, honesty –
but we have left them in the back of the boat, unused.
We pray that we may turn to these values
in this moment of need,
that like the apostles we may discover with awe
that these values can command the winds and the seas.

Lord, we thank you for the great people of faith we have known,
an uncle or aunt, a little tradesman in the village,
the granny of the community,
the kind of person who could sleep comfortably
because they trust in you.
How often we have been condescending towards them,
taking charge of them as the apostles took charge of Jesus,
and they went along with us.
Then it began to blow a gale, and we felt we were going down.
We turned to them and experienced their power.

Lord, modern people have confidence in brute force;
we look on trust as weak and ineffectual.
We thank you that you sent us someone like Gandhi.
He showed the world that trust is a mighty power,
one that could rebuke the wind and the sea, and say to them,
'Quiet now! Be calm!' and the whole world was in awe, saying,
'Who can this be? Even the winds and the sea obey him.'

Lord, we who are leaders in the church,
we talk easily about faith.
But every one in a while you say to us,
'Let us cross over to the other side'
and make us leave the crowd behind us
    - inviting us to make a retreat;
    - letting us experience failure or infidelity.
Then, on the open sea, without our usual supports,
we experience how frail we are, how easily we could go down.
That is a moment of grace for us as we realise
that we have been living on the surface of ourselves,
trusting in success and popularity,

and deep within ourselves, Jesus was asleep.
Now with him awake we have the resources
to calm the winds and the sea.

Lord, our rulers often act
as if the destiny of the country is in their hands.
Teach them that Jesus is in the little people
forgotten in the back of the boat
and if we turn to them we will discover to our surprise
that they have the resources to calm the storm
and we will get safely to the other side.

Thirteenth Sunday in Ordinary Time

Gospel Reading: Mark 5:21-43

21*When Jesus had crossed again in the boat to the other side, a large crowd gathered round him and he stayed by the lakeside.* 22*Then one of the synagogue officials came up, Jairus by name, and seeing him, fell at his feet* 23*and pleaded with him earnestly, saying, 'My little daughter is desperately sick. Do come and lay your hands on her and make her better and save her life.'* 24*Jesus went with him and a large crowd followed him; they were pressing all round him.*

25*Now there was a woman who had suffered from a haemorrhage for twelve years;* 26*after long and painful treatment under various doctors, she had spent all she had without being any better for it; in fact, she was getting worse.* 27*She had heard about Jesus, and she came up behind him through the crowd and touched his cloak.* 28*'If I can touch even his clothes,' she had told herself, 'I shall be well again.'* 29*And the source of the bleeding dried up instantly, and she felt in herself that she was cured of her complaint.* 30*Immediately aware that power had gone out of him, Jesus turned round in the crowd and said, 'Who touched my clothes?'* 31*His disciples said to him, 'You see how the crowd is pressing round you and yet you say, "Who touched me?"'* 32*But he continued to look round to see who had done it.* 33*Then the woman came forward, frightened and trembling because she knew what had happened to her, and she fell at his feet and told him the whole truth.* 34*'My daughter,' he said, 'your faith has restored you to health; go in peace and be free from your complaint.'*

35*While he was still speaking some people arrived from the house of the synagogue official to say, 'Your daughter is dead; why put the Master to any further trouble?'* 36*But Jesus had overheard this remark of theirs and he said to the official, 'Do not be afraid; only have faith.'* 37*And he allowed no one to go with him except Peter and James and John the brother of James.* 38*So they came to the official's house and Jesus noticed all the commotion, with people weeping and wailing unrestrainedly.* 39*He went in and said to them, 'Why all this commotion and crying? The child is not dead, but asleep.'* 40*But they laughed at him. So he turned them all out and, taking with him the child's father and mother and his own companions, he went into the place where the child lay.* 41*And taking the child by the hand he said to her, 'Talitha, kum!' which means, 'Little girl, I tell you to get up'.* 42*The little girl got up at once* *and began to walk about, for she was twelve years old. At this they were overcome with astonishment, and he ordered them strictly not to let anyone know about it, and told them to give her something to eat.*

Today's gospel comprises two distinct stories with no particular connection between them so you should decide to meditate on one or the other.

> - There is the raising of Jairus's daughter to life, which by a peculiar arrangement is told in two separate sections (verses 21 to 24, and 35 to 43);
> - and there is the healing of the woman with the haemorrhage (verses 25 to 43).

Remember that the miraculous cures by Jesus, while they record historical facts, are also lessons in how God works and invites us to enter with gratitude into his work of grace in our own lives and in the world today.

* * *

Lord, we thank you for Alcoholics Anonymous;
this great organisation reminds us
that to experience resurrection from the dead,
all of us, even if we are important officials,
have to come to the point where we are no longer in control
and fall at the feet of someone greater than ourselves,
pleading for help
and allowing ourselves to be carried along by a community.

Lord, we thank you for the great moments of grace in our lives:
> - we had struggled for years to give up a relationship that was harming us;
> - we went through months of depression;
> - we wanted to forgive but hurt was still eating us up.

We tried all kinds of remedies, got advice from many people,
without getting any better; in fact we were getting worse.
But there came a time when somehow or other
we knew deep down that all we needed was a little push,
a wise word, someone praying for us, a liturgy –
and sure enough, it happened.
It was all so simple that people around us could not understand,
but we were able to come forward, frightened and trembling

because we knew what had happened,
and we humbly told the whole truth. Thank you, Lord.

Lord, it sometimes happens
that we help people without realising it.
Some word we say, some gesture we make,
and they are deeply touched.
At such times we tend to be condescending
toward the people we helped.
We pray that we may be more like Jesus,
so that when we become aware of what has happened
we speak gently to them, encourage them to tell their story,
assure them that it was their faith that restored them to health,
and help them to go in peace, fully free of their complaint.

Lord, we pray for leaders, in our country and in the world,
leaders of church and civil communities,
especially those whose communities
are disillusioned or in despair.
As they go along, they will hear some people telling them
that things are too far gone
and there is no point putting themselves to further trouble;
they will see people weeping and wailing unrestrainedly,
and if they say that the community is not dead
but merely sleeping,
many will laugh at them.
But they must ignore all these voices
and surround themselves with people of faith and love,
so that they can take their communities by the hand
and tell them to get up and walk.

Lord, we thank you for kind, practical people like Jesus,
people who,
when others are weeping and wailing unrestrainedly,
can see that the one being mourned is not dead but asleep,
and who, when others are all excited
that a great miracle has been worked,
will tell them not to talk about it,
but to give the person healed something to eat.

Fourteenth Sunday in Ordinary Time

Gospel Reading: Mark 6:1-6

¹*Jesus went to his home town and his disciples accompanied him.* ²*With the coming of the sabbath he began teaching in the synagogue and most of them were astonished when they heard him. They said, 'Where did the man get all this? What is this wisdom that has been granted him, and these miracles that are worked through him?* ³*This is the carpenter, surely, the son of Mary, the brother of James and Joset and Jude and Simon? His sisters, too, are they not here with us?' And they would not accept him.* ⁴*And Jesus said to them, 'A prophet is only despised in his own country, among his own relations and in his own house,'* ⁵*and he could work no miracles there, though he cured a few sick people by laying his hands on them.* ⁶*He was amazed at their lack of faith.*

The gospel passage for this Sunday is St Mark's version of Jesus' return to his home town of Nazareth, accompanied by his disciples. He began to teach in Nazareth, and many were astonished by what they saw in him. They wondered where all this wisdom had come from. What they saw was very different from what others had seen. This man was one of them, in the deepest sense; they knew him and his family. The people of the town would not accept him; even though they had heard of his outstanding accomplishments in other places, they could not see what made him so special.

The story of what happened to Jesus when he decided to return to his town is a familiar story, one that happens to all of us: we achieve wonderful things far away from home – in another city, or perhaps in some other part of the world, where we are not well known; then the time comes when we know we must return to our own country and teach there, and we find that people at home do not see us in the same way.

As you reflect on this passage, you may find yourself identifying with the people who rejected Jesus because he was so well known to them. Or you may prefer to identify with Jesus, remembering times when you or others had an experience like his. If you are taking this approach you might like to read it as a necessary journey of 'returning to reality'. Feel free, also, to read the story symbolically, taking 'going home' to mean the journey to the deepest truth of ourselves.

'The false idealist skips over the real. He skips the mediation of time in order to land full-blown in the ideal, ultimate society where everything is taken care of. He dreams, he does not hope.' Jacques Ellul

Lord, we remember with gratitude
the time we had a deep experience of conversion
and then had to make a journey back to everyday life:
> - we made a Life-in-the-Spirit seminar;
> - we went to confession after a long time away from the sacraments;
> - we attended a meeting of our religious community and returned all fired up.

The time came when, like Jesus,
we had to leave that beautiful place and return home.
Naturally enough, people were astonished
when they heard us speak;
they asked sarcastically what was this new wisdom
that had suddenly been granted us,
what miracles did we expect to be worked through us.
We were no different from what we had been before,
they told us,
and our parents, our brothers and sisters
were there to remind us of this.
We were amazed to see that our own enthusiasm
was not universally shared.
But today, Lord, we thank you for that experience;
it taught us that we cannot work miracles overnight.
We may feel a lot of enthusiasm within ourselves,
but that does not mean we can get others to see things as we do.
Sometimes we have to be content, as Jesus was,
to cure a few sick people
by laying our hands on them.

'Humility is the virtue by which, knowing ourselves as we really are, we become lowly in our own eyes.' St Bernard

Lord, the biggest obstacles to conversion
always lie within ourselves.
We don't like facing up to this, but, like Jesus,
we must eventually leave the far away place and come home.
There, as Jesus did,

we will hear voices coming from deep inside,
and these voices will be questioning us:
> - do we really think that miracles can be worked through us?
> - are not our parents, our brothers and sisters there to show us
>   that we are not different from what we were?

A whole part of ourselves
rejects this new direction we are taking
and we are amazed at our lack of faith.
But Jesus taught us that a moment of grace is always resisted
by our long-standing relationships
and within our deeper selves.
Lord, help us to make our journey of grace with Jesus,
to accept that we cannot work any great miracles on ourselves,
and to be content that we can lay our hands
on some wounds and heal them.

*'If people regarded me as a Messiah they were living in a fool's
paradise. I have no miracles.'* Nelson Mandela
Lord, our leaders often prefer to play a role in foreign countries
where they are more respected than in their own.
So, too, church leaders
sometimes enjoy being present in other communities
where they are not well known.
Many of us feel more comfortable
away from our families or religious communities,
among people who only see part of who we are.
Help us to leave those far away places from time to time,
and to go to our home town,
like Jesus did, among our relatives and in our own homes,
even though we may feel despised.
We may not be able to work any great miracles,
but there are always a few sick people who need us
to lay our hands on them so that they may be cured.

*'God only comes to those who, in patience, love his fore-runners and
the provisional.'* K. Rahner
Lord, how often you have sent Jesus to us
in the form of someone we knew well,
but this person was just too ordinary for us.

All we could see was the carpenter, the son of our neighbour,
one whose brothers and sisters were there with us,
and so we would not accept him.
How true it is, as Jesus said,
that a prophet is only despised in his own country,
among his own relations and in his own house.
So the great miracle you had in store for us could not be worked.
Lord, have mercy.

'We all want to be famous people and the moment we want to be some-thing we are no longer free.' Krishnamurthi
Lord, we want to do great deeds.
Free us from all ambition,
so that when we cannot work miracles
we will be content to cure a few sick people
by laying hands on them.

Fifteenth Sunday in Ordinary Time

Gospel Reading: Mark 6:7-13

7Jesus summoned the Twelve and began to send them out in pairs giving them authority over the unclean spirits. 8And he instructed them to take nothing for the journey except a staff – no bread, no haversack, no coppers for their purses. 9They were to wear sandals but, he added, 'Do not take a spare tunic.' 10And he said to them, 'If you enter a house anywhere, stay there until you leave the district. 11And if any place does not welcome you and people refuse to listen to you, as you walk away shake off the dust from under your feet as a sign to them.' 12So they set off to preach repentance; 13and they cast out many devils, and anointed many sick people with oil and cured them.

This passage contains several separate sections. Each has an important message for us today.

1. Jesus summoned the Twelve. He selected a group of people who he felt would be able to represent him before the world. He called them by name so that he could send them into the world not merely as a group, but as individuals.

These disciples then received a mission from Jesus: to make the world a little more as Jesus wants it to be. This is always his work – to take the world as it is and make it the kind that he will be able to offer to God as a fragrant offering in his sight.

This work always has two dimensions. On the one hand it must help people become more committed to being closer to him as their Lord. As they develop within themselves an ever closer relationship with him, they must strive to become more and more like him.

A further purpose of the work is to help the world become more fervent in the Lord's service. The world must become a place where people will be able to do Jesus' work among their fellow men and women.

Jesus began to send them out in pairs. This was an important aspect of their mission – they must work together.

He also gave them authority over unclean spirits. They must go among those members of the human race who control and influence what is wrong in the world. The true spirit of God will always prevent us from looking at those different from ourselves as evil-doers or wrong in some way; an 'evil spirit' always works against this.

We as true disciples of Jesus are reminded of times when we too felt within ourselves a desire to 'summon' a group of disciples. We wanted them to be more like us. We wanted to send them out into the world to make it more as we would like it to be. The passage is telling us that when we feel like that we are closer to the spirit of Jesus.

2. Instructions: The first of these was very simple: they must take nothing for the journey 'except a staff'. This means two big things nowadays:

- that we must bring something of ourselves to the people we meet in the world; we come to others with our own opinions, our own view of the world;

- that this personal thing we are bringing must not be something for ourselves and against others.

The passage then tells us in some detail what this 'nothing extra' really means:

- 'no bread' – nothing extra to eat, nothing that we can claim as our own, nothing that we could draw on in case our method demands a special sacrifice from us;

- 'no haversack' – nothing that we could store for the next day in case things get rough; we must go as we are with no special requirements;

- 'no coppers for their purses', nothing that could be put in place for our personal 'source of sustenance'.

- they were to 'wear sandals' and 'not take a spare tunic' – have nothing extra to keep for a future day when things might be different.

Jesus then gives them additional instructions:

- Once they have entered a house they are to stay there until they leave the district, staying wherever people are willing to receive them and not moving around looking for a place where they will be even more welcome.

- If people refuse to listen to them, they must shake the dust off their feet: they must not hold on to a rejection as something that defines them from then on. They must move on in perfect freedom. This will be a clear sign to all as to what has really happened between the giver and the receiver of the message.

'Nowadays people know the price of everything and the value of nothing.' Oscar Wilde
Lord, in the world today it is taken for granted
that if we want to spread a message
we need an advertising campaign
with glamorous images on television,
catchy jingles on the radio, posters in public places.
Of course, this requires plenty of money.
We followers of Jesus seem to think
we too must adopt this way of spreading the message.
But for Jesus the truth of his message
was the most important thing.
This is why, when he summoned the Twelve and sent them out,
giving them authority over unclean spirits,
he instructed them to take nothing for the journey –
no bread, no haversack, no coppers for their purses;
they must wear sandals and not take a spare tunic.
Lord, help us to enter into the mind of Jesus.

Lord, forgive us for thinking we can do your work alone,
forgetting that we are all in need:
    - men and women must complement each other;
    - while each of us has gifts, we also have defects that others
    must make up for;
    - those who disagree with us bring a new dimension to our
    ideas;
    - our church needs the gifts of other churches.
Remind us that unless we are sent out in pairs
we will not have authority over the unclean spirits
of our society.

'Do not move from insight to insight, but let each one rest in your heart.' Theophane Venard, mystic of the early church
Lord, often when we read the Bible
we move quickly from one line to another,
from one thought to the next.
But you send your words as Jesus sent the Twelve,
to enter deeply into our inner dwelling and to remain there,
nourishing and reconciling everything in us.

Lord, when people reject us we feel a lot of anger,
anger that keeps us in bondage,
holding us back like mud on our feet.
Help us, Lord, as we walk away,
to shake the dust from under our feet,
so that we may be free to give ourselves to others.

'As a social force a university should enlighten and transform the society in which it lives and for which it should live.' Ignacio Ellacuria, one of the six Jesuits killed in El Salvador, December 1989
Lord, we pray for all those who work in teaching institutions.
Don't let us remain turned in on ourselves;
send us out as Jesus sent his disciples.
Many people are complacent –
help us to go out and teach them repentance.
There are terrible demons abroad:
materialism, individualism, racism, sexism –
help us to cast them out.
There are many sick people, the lonely,
the downtrodden, the victims of discrimination –
help us to anoint them with oil and to cure them.

'I have a great fear in my heart that one day, when they turn to loving, they will find we have turned to hating.' A black priest in Alan Paton's book about South Africa, *Cry the Beloved Country*
Lord, preserve us from rejecting the hand of friendship,
lest we find one day that those we want to love
have shaken the dust from under their feet as a sign to us.

Sixteenth Sunday in Ordinary Time

Gospel Reading: Mark 6:30-34

³⁰*The apostles rejoined Jesus and told him all they had done and taught.* ³¹*Then he said to them, 'You must come away to some lonely place and rest for a while,' for there were so many coming and going that the apostles had no time even to eat.* ³²*So they went off in a boat to a lonely place where they could be by themselves.* ³³*But people saw them going, and many could guess where; and from every town they all hurried to the place on foot and reached it before them.* ³⁴*So as he stepped ashore he saw a large crowd; and he took pity on them because they were like sheep without a shepherd, and he set himself to teach them at some length.*

Today's passage, like those of the last two Sundays, is an account of the ministry of Jesus and contains several messages that are important for us today. We can feel free to identify with one of the three characters in the story:
- Jesus,
- the apostles,
- the crowds.

Verse 30. Jesus highlights the contrast between two aspects of teaching:
- 'what we do,'
- 'what we teach'.

These are two distinct realities and in our teaching we should reflect on both. We need to share how we feel about things – within ourselves, with one another, and finally with our Lord and Saviour, Jesus Christ.

What we teach must include how we relate to what we have experienced. The emphasis is usually quite different and does not reflect how we ourselves respond. There are therefore two important conclusions. The words 'they returned to their master' remind us that we need to emphasise both of them in how we relate with Jesus.

On the part of Jesus, the passage is telling us that, like all good teachers, he wants us to look at the distinction we have made between the two. As regards ourselves, we need to share both what we do and what we teach with him, our Divine Master.

Verses 31 and 32 . Jesus makes another distinction, this time between
- our 'teaching'
- our 'going away to a lonely place' so that we can 'rest for a while'.
This 'resting' would include what we do on our own. These are the times when we know that no one is there to look after us or to see that we do nothing wrong. We all have to take time off for rest.

We take the verb 'eating' here in a very wide sense. It must include activities such as getting a good rest from our work, enjoying the good things of life. The fact that the apostles did not have time to eat is of course very significant. It means that the need to look after themselves has become very great. They must learn how to find rest for themselves.

Verses 33 and 34 . Jesus' plan is thwarted by the people. The passage stresses that the crowd gathered almost by chance; the people came by accident. And 'he took pity on them, because they were like sheep without a shepherd'. This is very important. We need to listen to what people are asking for. We must respond to them, remembering that they don't have people around them who can give them training or leadership. They have no one who can console them or give them a new direction to follow in their lives. And so he set himself to answer their great needs.

The passage stresses two important realities
- accommodating our need for rest, to get something to eat
- responding to the needs of others.
The passage also concerns 'the crowds'. We too can always expect that Jesus will be there to look after us. He wants to understand our needs and to respond to them.

We must make sure that our meditation is true to our experience. We must not move to a conclusion too quickly. We will then find, by the end of the passage, that we have been really helped to understand our lives better.

* * *

'The one who loves the community destroys the community; the one who loves the brothers and sisters builds community.'
Dietrich Bonhoffer
Lord, all of us work for people:
- at work we have school principals, heads of government, directors of firms;
- within our circle of friends there are those who organise functions;
- in the church community there are priests, choir leaders, youth group leaders.
We thank you that once in a way
you send us someone like Jesus,
someone who,
when we speak about all we have done for the organisation,
will notice that there is so much coming and going in our lives
that we have no time even to eat,
and will say to us that we must come away to some lonely place,
all by ourselves, and rest for a while.
Lord, we thank you that this is how you relate with us.

'God loves us too much to allow us to be satisfied and contented with mere images or signs of his presence.' Abhishiktananda
Lord, prayer is that moment in our lives
when we come into your presence
to tell you all we have done and taught,
and you see that with all the coming and going about us
we are not finding time to be nourished ourselves;
so you say to us that we need to come away
to some lonely place by ourselves,
even if when we step ashore
there is a large crowd waiting for us,
there is no need for us to panic
because eventually we will find
that we can teach them at some length.

*'The abbot is to temper all things so that the strong may still have
something to strive after and the weak may not draw back in alarm.'*
The Rule of St Benedict

Lord, great people are like Jesus
    - they know that it is necessary at times to go away
    to a lonely place and rest for a while;
    - but they know too that there are times
    when we have to forego our moment of rest
    because there are people out there
    who are like sheep without a shepherd,
    and we must take pity on them.
Help us to be more like your shepherd.

Lord, you know how difficult we find it
when we want to include our deep feelings into what we teach.
We would like to include both
but so often we neglect what we really believe
because we are afraid of betraying the deep teaching of Jesus.

*'The biggest mistake sometimes is to play things safe in this life
and end up being moral failures.'* Dorothy Day

Lord, the world is so complex that we feel to run away from it,
to take off in a boat where we can be safe.
Indeed, it is necessary to do that from time to time.
But that is dangerous too, because once we step ashore,
we will see that a large crowd has gathered there,
like sheep without a shepherd,
and your will is that we should be like Jesus for them
and set ourselves to teach them at some length.

Seventeenth Sunday in Ordinary Time

Gospel Reading: John 6:1-15

1Jesus went off to the other side of the Sea of Galilee – or of Tiberias – 2and a large crowd followed him, impressed by the signs he gave by curing the sick. 3Jesus climbed the hillside, and sat down there with his disciples. 4It was shortly before the Jewish feast of the Passover. 5Looking up, Jesus saw the crowds approaching and said to Philip, 'Where can we buy some bread for these people to eat?' 6He only said this to test Philip; he himself knew exactly what he was going to do. 7Philip answered, 'Two hundred denarii would only buy enough to give them a small piece each.' 8One of his disciples, Andrew, Simon Peter's brother, said, 9'There is a small boy here with five barley loaves and two fish; but what is that between so many?' 10Jesus said to them, 'Make the people sit down.' There was plenty of grass there, and as many as five thousand men sat down. 11Then Jesus took the loaves, gave thanks, and gave them out to all who were sitting ready; he then did the same with the fish, giving out as much as was wanted. 12When they had eaten enough he said to the disciples, 'Pick up the pieces left over, so that nothing gets wasted.' 13So they picked them up, and filled twelve hampers with scraps left over from the meal of five barley loaves. 14The people, seeing this sign that he had given, said, 'This really is the prophet who is to come into the world.' 15Jesus, who could see they were about to come and take him by force and make him king, escaped back to the hills by himself.

This famous chapter, which presents Jesus as the Bread of Life, starts with the story of the miraculous feeding of the people by Jesus. Take the story very slowly, watching how it unfolds and stopping at whatever point you find touches you.

It can be divided up into sections:

> * Verses 1-3: The stage is set. Jesus takes up his position on the other side of the sea, sitting on the hillside with his disciples. He lets the people come to him of their own accord.
> * Verses 10-12: The miracle of the feeding.
> * Verse 13: The command to pick up the scraps, which has its own deep symbolism.
> * Verses 14-15: The confrontation between Jesus and the people.

Right through the story you will find yourself identifying either with Jesus or with the people. Jesus is the great leader and teacher; the people are symbolic of ourselves being led to experience grace in a deep way, with the blessing that this implies, and also the wrong responses that we easily fall into.

The dialogue between Jesus and the apostles is also very significant, and you may want to focus on that aspect of the story.

* * *

Lord, we thank you for leading us
to a deeper relationship with you:
  - we joined a prayer group or a religious community;
  - we gave up a relationship that had been harming us for
  many years;
  - we returned to confession and Eucharist after a long break.
It was a journey you led us on,
as you led the people in the wilderness.
It began when we were impressed
by the signs you gave in curing the sick;
several people we knew had turned to you
and found new meaning to their lives.
For a time, we were just following,
not sure where we would end up;
others worried about how we would satisfy our needs,
but you knew exactly what you were going to do.
Then came the great moment of grace:
we felt that you had given us all the nourishment we wanted;
in fact, we had enough
to fill countless hampers with the leftovers.
Thank you, Lord.

Lord, we pray for parents
who see their children following Jesus into new places.
Naturally, they are concerned,
worrying about where the children will get bread to eat,
how they will make a living, or raise their families,
or enjoy their recreation.
But you are letting them feel this concern only to test them;
you know exactly what you are going to do for the children.

Lord, often leaders don't believe in their people.
They think the problem is finding money to buy bread for them,
and, of course, there is never enough
even to give them a small piece each.
If only they would seek out the little people
with five barley loaves and two fish,
take the loaves and give thanks
and give them out to all who are sitting ready,
and then do the same with the fish,
giving out as much as is wanted,
they would find that all would have enough
and they would even pick up leftover scraps
to fill twelve hampers.

*'One act is required, and that is all. For this one act pulls everything
together and keeps everything in order. This one act is to stand with attention in your heart.'* Theophane the Recluse
Lord, we thank you for our parents,
teachers, those who have guided us.
They allowed us to come to them of our own free will,
like Jesus sitting on the hillside with his disciples.
They tested us, as Jesus tested Philip
when he knew exactly what he was going to do;
and they waited for us to see the way forward,
as Jesus waited for Andrew to point out the little boy
with the five barley loaves and the two fish.

Lord, the sign that we receive food as a gift from you
is that we pick up the pieces left over,
so that nothing gets wasted.
We thank you for those who taught us this deep truth.

*'We have no vision, no models or metaphors to live by. Only saints and
mystics live well in a time like this.'*
Denys Arcand, Canadian film director
Lord, when people impress us,
we see the signs they have given and immediately we say,
'This is the prophet who is to come into the world,'
and we want to take them by force and make them king.

But they always escape from our grasp.
If we had experienced you,
we would know that you are the only king
and we cannot possess you.

'One who knows his own weakness is greater than one who sees the angels.' Isaac of Nineveh, Syrian monk of the 7th century
Lord, it is so important that we who are in authority
or have power over others should develop our inner life;
that, like Jesus, we should know how to leave people
and go to the other side,
and there climb a hillside to be alone with our companions.
Then we will have inner freedom
so that when people come to take us by force
and make us what we cannot be
we will be able to escape back to the hills by ourselves.

Eighteenth Sunday in Ordinary Time

Gospel Reading: John 6:24-35

24When the people saw that neither Jesus nor his disciples were there, they got into boats and crossed to Capernaum to look for Jesus. 25When they found him on the other side, they said to him, 'Rabbi, when did you come here?' 26Jesus answered: 'I tell you most solemnly, you are not looking for me because you have seen the signs but because you had all the bread you wanted to eat. 27Do not work for food that cannot last, but work for food that endures to eternal life, the kind of food the Son of Man is offering you, for on him the Father, God himself, has set his seal.' 28Then they said to him, 'What must we do if we are to do the works that God wants?' 29Jesus gave them this answer, 'This is working for God: you must believe in the one he has sent.' 30So they said, 'What sign will you give to show us that we should believe in you? What work will you do? 31Our fathers had manna to eat in the desert; as scripture says: He gave them bread from heaven to eat.' 32Jesus answered: 'I tell you most solemnly, it was not Moses who gave you bread from heaven, it is my Father who gives you the bread from heaven, the true bread; 33for the bread of God is that which comes down from heaven and gives life to the world.' 34'Sir,' they said 'give us that bread always.' 35Jesus answered: 'I am the bread of life. He who comes to me will never be hungry; he who believes in me will never thirst.'

With this gospel we begin the series of teachings of Jesus which draw lessons from the miraculous feeding, all under the general theme of Jesus as Bread of Life.

The language in these passages comes across as vague and abstract, and we must make a special effort to let the passages speak to our experience as all gospel passages are meant to do.

We can refer back to the story of the miraculous feeding and see the teaching fulfilled there in practice; but it is also important to understand the biblical language as being true to our life experience. For example, the expression 'seeing the signs' (verse 26) is the process by which we go beyond some event and discover that it tells us about life, a person, the movements of sin and grace, and so on. It is the same process that Pope John XXIII called 'interpreting the signs of the times,' when he urged us to understand the significance of modern social and political movements for the gospel message. So too God 'sets his seal' on a person (verse 27) means that he is acting within that person, using the person as his instrument.

The expression 'eternal life', which occurs in verse 27 and several times in later passages, tends to remain especially abstract. People often take it to mean merely 'the next life,' and it does include that, but it means more. The best approach is not to try and understand it all at once, but to enter gradually into what it means.

Think, for example, of deeply spiritual people, the kind of people that neither sickness nor failure nor death itself can stop from living creatively: they are living 'eternal life.'

Or you might remember a time when you felt so close to God that you felt you could face anything – that too is an experience of 'eternal life.' By referring back to experiences like these you will be touched by the teaching of Jesus.

Today's teaching takes the form of spiritual journeys that Jesus leads the people to take. We can identify three:

- verses 24 to 27: Jesus leads them to move from looking to him for material food to looking for something more spiritual; you can interpret that at many different levels – our relationship with God, for example, or with one another, or with some movement that we have joined;

- verses 28 to 33: Jesus invites the people to give up all forms of human security and put their trust in God alone: in verses 28 and 29 they are looking for the security that comes from knowing that they are doing 'the right thing'; in verses 30 and 31 it is the security of pointing to favours received or of having great leaders like Moses;

- verses 34 and 35: the people express good desires, but they are looking for the miraculous bread in some vague place; Jesus brings them back to reality: this bread is present in his own person.

* * *

Lord, true friendship is a journey into a deeper kind of living, like the journey Jesus invited the people to make with him. When we first love someone, we are all excited about it; we want to be with our newly found friend all the time. 'When did you come here?' we are always asking.

We are still at the stage of satisfying some need of ours,
working for food that cannot last.
Gradually we realise that there is something sacred
about this relationship,
that you have set your seal on it
and it is offering us an opportunity
to live at a deeper level than we have done.
We still have a way to go:
we want to do many things to please our friend,
when it isn't a matter of doing anything, but of trusting.
So, too, we must stop looking for signs that we are loved,
the kind of signs that others have got,
and just keep on being grateful
for this person whom you have sent to us.
Truly, such a relationship calms our restlessness and gives life.

Lord, when people come to us asking what they must do
if they are to do the work you want,
it is tempting to give them easy answers,
'Do this and do that, and you will be doing what God wants.'
But you want us to be honest, like Jesus,
saying clearly that there is no such security for us,
that the 'work' we have to do is
to give ourselves to the present moment,
as your gift coming down from heaven,
and this is the only thing that will set us free
from the hungers and thirsts which keep us in bondage.
This is the meaning of incarnation.

Lord, forgive us for becoming complacent
when people flock around us.
Give us the wisdom of Jesus to see that
    - children come to our schools, but it is to be successful in
    their examinations;
    - people vote for us at elections because we have got them
    favours;
    - we are often praised by some who are afraid to hurt us.
Help us to be like Jesus
and to offer those whom you have given to our care

the kind of food that endures to eternal life;
for it is for this that you have set your seal on us.

Lord, we often feel deeply hurt
when we realise that people are coming to us
because we have given them something;
they haven't got the message
that we need to be loved for our own sake.
We thank you that Jesus can understand,
because he had the same experience.

Lord, we thank you for moments of deep prayer
when we know that we have eaten bread from heaven
and feel a great calm,
as if we will never be hungry or thirsty again.

Lord, great leaders are like Jesus – they do not give in
to those who are looking for quick answers to the question
'What should we do?'
Nor are they intimidated by the challenge,
'What sign will you give to show us
that we should believe in you?'
Nor do they try to emulate some Moses of the past
who people say gave them bread from heaven to eat;
they trust in the truth of their message
and the sense that they are doing your work.

Lord, we think of young people today
hungry and thirsty for happiness,
deep friendships, meaningful work, prosperity.
If someone promises them these things, they hope for a miracle
and cry out excitedly as the people did to Jesus,
'Sir, give us that bread always.'
Help them, Lord, to see that it isn't as easy as that;
they must put aside their own desires,
putting all their trust in his values, and then, paradoxically,
their hungers and thirsts will be satisfied.

Lord, there are millions of people going hungry today,
and we Christians accept this as inevitable.
We forget your promise that if we came to Jesus
and believed in his teachings
the world would never be hungry or thirsty again.

Lord, we long for miraculous bread
that will come down from heaven and give life to the world.
You call us back to the reality
that bread from heaven is here before our eyes,
as truly as Jesus was present to the people.

Nineteenth Sunday in Ordinary Time

Gospel Reading: John 6:41-51

[41]Meanwhile the Jews were complaining to each other about Jesus, because he had said, 'I am the bread that came from heaven.' [42]'Surely this is Jesus son of Joseph,' they said. 'We know his father and mother. How can he now say, "I have come down from heaven"?' [43]Jesus said in reply, 'Stop complaining to each other. [44]No one can come to me unless he is drawn by the Father who sent me, and I will raise him up at the last day. [45]It is written in the prophets: "They will all be taught by God," and to hear the teaching of the Father, and learn from it, is to come to me. [46]Not that anyone has seen the Father, except the one who comes from God; he has seen the Father. [47]I tell you most solemnly, everybody who believes has eternal life. [48]I am the bread of life. [49]Your fathers ate the manna in the desert and they are dead; [50]but this is the bread that comes down from heaven, so that a man may eat it and not die. [51]I am the living bread which has come down from heaven. Anyone who eats this bread will live for ever; and the bread that I shall give is my flesh, for the life of the world.'

In this passage, Jesus again draws lessons about life from the feeding of the five thousand.

I remind you that all teaching of Jesus recorded in the gospels is intended to speak to experience, and we must therefore appeal to our experience to discover its truth. This can be difficult with passages like these: one reason is that the language is not the kind that we use ordinarily. Some expressions – such as 'eternal life,' 'being drawn by the Father,' 'living bread,' 'flesh' – you will have to bring down to earth for yourself, applying them to what you have lived yourself.

There is, however, a more important reason why we may find this passage difficult to relate to experience: it contains deep teaching, speaking of a level of experience that we seldom reflect on because we all tend to live at the surface of ourselves.

In meditating on these passages then, you must remember deep experiences. You will naturally think of deep conversion – for example, a retreat that changed your life, a Life in the Spirit Seminar, or a prayer moment that you have never forgotten.

But you need not stay with prayer moments. You could think

of other deep experiences – a movement, for example, or a leader who touched your life. The passage will help you understand these experiences and put them in the context of your growth as a person.

As always with gospel stories, you can focus on the person of Jesus, letting him remind you of someone very important to you and in the process, of the kind of person you yourself would like to be; or then you can focus on the journey the people were called to make, recognising a journey that you or people you love are making or have made.

Remember also that the fruit of your meditation is that you find yourself repeating the actual words of the passage prayerfully and with great gratitude to God for his grace.

It is not possible to meditate deeply on a passage like this all together – divide it up and take one section at a time. You will usually find that one section is all you can go into over a week, although you may be able to connect the other sections after a time. I would suggest dividing the passage as follows:

Verses 41 to 44 describe a journey that Jesus invites the people to make.

- In verses 41 and 42 they are 'complaining': their lives are so ordinary that God could not possibly be with them. All they can see is 'the son of Joseph' whose father and mother 'they knew'.

- In verses 43 and 44 Jesus asks them to look beyond that same ordinary reality and recognise two things: a) that the meeting with him is not by chance but by God's grace; and b) that it is a meeting that has great significance, not merely here and now, but for all eternity.

What encounter in your own experience resulted in your making that kind of journey? What kind of leader is able to challenge people to make such a journey?

- Verses 45 and 46 speak of a similar journey, this time as one of 'hearing' or 'being taught' or 'learning'. We can know right teaching, but in an abstract way; when we come to Jesus, we learn God's lessons personally as if he had taken us aside and given us individual tutoring. Identify a moment when you made that journey and who was the Jesus you 'came to'. Verse 46 makes an interesting comment on the process: we don't have to have seen God, only the one who came from God.

Verse 47. Take this verse by itself, as a reflection on a fact of life. 'Believes' is left vague, and so you are free to take it in as wide a sense as you want, of any act of faith. On the other hand, you can also take it to refer to real faith.

Think of people who have risked their lives, their careers or friendships for the sake of non-violence or for the liberation of oppressed people, or for honesty. Remembering them, you gradually discover the meaning of 'having eternal life' and you will feel a kind of awe as he reflected on the power of that kind of faith, 'I tell you most solemnly'.

Remember world-famous people, but don't limit yourself to them: remember members of your own family or your village community.

A negative way of appreciating this powerful verse would be to reflect on the emptiness of a life without faith. 'If a man has not discovered something that he will die for, he isn't fit to live' (Martin Luther King).

In verses 48 to 50 Jesus speaks of himself as bread. This is a metaphor that is quite frequent in the Bible to describe the teaching of a leader. Jesus makes a distinction between two kinds of teacher or leader. There are those who when they find people in the wilderness are content to give them manna after which they die. Jesus is a different kind of teacher: through his teaching people are set free from within themselves so that they live. His teaching gives unlimited depth to a person's life.

In verse 51 the teaching is repeated but Jesus makes a new point which he will make clearer in the following passage: the bread he gives is his flesh. Make sure you bring this expression down to experience. 'Flesh' in Bible language means various things. Here it clearly stresses that Jesus is a source of life by giving himself, not abstract teaching but his own self-sacrificing love. The word goes deeper and says that Jesus did not give himself in power but in weakness, and this of course is a tremendous lesson about giving life to others.

* * *

Lord, we often complain about
- our bad health, our failures
- the friends who let us down, our parish community
- society today with its materialism, its selfishness, its crimes.
How can anybody say that you are with us?
But Jesus tells us to stop complaining;
unless you were drawing us we would not be where we are.
The people we live with, the situations we find ourselves in,
all are your gift to us and they can raise us up to your presence.
In fact they can raise us up on the last day.

'Our prayer has had a beginning because we have had a beginning. But it will have no end. It will accompany us into eternity and will be completed in our contemplation of God.' Carlo Carretto
Lord, we thank you for moments of deep prayer;
we can only come to them because you draw us there
and we know that they will take us beyond the last day.

Lord, we thank you, those of us who preach the Word,
for calling us to be part of this mystery.
People are there, listening to us as they listen to other speakers,
but they cannot really come to us unless you draw them.
On the other hand, those words of ours,
poor though they may be,
can raise them up so high
that they are beyond the reach of death
and of all that can harm them.

Lord, we have known Jesus all our lives,
but for a long time he was someone far away
who taught abstract truths.
Then, one day, we experienced conversion
and it was as if we understood life for the first time.
We understood, then, what was written in the prophets:
'They will all be taught by God.'
Teachings that had seemed abstract
we now heard addressed personally to us,
and we really learned from them.
That is what it means to come to Jesus.

We know that no one has seen you,
but we have met the one who came from you and has seen you.

'Gandhi's impact is not measured over two years, or four years or
twenty years; the ideas he has given us are imperishable.'
A disciple of Gandhi
Lord, how true it is that one who believes has an eternal life.
When we put our trust in absolute values
– truth, justice, the equality of all men and women,
the care of little ones –
we are taken out of ourselves, out of our present history
and become part of eternity.

Lord, many people take it for granted
that their destiny is to be inferior to others;
they are convinced that
    - they will always fail,
    - they will never overcome their faults,
    - they will remain forever in bondage.
There are leaders who encourage this attitude,
content to give people bread in the wilderness
and let them die there.
Lord, send us leaders, spiritual guides, like Jesus
who will give us a different kind of teaching,
feeding us with another kind of bread, one that comes from you,
and help us to experience that we have it within us
to be free and creative,
that we are born not to die in bondage but to live forever.

Lord, our culture leads us to think
that people can only help others
by their power, their wealth or their achievements.
We have even come to think that Jesus helped people like that.
But the bread that he gave others to eat
was his weakness, his flesh:
    - he made himself vulnerable to children
    - he asked the woman at the well for water and Zacchaeus for
    hospitality
    - on the cross he was so human, so much 'flesh'

that the good thief could speak words of encouragement to
him.
It is by sharing our weakness that we give life to others.

Lord, we thank you for our mothers:
they gave us their flesh that we might live.

Lord, our churches are big and beautifully decorated,
with imposing statues.
But the heart of all is Jesus under the form of simple bread.
It is still true that he gives his flesh for the life of the world.

Lord, we pray for our leaders, in the church and in the state.
Teach them that they cannot give life to others by their words,
but only by giving their flesh.

Twentieth Sunday in Ordinary Time

Gospel Reading: John 6:51-58

⁵¹*Jesus said to the crowd: 'I am the living bread which has come down from heaven. Anyone who eats this bread will live for ever; and the bread that I shall give is my flesh, for the life of the world.'* ⁵²*Then the Jews started arguing with one another: 'How can this man give us his flesh to eat?' they said.* ⁵³*Jesus replied: 'I tell you most solemnly, if you do not eat the flesh of the Son of Man and drink his blood, you will not have life in you.* ⁵⁴*Anyone who does eat my flesh and drink my blood has eternal life, and I shall raise him up on the last day.* ⁵⁵*For my flesh is real food and my blood is real drink.* ⁵⁶*He who eats my flesh and drinks my blood lives in me and I live in him.* ⁵⁷*As I, who am sent by the living Father, myself draw life from the Father, so whoever eats me will draw life from me.* ⁵⁸*This is the bread come down from heaven; not like the bread our ancestors ate: they are dead, but anyone who eats this bread will live for ever.'*

This is the fourth passage from chapter six of John's gospel. It is the third in which Jesus gives the people a teaching based on their experience of the miraculous feeding.

Some themes are repeated in all these passages, and yet each passage has its own dominant theme running through it. In the two previous passages Jesus presented himself to the people as 'bread come down from heaven'. In this one, he pushes the metaphor further: he gives them his flesh to eat and his blood to drink.

You may find the metaphor strange, but you should try to enter into it, so that it becomes part of your prayer. Remember that in Bible meditation it is not sufficient to get the meaning of a passage; you must get into the words themselves and grow to love them so that you feel moved to repeat them many times.

The metaphor has its origins in 'flesh and blood', the biblical expression that means the reality of a human being, with a special stress on his or her weakness or limitations. For example, when in chapter 16 of Matthew Peter made his act of faith, it did not come from 'flesh and blood', but as a gift from God. So, too, St Paul warned the Ephesians that their struggle was not merely against 'flesh and blood', but against heavenly forces.

When Jesus says that he gives his flesh to eat and his blood to drink, he is saying three things.

The first is that he gives himself totally to others; every part of his being is at their service. It is the same as saying 'This is my body given for you.'

Secondly, he is inviting people to deep union with himself, to 'have his spirit coursing through their souls so that they can know the passion of his love for every one', as we sing in the hymn 'To be the Body of the Lord.'

Thirdly, he wants them to unite their weakness and their sufferings with his so that they can experience his strength and his courage. As he would say to them at the Last Supper, 'In the world you will have trouble, but be brave, I have conquered the world.' When we eat his flesh and drink his blood, our own flesh and blood are ennobled. St Paul says it in 2 Corinthians: 'We carry with us in our body the death of Jesus so that the life of Jesus too may always be seen in our body.'

The passage is therefore a meditation on Jesus as teacher, leader and guide. In all three roles he does not stand outside of people – he wants to share their lives and to have them share his.

Now this tells us something about God. Whereas we tend to imagine God in heaven looking down on us but not getting involved in the movement of our history, Jesus shows God entering into flesh and blood with us.

But the passage also tells us about human relationships. In your meditation remember with gratitude people who have been Jesus for you – a parent, a spiritual guide, a friend, a national leader. Naturally you will feel the passage calling you to grow in your own relationships.

Finally, a good meditation on this passage will help you to appreciate the Eucharist. It will show you why Jesus chose to be present in the church under the form of bread and wine.

It is not possible to meditate on a passage such as this one all together: take one section at a time and enter into it, letting it speak to your experience. I suggest dividing the passage as follows:

- Verses 51 and 52: the people are questioning the very possibility of someone giving himself totally, as Jesus claims to do. Their response is cynical, but is it not typical of the way many would respond today?

- Verse 52 invites us to think of people who have no life in them, and to go to the root cause – they have never experienced, or perhaps have never let themselves experience, the kind of selfless love that Jesus gives.

- Verse 54 introduces the theme we have met several times in the chapter: deep relationship with God in Jesus lifts us up beyond the limitations of time and history.

- In verse 55 we remember that there is false food and drink and to recognise them we can look at what relationship with Jesus does to us.

- Verse 56 teaches us the effect of love, the love of Jesus, as well as of all those who love selflessly.

- In verse 57 we see another effect of selfless love. Here, as frequently in St John's gospel, Jesus' relationship with his followers is similar to his relationship with his Father – 'as the Father has sent me so I am sending you'; 'as the Father loves me so I have loved you.'

- In verse 58 we see again the theme of the newness of Jesus' teaching.

* * *

Lord, we remember with gratitude
the day when we realised for the first time
that following Jesus meant eating his flesh
and drinking his blood.
Up to then it was a matter of believing abstract truths –
that Jesus was truly God and truly man,
that there are three persons in God and seven sacraments.
That kind of faith was not a source of life for us.
Then one day we knew that we had to lay down our lives
    - caring for a wayward child,
    - working for reconciliation in the workplace and being attacked by both workers and employers;
    - forgiving someone who had hurt us deeply.
At that moment we knew
that Jesus on the cross was present within us,
and the strange thing was
that we felt an inner strength and freedom,
and we were certain that no matter how low we fell
he would raise us up.

Lord, self-centredness has become
like a first principle of living today.
People will argue with one another that it is not even possible
for us to give our flesh to be eaten,
and yet there can be no life in the world without selfless giving,
not in nature, not in families, not in any society.

Lord, we pray for those who are mourning for a loved one.
Remind them that Jesus gave them his flesh to eat
and his blood to drink
and he will raise them up on the last day.

*'I should like to set down here my own belief. In so far as I am willing to
be made an instrument of God's peace, in that far have I already entered into eternal life.'* Alan Paton
Lord, we thank you for those who eat the flesh
and drink the blood of Jesus
and therefore already have eternal life.

*'We need the eyes of deep faith to see Christ in the broken bodies and
dirty clothes under which the most beautiful one among the sons of
men hides.'* Mother Teresa
Lord, help us to receive Jesus
when he comes to us in flesh and blood.

Lord, you give us food and drink
so that we might live more freely and creatively.
Yet we nourish ourselves with many things
that are not life-giving at all,
but rather clutter up our lives and keep us in bondage.
We pray that your Christ may be Jesus today,
giving the world real food and drink.

Lord, we thank you for the people who have touched our lives;
when we read the story of Jesus we see them living in him,
and when we remember their stories,
we see Jesus living in them.
Truly they have eaten his flesh and drunk his blood.

Lord, we talk too much when we pray.
Teach us to remain silent,
so that we become conscious of Jesus present within us
and the life he draws from you may well up in us too.

Lord, we think today of those
who see their spouses destroying themselves
with bitterness, envy or false pride.
With anguish in their hearts, they say to them,
as Jesus said to his followers,
'Unless you allow yourself to receive selfless love,
you will not have life within you.'

Lord, we pray for the people of South Africa,
 Afghanistan, Sri Lanka, Ethiopia.
For generations their ancestors ate the bread of suspicion,
fear and hatred, and they are dead.
We thank you that you are raising up new leaders
in those countries,
and they, like Jesus,
are offering their people a different kind of nourishment,
based on reconciliation and sharing,
bread come down from heaven,
so that they can eat it and live.

Twenty-first Sunday in Ordinary Time

Gospel Reading: John 6:60-69

60*After hearing his doctrine many of the followers of Jesus said, 'This is intolerable language. How could anyone accept it?'* 61*Jesus was aware that his followers were complaining about it and said, 'Does this upset you?* 62*What if you should see the Son of Man ascend to where he was before?* 63*It is the spirit that gives life, the flesh has nothing to offer. The words I have spoken to you are spirit and they are life.* 64*But there are some of you who do not believe.' For Jesus knew from the outset those who did not believe, and who it was that would betray him.* 65*He went on, 'This is why I told you that no one could come to me unless the Father allows him.'* 66*After this, many of his disciples left him and stopped going with him.* 67*Then Jesus said to the Twelve, 'What about you, do you want to go away too?'* 68*Simon Peter answered, 'Lord, who shall we go to? You have the message of eternal life,* 69*and we believe; we know that you are the Holy One of God.'*

This is the final extract from chapter 6 of John's gospel that the church invites us to meditate on at this time. We have had three rather abstract passages and, no doubt, you will be relieved to find that we have a story again, just as we had at the opening of the chapter.

The story has several characters. In your meditation, listen carefully to yourself and you will find that you are reading the passage from the perspective of one of them; stay with that perspective so that you enter the story personally.

There is, first of all, Jesus, and you might like to focus on him as he relates with the other characters. Watch his inner freedom. Already in the account of the feeding we saw him sitting on the hillside allowing the people to come to him out of their own freedom. So, too, here he gives each group their space, those who reject him as well as the twelve – including the betrayer.

He also tells us the secret of his inner freedom: he knows he is in his Father's hands and no one can come to him unless the Father allows it. This inner freedom gives him space to see others clearly, so that he is not deceived by people.

Let your memories of great people who have touched your

life confirm the truth of St John's account of Jesus, and of course, let him reveal to you how God wishes to relate with us.

Jesus' words in verse 62 are difficult, but you might want to remain with them. 'The Son of Man ascending to where he was before' probably refers to the painful journey through the passion which would test his followers to the utmost. Jesus, then, is the great leader who gives his followers a first test and judges whether they will survive the greater ones that lie ahead.

Every word of the great confession of Peter is important: the four statements are different aspects of the one deep commitment. What memories does this stir up in you? Make sure not to be self-righteous as you read of those who rejected Jesus. They symbolise us when we find some demand of God difficult to accept. The use of the word 'language' is significant. When our values go astray, we find the language of true believers alien to us.

The mention of the traitor might touch you. Judas is the symbol of the betrayal of Christian values that remains within every community and within each one of us.

Finally, there are the two sayings in verse 63 that are the kind of difficult sayings that occur several times in the chapter. As I have already urged you to do, be creative in your interpretation, asking yourself when you have experienced the truth of the sayings. 'Flesh' here is whatever in our lives or in our church lacks the true spirit of Jesus and therefore is not life-giving in the deepest sense.

The second saying invites us to remember 'words' that gave us life and to see how they could be considered 'spirit'.

* * *

Lord, it sometimes happens that
when we stand up for our values
our companions stop going with us
    - because we will not discriminate against people
    of a different race;
    - because we refuse to give expressions of love that are not
    appropriate to a relationship;
    - because we criticise those in authority.
Help us, Lord, when this happens, not to become bitter,
not to give up our values, but to understand, as Jesus did,

that we cannot force people to come to us
and that a relationship will only develop if you allow it to.

Lord, we thank you for all the times in recent years
when your church has spoken out
against injustice in different parts of the world,
even when many of its members found this language intolerable
and could not accept it.

Lord, we remember the time when we were upset
because, for the first time, Jesus asked something hard of us.
Now, looking back on it, we smile.
What if we had known then
how much is entailed in following him
on his way to you?

Lord, we live at the surface of ourselves,
and so we lack energy and creativity.
Give us the grace to withdraw, from time to time,
to the depths of ourselves.
Only if we go to the level of the spirit can we really live.

Lord, many preachers are content to repeat
what they have heard from others.
We thank you for those whose words have been life to us
because they speak from the depths of their experience.

Lord, forgive your church for taking pride
in our great achievements
    - the big numbers that attend our services
    - our influence with the rich and the powerful
    - our imposing buildings and prestigious institutions,
forgetting that the flesh has nothing to offer.
What will give life to the world is simplicity, truth, compassion,
reverence for little people –
all that we know to be the spirit of Jesus.

Lord, we thank you for the great moment
when we knew we had made a life commitment
  - we met the person we should spend the rest of our life with
  - we gave our whole selves to a movement
  - we read the life of a great person and were never the same
    afterwards.
We knew then that there was nowhere else for us to go;
this was, for us, the way to eternal life.
We believed and we knew that this was the Holy One of God.
It was like that when people met Jesus.

Lord, to achieve anything worthwhile in life
we have to take risks.
We must go ahead and choose twelve,
even though one of them eventually betrays us.

Lord, there was a time when we made a deep act of faith
and became complacent.
We thank you that you sent Jesus to us
  - a friend pointed out how self-righteous we had become
  - we fell into a sin we thought we had finished with.
This was Jesus reminding us
that the capacity to betray him is always part of us too.

Lord, send us leaders like Jesus
who will proclaim their message,
even if many of their followers find the language intolerable
and impossible to accept;
who will be free enough to turn
even to their closest companions and say,
'What about you, do you want to go away too?'.

Twenty-second Sunday in Ordinary Time

Gospel Reading: Mark 7:1-8, 14-15, 21-23

[1]The Pharisees and some of the scribes who had come from Jerusalem gathered round Jesus, [2]and they noticed that some of the disciples were eating with unclean hands, that is without washing them. [3]For the Pharisees, and the Jews in general, follow the tradition of the elders and never eat without washing their arms as far as the elbow; [4]and on returning from the market place they never eat without first sprinkling themselves. There are also many other observances which have been handed down to them concerning the washing of cups and pots and bronze dishes. [5]So these Pharisees and scribes asked him, 'Why do your disciples not respect the tradition of the elders but eat their food with unclean hands?' [6]He answered, 'It was of you hypocrites that Isaiah so rightly prophesied in this passage of scripture: "The people honour me only with lip-service, while their hearts are far from me. [7]The worship they offer me is worthless, the doctrines they teach are only human regulations." [8]You put aside the commandment of God to cling to human traditions.'

[14]He called the people to him again and said, 'Listen to me, all of you, and understand. [15]Nothing that goes into a man from outside can make him unclean; it is the things that come out of a man that make him unclean. [21]For it is from within, from men's hearts, that evil intentions emerge: fornication, theft, murder, adultery, [22]avarice, malice, deceit, indecency, envy, slander, pride, folly, [23]All these evil things come from within and make a man unclean.'

Today's passage contains several sayings of Jesus which are very well known; we must therefore make an effort to read the passage not as an abstract teaching but as a story, letting the message emerge from the interplay of characters.

There are three characters, all representing roles in a human community.

1. Jesus' disciples are humble people. They are not 're-spectable' or refined. They do not conform to social norms ('the traditions of the elders') in how they speak, dress or, in this case, 'eat with unclean hands'. In the gospels they are classified as 'sinners', those who 'break the law'. To judge from Jesus' remarks

in this passage, they are not malicious, their hearts are not unclean.

2. The 'Pharisees and scribes' are those who set the norms, in words and in practice. They observe and teach the rules of respectability, their etiquette is beyond reproach. But they are judgmental of those who do not conform; they do not take time to understand them and in the process they are blind to the fact that they go against basic virtues such as humanity and compassion.

Very significantly, the text says that they have 'come from Jerusalem'. The company of Jesus and his disciples is not their home territory; they are out of place among these new people.

3. Jesus as always is the protector of the poor. He sees the greatness and beauty that lie beneath their rough externals, defends them passionately against their oppressors. He is harsh with the scribes and Pharisees, but his harshness (as God's harshness in the Bible) is because of his concern for the poor.

The movement of the story shows the process by which the church, and every human community dedicated to noble ideals, gradually becomes set in its ways and ends up accepting the false values of the surrounding culture. The Bible always gives a simple criterion for recognising when this happens – the poor and the marginalised in a country end up being poor and marginalised in the Christian community as well.

The root problem lies with laws which exist originally to protect the weak but end up on the side of the powerful. Someone like Jesus must come on the scene and expose the 'hypocrisy' of the community by standing up for the lowly. The community is then forced to revisit its laws in order to distinguish the true ideals of the community ('God's commandment') from the 'human regulations' which maintain the *status quo*.

Every community and movement needs laws and customs, as Jesus always taught; but they must be constantly re-examined to see if they conform to God's laws.

The passage invites us to recognise God-in-Jesus at work in this way in our church communities and in the world.

We will recognise him at work within our individual selves too. Often we allow ourselves to be oppressed by so-called 'laws' that are not from God but are social taboos (gender or ethnic stereotypes, for example). Now they simply block our true selves ('the heart'). One day Jesus comes into our lives – through a friend, a spiritual guide or a moment of prayer – and rescues us from oppression.

Being God's instrument of liberation is often the principal role of the counsellor or spiritual guide. It is also the lofty vocation of the moral theologian in the church.

* * *

Lord, we remember times when we felt out of place,
  - among people wealthier or better educated than ourselves;
  - when we returned to church after staying away for many years;
  - because we were not as successful as our brothers and sisters;
  - in a strange country where no one understood what we said.
It was like when the Pharisees and some of the scribes
who had come to Jerusalem
gathered around Jesus and noticed that his disciples
were eating without first washing their hands.
We too were made to feel that we were unclean
because we did not respect the traditions of the elders.
We thank you for sending someone like Jesus who protected us
  - one of our parents, an uncle, an aunt or a grandparent,
  - a teacher or community leader,
  - a friend who understood what we were going through,
  - a book that touched us.
They taught us that what counts in life
are the things that come from within,
these are the things that make us unclean.
We were able then to recognise what is merely custom
and in fact keeps people far from the truth of themselves.

Lord, forgive us members of your church for focusing on
being loyal members of your church and keeping its laws,
while we put aside your first and only commandment
of universal love and compassion,
ignoring sexism, racism, elitism,
cultural imperialism and religious intolerance,

all these evil things which come
from within the worst of the human heart
and make humanity unclean.

Lord, we thank you for sending us Bernard Häring
and other great moral theologians of our time.
Church discipline had become set in its ways
and was reinforcing the false values of our culture
    - laws on divorce and remarriage were weighted against de-
    prived families;
    - liturgical rules reinforced the superiority of Western cult-
    ure;
    - seminary studies did not reverence traditional religions of
    Africa and Asia;
    - sexual morality favoured men;
    - the laity were deprived of our teachings on mysticism.
Bernard Häring and other prophetic figures
were the presence of Jesus among us,
showing that judgements were being passed by an elite,
isolated from the reality of people's experiences
like the Pharisees and scribes coming down from Jerusalem.
What were called the customs of the elders
were rules concerned with external cleanliness
which the humble could not live up to.
Doctrines were put forward as if they came from you
when in fact they were only human regulations;
your commandment of universal love
was put aside so that traditions could be upheld.
We thank you that Jesus was in them,
calling your church to listen – all of us –
and understand that nothing which comes to us from outside
can make us unclean;
only the things that come from our hearts make us unclean.

Lord, we pray that in our parish liturgies
we will give every opportunity to the marginalised,
    - allow those without much education to read
    - arrange processions in which the disabled can take part
    - ensure that foreigners can understand the homily

- give special welcome to those who cannot receive communion.
In this way we will not honour you only with lip service
but our hearts will be close to you,
our worship will be precious to you,
and we will be following your teachings,
not mere human regulations.

Lord, your will is that we should live
with people very different from us
    - those of other religions
    - ancestral cultures of Africa, Asia, and Latin America,
    - different ethnic groups
    - the world of high technology
    - the youth culture of today.
Help us not to become like Pharisees and scribes
coming to Galilee from Jerusalem,
noticing how others do things differently from us.
Help us to discern what in our culture
is merely human regulations
which do not make anyone clean or unclean,
so that we will repent of paying only lip service
to the lofty principles we proclaim
and recognise that so much of what we call holy is worthless.

Lord, we thank you that in our time
the Bible has become once more
the soul of your church's theology,
enabling us to recognise
that many of what we call biblical doctrines
are no more than human regulations.

Lord, we thank you for moments of deep prayer
when you showed us clearly that the laws we were breaking
did not make us unclean
because they were only human regulations,
that we could go beyond them and find our purity of heart.

Twenty-third Sunday in Ordinary Time

Gospel Reading: Mark 7:31-37

³¹*Returning from the district of Tyre, Jesus went by way of Sidon towards the Sea of Galilee, right through the Decapolis region.* ³²*And
they brought him a deaf man who had an impediment in his speech; and
they asked him to lay his hand on him.* ³³*He took him aside in private,
away from the crowd, put his fingers into the man's ears and touched
his tongue with spittle.* ³⁴*Then looking up to heaven he sighed; and he
said to him, 'Ephphata', that is 'Be opened.'* ³⁵*And his ears were
opened, and the ligament of his tongue was loosened and he spoke clearly.*
³⁶*And Jesus ordered them to tell no one about it, but the more he insisted,
the more widely they published it.* ³⁷*Their admiration was unbounded.
'He has done all things well,' they said; 'he makes the deaf hear and the
dumb speak.'*

We are given the context of today's story: it took place as Jesus
was 'returning from the district of Tyre'. He was passing 'by
way of Sidon towards the Sea of Galilee' and this brought him
'right through the Decapolis region'. This reminds us that we
must know how to leave our ordinary surroundings so that we
can meet people like this person.

Today's gospel passage is a healing story. We must be careful
to interpret these stories correctly. For example, we would be
wrong to draw the conclusion that since Jesus healed miracu-
lously, all his followers are called to do the same. That would be
to misunderstand the meaning of the miracles.

St John gives us the key to interpret Jesus' miracles. Whereas
the other evangelists refer to the miracles as 'wonders' or 'powers', John calls them 'signs'; for him the miracles point beyond
themselves to the 'kingdom of God'. This is the world as God
wills it to be. It is what Jesus lived and died for. The miracles
therefore are living lessons on the kingdom. They are also signs
that the kingdom is already present in the world. We can see
fleeting glimpses of it, its first fruits, its heralds.

Jesus' miracles are like the educational films made nowadays
which show the processes of nature speeded up. They are 'fast
forwarded'. For example, we see in one continuous movement a
seed germinate, become a bud then a beautiful flower, and then

spread new seeds. In somewhat the same way, Jesus' miracles display (and announce the arrival of) God's plan for the world. They 'go against nature' but only in the sense that in them God's kingdom comes instantaneously, whereas in real life it takes considerable time and plenty of painful effort.

The person in this story can neither hear nor speak and is therefore a truly touching symbol of those who cannot communicate. They cannot hear God's word of truth, wisdom and consolation, the words of those who would like to enter into communication with them. They cannot hear the life-giving words spoken by nature, the truth of themselves, the greatness or the weakness of their own beings.

The 'impediment' in his speech symbolises well our inability to initiate conversation – with God, other human beings, nature, oneself. The phrase 'the ligaments of his tongue were loosened' tells us that the power to communicate is within us all. It is kept in check by the negative forces within us, like fear, hurt and anger. 'He spoke clearly' is also a very telling phrase – it refers to the great wonder of good communication, a power we have within us, if we can only do it right.

Jesus takes the man 'aside in private'. This is surely an indication that his healing often requires intimacy. When we try to do it publicly, we run the risk of using persons to bolster our ego or for our personal ambition.

The healing process in this story is very physical. Jesus 'puts his fingers into the man's ears' and 'touches his tongue with spittle'. This reminds us that the meeting of bodies is very important in the ministry of healing. Jesus also 'sighs'; this is telling us that he takes on himself the pain of the man. He 'looks up to heaven'– a sign that he knows the source of his healing power is there. It is also a sign of a deep respect before the person's vulnerability.

The passage concludes with one of the several stories of Jesus imposing what biblical scholars have called the 'messianic secret.' At present, scholars are divided on the issue. Some think of the deep significance of this mysterious aspect of Jesus' ministry, a meaning which is always manifested slowly. We need to enter into this mystery as we can.

My own feeling, however, is different. I take it to mean that the 'secret' of Jesus reminds us that as always we must interpret the story of Jesus from our own experience. Jesus is then the model of those who choose to minister from the truth of who they are. They do not start from the false idea of what status society finally confers on them.

The text brings out the important aspect of what Jesus really achieved. It notes that the people 'published widely' what he had achieved; their 'admiration was unbounded'. It then adds, 'He has done all things well', and specifies further, 'he makes the deaf hear and the dumb speak.'

This is always Jesus' point of view. He is always there to help people, to make sure that the deaf hear and the dumb speak. Those who had little or no capacity for communication are now able to speak clearly.

* * *

Lord, nowadays, when people need to have hands laid on them they are often treated impersonally:
　　- doctors and nurses see the sick as objects rather than people,
　　- parents are too busy to spend quality time with their children,
　　- teachers prefer classroom lectures rather than one-to-one sessions,
　　- pastors in your church no longer sit and converse with members of their communities,
　　- the confessional has been replaced by the office with secretaries and answering machines,
　　- spiritual guides approach their work like busy professionals.
Our Western culture needs care-givers like Jesus
who take people aside in private, away from crowds,
put their fingers into the ears of those who have not heard words
of forgiveness and encouragement,
make personal contact with them
as intimate as Jesus putting spittle on the tongue of the man
who had an impediment in his speech;
people who feel very deeply
the pain of the person entrusted to them
so that in communion with them
they will raise their eyes to heaven and sigh.

Only then will those whose ears are blocked be able to hear
that they are worthy of love and friendship,
the ligaments of their tongues will be loosened
so that they will feel able to speak clearly
the truth of what they feel.

Lord, we bring to you the many people who cannot hear
and have an impediment in their speech
and therefore do not experience the joys of human communion:
- they have heard so many negative things about themselves
that compliments do not get through to them;
- they are fearful of being rejected and cannot risk saying
what is within them.
Send them people like Jesus to lay healing hands on them,
people who recognise how deep-seated their problems are
and take them aside in private, away from the crowd,
where they can say what is in their hearts;
people who will make a human contact with them,
almost putting their fingers into their ears
and touching their tongues with spittle;
not arrogant people,
but the kind who will look humbly to heaven
for the wisdom to say and do the right things;
who will not be aloof either,
but will sigh as they feel the pain of those they are listening to.
They will say, 'Be opened,' and people's ears will be opened;
at their touch, ligaments of tongues will be loosened
and speech will flow.

Lord, we think today of the many people
who live in their own world,
unable to communicate with those around them:
- the elderly abandoned by their families and residing in
homes with strangers,
- young people isolated from both peers and elders,
- immigrants who cannot hear what is being said to them and
cannot speak in their own language,
- people of deep faith categorised by majority religions as
pagans or idolaters.

They have heard no words of love or even of respect
and are impeded from sharing what is most important to them.
We ask you to send them people to whom they can be brought,
as the man in the gospel was brought to Jesus,
to have hands laid on them
so that they can hear the liberating words, 'Ephphatha'
and their ears can be opened to hear a voice they can recognise
and they can feel a human presence
which will loosen the ligaments of their tongues.

Lord, we thank you for Charismatic Renewal in our church.
Through Life-in-the-Spirit seminars
many have been brought to Jesus
to have him lay hands on them.
Their ears were opened so that they heard your word
spoken personally to them,
the ligaments of their tongues were loosened
and they who up till then were silent in your presence
as if they had an impediment in their speech
now speak clearly and freely in joyful praise.

Lord, we thank you for the humility showed by your Son Jesus
when he ordered those he healed to tell no one about it.
Help the leaders of your church to walk in his steps,
not relying on their status as bishops,
priests, deacons or lay ministers,
but on their willingness to meet people at their level,
in private away from the crowds,
sharing their common humanity and feeling their pain.

Lord, we pray today for societies
divided on grounds of ethnicity, race and culture,
religious belief and practice, long-standing territorial disputes.
Their history of mutual suspicion has made them incapable
of communicating with each other.
Like the man in the gospel story their ears are blocked
and they have an impediment in their speech
– neither side can hear what the other is saying,
and they cannot speak without being misunderstood.
We pray that Jesus will lay hands on them

and do all things well for them
so that their ears will be opened
and they will be able to speak clearly.

Twenty-fourth Sunday in Ordinary Time

Gospel Reading: Mark 8:27-35

27Jesus and his disciples left for the villages round Caesarea Philippi. On the way he put this question to his disciples, 'Who do people say I am?' 28And they told him. 'John the Baptist,' they said, 'others Elijah; others again, one of the prophets.' 29'But you,' he asked 'who do you say I am?' Peter spoke up and said to him, 'You are the Christ.' 30And he gave them strict orders not to tell anyone about him. 31And he began to teach them that the Son of Man was destined to suffer grievously, to be rejected by the elders and the chief priests and the scribes, and to be put to death, and after three days to rise again; 32and he said all this quite openly. Then, taking him aside, Peter started to remonstrate with him. 33But, turning and seeing his disciples, he rebuked Peter and said to him, 'Get behind me, Satan! Because the way you think is not God's way but man's.' 34He called the people and his disciples to him and said, 'If anyone wants to be a follower of mine, let him renounce himself and take up his cross and follow me. 35For anyone who wants to save his life will lose it; but anyone who loses his life for my sake, and for the sake of the gospel, will save it.'

This passage is in three sections, each of which has deep implications for our life of faith. The passage as a whole helps us understand and celebrate our own journey to commitment, or that of someone who has touched our lives. We start, as always, from experience, remembering a time when we got a better insight into the truth of Jesus, we realised for the first time that God truly became a human being among us.

Verse 27a: In this verse Jesus takes the decision to 'leave for the villages round Caesarea Philippi'. It was on that journey that he put his question to the disciples. He made a conscious decision, and brought out a new profession of faith from them.

Verses 27b-29: 'Who do people say I am?' We can identify with Jesus. There have been times when we have been in leadership positions in a community and have stopped to look at our work, to evaluate our impact on those around us. 'Who do people say I am? Do people understand what I am doing, what I am trying to communicate?' Nowadays we do this systematically with surveys and evaluations.

As Christians entrusted with the mission to proclaim the Good News we often ask the question: when people look at us, who do they say we are?

We can also identify with the disciples. Every so often we look at the image of Jesus we carry within us – who is he for us? We may find that our image of him has changed over time, become more concrete, more real, and more coherent with our experiences. We celebrate the moments when we have become conscious of our journey to him.

Verse 30: Jesus often instructs his disciples not to tell others what they have 'seen'. We celebrate wise teachers who warned us not to share our deepest insights with those who have not yet made the journey. We would be robbing them of the joy of making their own discovery with its own particular twists and turns. We thank God for the times when we have waited respectfully for others to know Jesus – and learnt something new about him from them.

Verses 31-33: We remember a time when someone we loved dearly – a friend, a child, a spouse – made a decision which they dreaded and yet accepted as necessary. We knew it would cause them pain, and we wanted so much to spare them! We tried to dissuade them, urging them to compromise and chose an easier path. They refused, and today we are grateful for their integrity.

Or it may be that we ourselves have made that journey, and today we thank God that we were able to.

Verses 34 and 35 are a meditation on the preceding incidents. We must make sure that we do not read them in a vague or abstract way, or as moralising. We recognise each statement as true, corresponding to experience.

Verse 34 must remind us of concrete ways in which we (or others) 'renounced ourselves' and as a result became better 'followers of Jesus' – forgiving a person (or group) for whom we felt resentment, not accepting a high position, giving up an addiction, etc.

Verse 35 evokes things that we have risked 'losing' and then 'found' again in a deeper way – a friendship, prestige, inner peace, a harmonious community or workplace.

* * *

Lord, we thank you for the quiet times we have taken,
away from the busyness of daily life,
to be with you and take stock of our lives:
long walks on the beach, retreats, quiet holidays.
Away from the pressures of family, co-workers and friends,
those who wish us to conform
to whatever image they have of us,
we asked you, Lord, 'Who do you say I am?'
and slowly we began to understand our own special vocation,
the life of Jesus within us.

'True love is self-sacrificing because it is about making choices, and some of these will always be made at personal cost to ourselves. In the name of the God of costly love we take up the daily burden of being open to costly choices. In this way we too will be broken, but broken as bread is broken, in order to be shared.' Lavinia Byrne
Lord, we thank you for friends who,
at major turning points in their lives,
spoke openly to us as Jesus spoke to his disciples.
They asked us whether we understood
what their destiny called them to.
They shared with us quite openly that what they had to do
would entail being rejected by elders, chief priests and scribes,
and even being put to death.
They asked us to have faith that ultimately
their suffering would result in resurrection and new life.
They were laying down their lives
for the sake of something higher,
knowing that only by being true to what they believed
could they save their lives.
Forgive us that when we did not understand
we took them aside and started to remonstrate with them.
We thank you that when they heard us
they rebuked us and told us,
'Get behind me, because the way you think is human,
not divine.'

'Death as an image for the path of transformation points to a dying to the world of conventional wisdom as the centre of one's security and identity and a dying to the self as the centre of one's concern. The path of death is also, for Jesus, the path to new life. It results in rebirth, a resurrection to a life centred in God.' M. J. Borg

Lord, we know you are asking us once again,
as you did when we first became your disciples,
'Who do you say I am?'
Our childhood images no longer make sense to us,
they seem to have disintegrated,
and we are frightened of being rejected
by the elders, chief priests and scribes within us.
Remind us that we need not be afraid of being put to death
because after three days we will rise again.
How true it is that if we are too anxious
to save things that are precious to us we lose them,
whereas if we are prepared to lose them
for the sake of the higher values of honesty and truth,
we will save them.

'It is evident that women are meant to form part of the living and working structure of Christianity in so prominent a manner that perhaps not all their potentialities have yet been made clear.'
Pope Paul VI, *On the dignity and vocation of women*

Lord, there are women all over the world today
who feel called to the priestly ministry,
but they are destined to suffer grievously,
to be rejected by elders, chief priests and scribes.
Help them to take up their destiny as Jesus took up his cross,
understanding the concerns of those who oppose them,
while remaining true to his Spirit within them.
Whatever they lose for his sake and the sake of the gospel
they will save it.

Twenty-fifth Sunday in Ordinary Time

Gospel Reading: Mark 9:30-37

30After leaving the mountain Jesus and his disciples made their way through Galilee; and he did not want anyone to know, 31because he was instructing his disciples; he was telling them, 'The Son of Man will be delivered into the hands of men; they will put him to death; and three days after he has been put to death he will rise again.' 32But they did not understand what he said and were afraid to ask him.

33They came to Capernaum, and when he was in the house he asked them, 'What were you arguing about on the road?' 34They said nothing because they had been arguing which of them was the greatest. 35So he sat down, called the Twelve to him and said, 'If anyone wants to be first, he must make himself last of all and servant of all.' 36He then took a little child, set him in front of them, put his arms around him, and said to them, 37'Anyone who welcomes one of these little children in my name, welcomes me; and anyone who welcomes me welcomes not me but the one who sent me.'

Today's passage is in two sections:

- a narrative which gives the context of the entire passage (verses 30-32);
- two teachings on humility, both woven into dramatic narratives (verses 33-35 and 36-37) which flow from the previous teaching.

As usual, we are free to take each section separately, or then we can see an inner logic between them.

The narrative: St Mark gives a deeply moving account of Jesus at a new and decisive stage in his life's journey. His glory days are over; the opposition has become more pronounced, he has decided that it is time to leave the relative safety of Galilee and go to Jerusalem where he will confront the powers of the nation, 'the elders, chief priests and scribes' of last Sunday's passage. So he begins his fateful journey, 'making his way through Galilee,' as the text notes.

This is a moment of truth then, not a time for miracles but for facing up to harsh reality. Speaking to large crowds would be inappropriate; it is the time for being alone with his faithful disciples and 'instructing them' with his deep teaching.

We think of similar moments in our experience (or the experience of great people who have touched our lives). The time for compromise passes, and the time for confrontation arrives. Being 'delivered into the hands of men' means laying oneself open to one's opponents. The confrontation is public, there is no hiding from it.

We can identify with Jesus, the courageous leader who is fully conscious of the consequences of his decision to confront. He is now at peace with himself. He doesn't have to work out problems of fear or hurt or resentment. He is therefore free to focus on training those who will carry on the work after he is gone and will have to hand it on to future generations, like ours today.

We can also identify with the disciples. They are truly blessed to have a leader like Jesus. They will always look back on this time of spiritual formation with deep gratitude that they went through it. They will naturally feel some regret at how slow they were to understand what he truly meant.

The teachings: In the first teaching on humility (verses 33-35), the disciples are unable to face the issues raised by Jesus. They are too frightened and (as we all do in such situations) they take refuge in arguing about unimportant issues – greatness, status and power.

Jesus, on the contrary, is unambiguous. His body language conveys the seriousness of the teaching. The text says that this happened, 'when he was in the house'. It adds that the following happened, 'when he sat down'; he then 'called the Twelve to him'. He clearly wanted to speak seriously to them about a crucial point in his teaching.

A teaching on humility is very appropriate in the context of Jesus' decision to go to Jerusalem. Only humble leaders who are not concerned about 'who is the greatest' can face calmly the prospect of being 'delivered into the hands of men'. They can then take what is offered to them and make the best of it.

The second teaching (verses 36-37) is also woven into a dramatic story and we must enter into the symbolism of the gestures. 'Welcoming' by itself can be vague. We must fill it out with the details provided by St Mark. He 'took a little child' and 'set him in front of them' and 'he put his arms around him'.

The expression 'little child' can be taken literally. As often in the gospels, however, we can give it a wider meaning. We can apply it to those who are 'little' in any sense at all. These are society's (or our community's) drop-outs. They are what the Bible calls 'tax collectors, prostitutes and sinners'.

The gospels have several teachings of Jesus on little children and each makes its own particular point, so we must focus on the angle being taken in the text before us. In this passage, the point Jesus is making is that leaders who 'make themselves last of all and servants of all' have the capacity to 'welcome' (in the sense noted above) 'little ones'. They approach them not as objects of pity, as 'the less fortunate', but rather as precious gifts sent by God, 'the one who sent Jesus'. He has much to offer and to teach us through them.

Those who are concerned about who is 'the greatest' are not able to see the greatness of the humble people of the world. We must all find ourselves in this wonderful text. It is certainly addressed to us. If we can't recognise ourselves in it, it means that we have not really accepted that it is directed to all. Yet this is clearly what it is meant to be.

* * *

'The future belongs to those who have nothing to lose.'
Herbert Marcuse
Lord, we remember a time
when we realised that being true to our values
required that we come out of our obscurity
and take a public position:
    - quit a job, break a relationship, speak up before someone in
    authority,
    - join a political party or a social movement.
Like Jesus, we knew
that we would be delivered into the hands of men
and would be put to death in some way.
We had to protect ourselves against pressure from outside
so we did not want anyone to know where we were,
and we concentrated on explaining ourselves
to those closest to us.
They did not understand, and were afraid to ask questions,

but we sat calmly with them, called them to us and explained
that, for us, being great in the eyes of others
was not worth arguing about;
the only important thing in life
was to carry out the service you entrusted to us.
We thank you, Lord,
for giving us the grace to follow in the footsteps of Jesus.

*'A great disaster reminds us of the big things in life that we forget and
the small things of which we have thought too much.'* Nehru
Lord, there was a time when we were afraid to think of failure.
Like Jesus' disciples, we preferred not to ask questions
but focused on being greater than anyone else.
Then one day we experienced death and resurrection:
   - a cause we believed in collapsed and rose again;
   - people in whom we had faith disappointed us,
   but we got to appreciate them better for who they were;
   - we admitted a secret addiction to ourselves and to others,
   and felt free for the first time.
That was Jesus whom you had sent us,
teaching us that life is a cycle of death and rebirth.
Now we give ourselves to the present,
we welcome the little children you set in front of us
and put our arms tenderly around them.
Thank you, Lord.

Lord, send us church leaders
who make us conscious of how much energy we waste
arguing with members of other churches and religions
as to which of us is the greatest;
who will sit down as our teachers, call us and tells us clearly
that we are your greatest disciples to the extent that
we make ourselves the last of all and the servants of all.

*'The longer I live the more I see God at work in people who don't have
the slightest interest in religion.'* Dorothy Day
Lord, we thank you for the many times that you touch us
through people we had looked down on.
You take them and set them in front of us

and we see them in a new light;
we are so moved that we put our arms around them
and welcome them as your messengers to us.
They make us aware that being great is so important to us
that we spend our time on the road arguing about it.
They are the presence of Jesus,
sitting down and calling us to him,
reminding us that we are truly great
when we are the servants of all.

Lord, we thank you for Alcoholics Anonymous
and other organisations which follow their healing method.
Like Jesus, they call addicts to their communities,
help them to present themselves
not as the greatest but as the least of all,
set them in front of the others
who then put their arms around them
and welcome them as your precious gift.

'The poor are the judges of the democratic life of a nation.'
The bishops of Brazil
Lord, our modern Western culture
is interested only in the greatest
– good customers,
– those who draw crowds, winners.
We thank you that in many countries of the world
leaders of your church are following in the footsteps of Jesus,
setting the little ones in the forefront,
putting their arms around them
and reminding all that in welcoming them they welcome you.

Twenty-sixth Sunday in Ordinary Time

Gospel Reading: Mark 9:38-43, 45, 47-48

38John said to Jesus, 'Master, we saw a man who is not one of us casting out devils in your name; and because he was not one of us we tried to stop him.' 39But Jesus said, 'You must not stop him; no one who works a miracle in my name is likely to speak evil of me. 40Anyone who is not against us is for us. 41If anyone gives you a cup of water to drink just because you belong to Christ, then I tell you solemnly, he will most certainly not lose his reward. 42But anyone who is an obstacle to bring down one of these little ones who have faith, would be better thrown into the sea with a great millstone round his neck. 43And if your hand should cause you to sin, cut it off; it is better for you to enter into life crippled, than to have two hands and go to hell, into the fire that cannot be put out. 45And if your foot should cause you to sin, cut it off; it is better for you to enter into life lame, than to have two feet and be thrown into hell. 47And if your eye should cause you to sin, tear it out; it is better for you to enter into the kingdom of God with one eye, than to have two eyes and be thrown into hell 48where their worm does not die nor their fire go out.'

Today's passage is in two sections:
- a narrative: verses 38-40;
- a series of five sayings: verses 41-48.

Modern Bible scholarship has shown that the different sections of a gospel passage were often written at different times and their juxtaposition may be a matter of chance. But coming to a passage in faith, we take it that divine inspiration brought the sections together, and therefore look for the inner logic linking them, and also linking the individual sayings. This inner logic is then a Word of God for us.

I suggest the following logic in this passage:

1. The basic theme of the passage is expressed in the three sayings in verses 41 to 48. Using different images they all say that in order to 'enter into life' we must from time to time make the painful choice to renounce something that is very dear to us.

2. Making this choice sets us free is two ways:

a) from pettiness, illustrated by contrasting attitudes of the disciple John who is not free and Jesus who is (verses 38-40);

b) from ego-centredness, as a result of which we can give ourselves totally to the cause of the 'little ones':

- positively: we are deeply touched by those who show them the smallest sign of compassion, e.g. 'give a cup of water'; we affirm that 'they will most certainly have their reward (verse 41);

- negatively: we are extremely angry against those who put obstacles which bring them down – 'they would be better thrown into the sea with a great millstone round their necks (verse 42).

Making the connection in this way reminds us that Jesus never gave abstract teachings. His teachings are always his reflections on his personal spiritual journey. Correspondingly, we who receive those teachings see in them the story of his life.

Verse 42 is a precious jewel in that it repudiates conclusively the error of contrasting the 'vengeful God' of the Old Testament with the 'loving God' of the New. This false opposition has bedevilled Catholic spirituality for many centuries and continues to do so today. Both Testaments reveal the one true God who is passionately committed to the cause of his lowly people. Woe to those who keep them down in any way whatsoever! Far from wanting to 'curb his anger' (or asking the Blessed Virgin Mary to do it for us!) we enter into his anger (as Mary did in her Magnificat).

We must be careful therefore not to 'interpret' Jesus' words in a way which downplays his passion – what our Catholic tradition has called his 'righteous indignation'. God's passionate commitment to the poor spells salvation for us all, even those of us who are oppressors – we will be brought low and so be lifted up.

We must identify the 'obstacles' referred to by Jesus, starting from our experience. We think of the various things in the world today which prevent the lowly from realising their full potential – the lack of material goods, of opportunities for education and health, of credit facilities; the lack of a sense of self-worth, of access to sources of grace, spiritual formation. The 'obstacles' can be put by individuals or they can be embedded in the culture (English society recognised recently that it suffers from 'institutional racism'). They may be caused by selfishness or by social and economic structures.

Verses 43-48 contain dramatic language which we must enter into, getting a feel for the painful choices we must make. We also enter fully into the two possibilities open to us, allowing them to come alive for us – 'life' on the one hand, 'hell' on the other. Experience (our own or that of people whose lives have touched us) will reveal the meaning of 'the fire that does not go out' and 'the worm that does not die'.

* * *

Lord, we thank you for great moments of grace
when we decide to renounce something that is precious
in order to be true to a higher value:
    - take a lower paying job in order to have quality time for our
    family;
    - terminate a relationship that is destroying our marriage;
    - refuse a post in the workplace which would compromise
    our integrity;
    - accept that our marriage is destroying us and move on;
    - lose an election rather than appeal to racism;
    - take the risk of confronting authority in the church.
Before making the decision, it seems impossible,
almost like cutting off a hand or a foot or tearing out an eye;
but once we make the choice, everything flows spontaneously,
we just know that it is better to enter into life crippled
or lame or with one eye,
rather than continue living in hell,
being burnt up by fire that cannot be put out,
and eaten by a worm that does not die.
Now we find that we have become free of spirit,
we are no longer worried
about whether other people are one of us,
or whether we are personally popular or influential.
As long as the devils of racism, sexism
and elitism are driven out,
we don't stop those who are doing it,
we know that those who are not against what we stand for
are for us.
We feel an overwhelming compassion
for the little ones of the world,

Jesus' special people,
we will do anything to reward those
who give them even a cup of water,
and feel anger at those who put up obstacles
which bring them down.

Lord, we thank you
that so often in our time you have sent us someone
who was not one of us but cast out the demons
which afflicted our community:
- Gandhi preached the non-violence of Jesus;
- Marxist atheists put us believers to shame in their commitment to the poor;
- warring communities in our country were brought to the negotiating table by foreigners;
- the World Council of Churches committed itself to ecumenism long before our church joined in;
- the biblical renewal arose among other Christian churches.
Some people tried to stop them, but you brought them to realise
that no one who works a miracle in your name
is likely to speak evil against you,
and that those who are not against you are for you.

Lord, remind us that the poor don't need long speeches
or grand gestures;
what they want is to experience that they belong to you
and therefore are entitled to have a cup of water to drink.

Lord, we pray that your church throughout the world
will not be afraid to renounce the things that give us security,
- customs and rituals that have sprung up over the centuries;
- large numbers;
- beautiful churches;
- prestigious health and educational institutions;
- the patronage of the powerful.
We pray that once we recognise
that any of these things is an obstacle
bringing down little ones who have faith,
we will not be afraid to throw it into the sea

with a great millstone around it.
It may be something that is as precious to us as a hand,
a foot or an eye,
but we must not be afraid to tear it out
so that we can enter into the glorious life of being your church,
experience your kingdom here on earth,
rather than living far from your presence,
burning with desires that can never be satisfied,
eaten by the worm of jealousy that never dies.

Lord, we think with great compassion
of those who are paying the penalty
for wrong choices made earlier in their lives;
    - parents who were afraid to give up a high lifestyle in order
    to give time to their children and are now consigned to senior
    citizens' homes with no one to visit them;
    - public figures who compromised their integrity in the
    search for power and were eventually discarded by the pow-
    erful;
    - those who feel isolated because they neglected their neigh-
    bours who were poor.
Deliver them from the hell of loneliness
and remorse they now live in,
the fire that never goes out and the worm that does not die.

Twenty-seventh Sunday in Ordinary Time

Gospel Reading: Mark 10:2-16

2Some Pharisees approached Jesus and asked, 'Is it against the law for a man to divorce his wife?' They were testing him. 3He answered them, 'What did Moses command you?' 4'Moses allowed us,' they said, 'to draw up a writ of dismissal and so to divorce.' 5Then Jesus said to them, 'It was because you were so unteachable that he wrote this commandment for you. 6But from the beginning of creation God made them male and female. 7This is why a man must leave father and mother 8and the two become one body. They are no longer two, therefore, but one body. 9So then, what God has united, man must not divide.' 10Back in the house the disciples questioned him again about this, 11and he said to them, 'The man who divorces his wife and marries another is guilty of adultery against her. 12And if a woman divorces her husband and marries another she is guilty of adultery too.'

13People were bringing little children to him, for him to touch them. The disciples turned them away, 14but when Jesus saw this he was indignant and said to them, 'Let the little children come to me; do not stop them; for it is to such as these that the kingdom of God belongs. 15I tell you solemnly, anyone who does not welcome the kingdom of God like a little child will never enter it. 16Then he put his arms round them, laid his hands on them and gave them his blessing.

Today's reading follows a previous summary of Jesus' teaching. It reminds us that this was part of his teaching at this point of his life: 'And again crowds gathered round him and again he taught them as his custom was.' All this teaching was very appropriate once he had made up his mind to head for Jerusalem and face the consequences of what he had achieved up to now. This was especially 'his custom' at this stage.

Our text for today is clearly divided into two sections.

Verses 2 to 12 are a teaching on marriage.

Verses 13 to 16 are a teaching on Jesus' attitude to children. The juxtaposition reminds us then that Jesus' teaching on marriage must not remain focused on this aspect of life alone. We must therefore look on his teaching as a wide concept.

This is the glory and the richness of the method of *lectio divina* and today's passage is not an exception. In this method, every text of the Bible is spoken to the whole world. Every Christian, no matter what his own vocation may be, is set to find within the context of the story before us something they can learn from it. It is always a wonderful message of new life, a way of being truer to what is deep within ourselves.

Jesus shows himself as a wise person. He points out how in the course of every period, a community always tends to take the easy way out. This is a normal turn of events. Then eventually some one like Moses arises on the scene. He makes something official although it was originally just a spontaneous compromise. It was intended to suit a particular circumstance. Now all of a sudden it takes on the force of a law.

The relationship between man and woman is a very good example. The ancient text of Genesis reminds us that man and woman were intended by God to live on equal terms. There was to be no great difference between them. They are both human beings, created by God to live in harmony.

Jesus then is the typical 'wise person'. He is able to move beyond the here-and-now problem and see how things were 'at the beginning of creation'. This is why he can see that 'they were testing him'. It was not a small question but a great one.

We can read the passage then of other realities which God made to be complementary and we have allowed to become opposed or even in competition. Jesus is the great teacher who restores harmony that was there in the 'beginning'. He brings about that what had become two should once more be found as 'one body', always in harmony, never in opposition.

We remember being able to give ourselves to work of different kinds, whatever it may be. The work often seems to be intolerable to us. But we need to be comfortable with ourselves. We must give ourselves as we are – not as we think we should be.

We remember our own country for example. Our people have been brought up to be well able to get over the disagreements among themselves and continue to find a harmonious relationship with each other. In this way, our country can be an outstanding example to many others in the rest of the world. We are called to live in good relationships in spite of our religious disagreements which may appear to be serious but do not prevent us from living in harmony.

We will notice that verses 10 to 12 are separate from the rest of the passage. In fact they don't occur in the other versions of the story at all. They serve as an important addition to the passage. Jesus adds a new element to the usual breakdown between husband and wife. He says, 'If a woman divorces her husband, and marries another, she is guilty of adultery too.' This is a remarkable addition telling us that in the Christian Church women have their rights and privileges too. Men have them and so do women. We must insist that this is the right approach to the problem – at every level.

In general we interpret both passages as moments when we find that we come to a deeper insight into a truth. We thought we had it well received. Now we realise that it means more to us than we had originally thought. We accept this with great joy and recognition.

The story of Jesus and the children must not be limited to one meaning of literal children. In the New Testament, children are always to be taken as examples of the 'little ones'. They are those who are not considered important or worthy of serious consideration in our community.

We can apply it to situations where they include people who are called in the Bible 'tax collectors and sinners'. These are those who are rejected by most people but whom we now recognise as our equals. There are many of them as life teaches us.

We may identify with the disciples, or more probably with Jesus. His attitude is at three levels.

i) He is welcoming of those whom society has tended to reject as unreasonable.

ii) He shows the children reverence. He 'lays hands on them and blesses them', treating each of them as very important.

iii) He sees that each of them has something unique to teach the rest of us.

All children, and this includes all those in our community we tended to neglect, have a deep lesson to teach us. They tell us how we should relate to those in our community whom we tended to neglect.

* * *

'Able to approach the future as a friend,
Without a wardrobe of excuses.' W. H. Auden
Lord, there are many things in life
which you have made complementary,
not two, but together forming one reality:
- young and old in a community;
- men and women in relationships;
- people of different cultures in our one world;
- body and soul within each of us.
It is difficult to make this unity,
and so we allow ourselves
to divorce these things from each other.
We see them as opposed and even in competition.
We thank you for people like Jesus
who teach us that it was not so at the beginning of creation,
and what you have united
we human beings have no right to divide.

Lord, we who have been happily married
thank you today for the great gift
by which two people whom you have made male and female
left their mothers and fathers
and the two then became one body,
so that we are no longer two but just one body
in a bond so strong that no one could ever break it.

Lord, we pray that your church
may remain faithful to the teaching of Jesus,
so that even though we come back
and question one another over and over again,
we may continue to say, as he did,
that not only is the man who divorces his wife
and marries another
guilty of adultery against her,
but the woman who divorces her husband and marries another
is guilty of adultery too.

Lord, we remember the time when little children
were not allowed to go to Holy Communion.

We thank you that you sent us a great pope like Pius X.
He was rightly indignant that they were being turned away;
he allowed them to come to Jesus
and would not let them be stopped any longer.

*'The incarnation is the mystery in which each of the thousand million
human beings living on our planet has become a sharer from the
moment he is conceived beneath the heart of his mother.'*
Pope John Paul II
Lord, when we become professionals,
doctors, lawyers, consultants, bankers, principals of schools,
we tend to isolate ourselves in our air-conditioned offices
with efficient receptionists who turn away people
when they bring small problems to us.
We pray that we may feel indignation at this
and that in our presbyteries and church offices
we may rather put our arms round the little people,
lay our hands on them and share our blessings with them.

'To understand scripture we must stop acting like mere spectators.'
Karl Barth
Lord, sometimes at our church services little children distract us;
they make noise, run up and down the aisle
and make comments.
We block them from our minds
so that we can concentrate on our prayers
or on the sermon.
But they are teaching us a precious lesson,
that if we do not feel at home with them
we can never enter into your presence.

'How much better to carry relief to the poor than send it.' John Wesley
Lord, when we were young we said foolish things,
or expressed ourselves awkwardly,
and most adults dismissed us.
Today we remember with gratitude
that one person who welcomed us
as Jesus welcomed little children, and took us seriously,
showing us that what we were saying
was in fact very important, and so gave us a blessing.

Twenty-eighth Sunday in Ordinary Time

Gospel Reading: Mark 10:17-30

[17]*Jesus was setting out on a journey when a man ran up, knelt before him and put this question to him, 'Good master, what must I do to inherit eternal life?'* [18]*Jesus said to him, 'Why do you call me good? No one is good but God alone.* [19]*You know the commandments: You must not kill; you must not commit adultery; you must not steal; you must not bring false witness; you must not defraud; honour your father and mother.'* [20]*And he said to him, 'Master, I have kept all these from my earliest days.'* [21]*Jesus looked steadily at him and loved him, and he said, 'There is one thing you lack. Go and sell everything you own and give the money to the poor, and you will have treasure in heaven; then come, follow me.'* [22]*But his face fell at these words and he went away sad, for he was a man of great wealth.* [23]*Jesus looked round and said to his disciples, 'How hard it is for those who have riches to enter the kingdom of God!'* [24]*The disciples were astounded by these words, but Jesus insisted, 'My children,' he said to them, 'how hard it is to enter the kingdom of God!* [25]*It is easier for a camel to pass through the eye of a needle than for a rich man to enter the kingdom of God.'* [26]*They were more astonished than ever. 'In that case,' they said to one another, 'who can be saved?'* [27]*Jesus gazed at them. 'For men' he said 'it is impossible, but not for God; because everything is possible for God.'*

This passage, like last Sunday's, is in two clearly distinct sections:
- verses 17 to 22: the story of Jesus and the wealthy man;
- verses 23 to 27: a teaching of Jesus on wealth, although the phrase 'he looked around' invites us to read this second section as a commentary on what happened in the first section.

Be creative in interpreting the words 'inherit eternal life' as entering into a deeper kind of life through prayer and the following of Jesus, but also through deep relationships with other people, or involvement with some noble cause.

The wealthy man is the model of the one who wants to enter into this deeper life the easy way, by drawing up a list of commandments – things to do and things to avoid – but eventually learns that the only way is to take the risk of leaving all and following one's Lord. Feel the pathos of the ending of verse 22, remembering those who live with regrets for not having taken the risk at a certain point in their lives.

Jesus is the teacher, the leader or spiritual guide who is humble but firm and invites the man to make the leap of faith, not coldly or objectively, but himself getting emotionally involved with the man and taking the risk of rejection.

The wealthy man can be for you a model of a community as well as a person; a nation, perhaps, or our modern civilisation. Jesus can be a model of a great national leader or of the church as a whole.

Enter into the teaching on wealth as a journey, the first statement causing consternation, the second even more, and the third more still. Focus on the disciples, remembering when you understood for the first time how you had let yourself be influenced by the false values of the world; or then focus on Jesus, free in himself and his vision clear, so that he can stand by his values in the face of any opposition. Note however his gentleness and compassion even as he makes demands on others.

* * *

Lord, we thank you for the deep relationships
we have entered into through your grace –
with one of our children, a spouse, an intimate friend, a leader –
the kind of relationship that has given a new quality to our lives.
People sometimes think they can run and kneel before someone
and say, 'You are a good person;
what must I do to have a deep relationship with you?'
But as we know, it cannot happen like that;
it isn't a matter of someone being good,
because only God is good;
nor of learning off by heart a list of things to do.
Something is still lacking:
to experience that someone is looking deep into our souls
and loving us,
to feel that we could sell everything we own
and distribute the money to the poor,
because nothing in the whole world
is more important than being with that person.
Of course, many people's faces fall at this point,
because they have things which they cannot let go,

and so they go away sad,
with a sadness that nothing will ever cure.

*'If a man has not discovered something that he will die for, he isn't fit to
live.'* Martin Luther King
Lord, how many people go away sad
because they have never left everything to follow a noble cause?

A modern poet once said, 'Traveller, there is no path:
paths are made by walking.'
Lord, forgive us for using the commandments as an excuse
for not stepping out in faith.

Lord, help those of us who have authority in the church
to be more like Jesus.
When people run up and kneel before us
asking what they must do to inherit eternal life,
we let our authority go to our heads;
we rattle off a list of commandments
that Christians have learnt from their earliest years,
when, like Jesus, we should invite them simply to walk with us.
But that requires an inner freedom on our part,
because the faces of some will fall when they hear our words,
especially those who have great wealth.

Lord, we thank you for the spiritual journey
you have led us on.
When we first began to follow Jesus seriously
we were anxious to acquire many virtues.
Then, one day, quite suddenly,
we realised how self-righteous we had become:
    - we found ourselves condemning others;
    - we heard a sermon on humility which touched us;
    - someone we had thought of as a sinner appeared to us as
    deeply spiritual.
It was as if Jesus had looked round at us and said to us,
'How hard it is for those who have riches
to enter the kingdom of God!'
It was an insight that astounded us

and it took us several weeks to accept it.
Lord, we thank you that you insisted.

Lord, when we see the pitfalls in the way of true holiness,
and how even the virtuous find it difficult to enter there,
we wonder, can anyone be saved.
But that is a moment of grace
because we understand then that spiritual growth is your work,
and everything is possible for you.

Lord, some nations in the world today
have become very wealthy;
no nation in history was ever as wealthy as they are.
Yet their very wealth makes it impossible for them
to become caring and sharing communities,
and they go away sad because they cannot give up
their present lifestyle.
We thank you that our Pope and many other religious leaders
have watched carefully what is happening there,
and have turned round to warn us of the dangers
of making economic growth our primary goal.
Many are astounded because their own deepest aspiration
is to become wealthy nations in their turn;
but our leaders must insist
that it is easier for a camel to pass through the eye of a needle
than for a wealthy nation to enter your kingdom.
Not that it is not possible – because all things are possible to you.

Twenty-ninth Sunday in Ordinary Time

Gospel Reading: Mark 10:35-45

35*James and John, the sons of Zedebedee, approached Jesus. 'Master,'
they said to him, 'we want you to do us a favour.' 36He said to them,
'What is it you want me to do for you?' 37They said to him, 'Allow us to
sit one at your right hand and the other at your left in your glory.'
38'You do not know what you are asking,' Jesus said to them. 'Can you
drink the cup that I must drink, or be baptised with the baptism with
which I must be baptised?' 39They replied, 'We can.' Jesus said to them,
'The cup that I must drink you shall drink, and with the baptism with
which I must be baptised you shall be baptised, 40but as for the seats at
my right hand or my left, these are not mine to grant; they belong to
those to whom they have been allotted.' 41When the other ten heard this
they began to feel indignant with James and John, 42so Jesus called
them to him and said to them, 'You know that among the pagans their
so-called rulers lord it over them, and their great men make their authority felt. 43This is not to happen among you. No; anyone who wants
to become great among you must be your servant, 44and anyone who
wants to be first among you must be slave to all. 45For the Son of Man
himself did not come to be served but to serve, and to give his life as a
ransom for many.'*

There are two distinct sections in this passage:
- verses 35 to 40: the encounter between Jesus and the sons of
Zebedee; and
- verses 41 to 45: his teaching on service.
The dialogue with the sons of Zebedee is very dramatic, with
plenty of significant details. As usual with gospel stories, feel
free to focus either on Jesus or on the people who come to him.

James and John are typical of young, enthusiastic followers
of any cause – very ambitious, but also very committed and
ready for everything. Note how they are confident: they can
accept the challenges, even if they do not see clearly what they
entail.

The portrayal of Jesus is very touching: his respect for the
young men, the way he takes them seriously, the way he challenges them and reassures them simultaneously. His humility is
remarkable as he disclaims the authority to give final rewards.

As in last week's passage, Jesus is the model for civil as well as religious leaders, and the two brothers can be the church community or the nation.

Verse 45 is very deep and can be read by itself. Enter into the metaphor of the ransom, asking yourself how this ancient practice of buying back slaves is lived today when people give themselves to the work of human liberation, with the life of Jesus as the model.

* * *

Lord, we remember with gratitude
the spiritual journey we have made.
At first we were like the sons of Zebedee,
very anxious to become loyal and to do great things for you.
Truly we did not know what we were asking.
You did not reject us, but rather guided us gently,
  - some of us through prayer and Bible reading;
  - others through a guide who was Jesus for us.
You made us understand that spiritual growth
is setting out on the path of Jesus,
drinking whatever cup of suffering you send us,
and entering deep waters as he did.
As the challenge came, we said 'Yes',
and you certainly took us at our word.
Today we find that we are not interested in success of any kind.
We know that sitting at your right hand
or at your left in your glory
is not something that any one can give us,
or that we can earn for ourselves,
and we leave that to you to allot to whoever you will.

Lord, we thank you for young people,
especially those of us who work with youth in schools,
church communities or families.
We thank you for their enthusiasm and their great desires.
Don't let us become cynical
just because they do not know what they are asking.
Help us rather to be like Jesus and walk with them,
challenging them, but also reassuring them

that they can in fact make the sacrifices
which their desires imply.
Lord, leaders are afraid to ask sacrifices of their people;
they like to promise great rewards in some future kingdom
even though these rewards are not theirs to give.
We pray that they may be like Jesus, honest with their people.
But of course, if they ask a sacrifice of their followers,
they must go that way themselves,
the cup they ask others to drink
must be one they drink themselves,
and if they ask others to receive a baptism
it should be one they have received themselves.

Lord, forgive us that as a church
we promise people heavenly rewards
if they fulfil certain requirements.
Remind us that places at your right hand or your left
are not ours to give
but belong to those to whom they have been allotted.

Lord, it is not easy to work
for the liberation of oppressed people.
We would like to do it the easy way,
giving handouts or making nice speeches.
But Jesus has shown us that this kind of work is always costly.
It is like the ancient practice of buying back slaves,
except that for us
the money we have to put out is our own selves,
our security and our need to be successful,
allowing ourselves to be hurt
and in that way healing the hurts of others
and helping them go free.

Lord, we remember the time
that jealousy arose in our church community,
our parish council, the choir, the youth group,
some trying to get places of honour
and others indignant with them.
Then you sent someone who called us together

and showed us how we were no different
from the other rulers in our society,
or other important people who like to make their authority felt.
We realised at that moment
that this should never happen among us
because for us to be great or important
is to be at the service of all.

Lord, we pray for those who are about to get married,
that they may understand what they are asking of each other,
which is that whatever cup of suffering one has to drink
the other must drink it too,
and whatever baptism life demands of one
the other must enter into that baptism too.

Thirtieth Sunday in Ordinary Time

Gospel Reading: Mark 10:46-52

⁴⁶*As Jesus left Jericho with his disciples and a large crowd, Bartimaeus (that is, the son of Timaeus), a blind beggar, was sitting at the side of the road.* ⁴⁷*When he heard that it was Jesus of Nazareth, he began to shout and to say, 'Son of David, Jesus, have pity on me.'* ⁴⁸*And many of them scolded him and told him to keep quiet, but he only shouted all the louder, 'Son of David, have pity on me.'* ⁴⁹*Jesus stopped and said, 'Call him here.' So they called the blind man. 'Courage,' they said, 'get up; he is calling you.'* ⁵⁰*So, throwing off his cloak, he jumped up and went to Jesus.* ⁵¹*Then Jesus spoke. 'What do you want me to do for you?' 'Rabbuni,' the blind man said to him 'Master, let me see again.'* ⁵²*Jesus said to him, 'Go; your faith has saved you.' And immediately his sight returned and he followed him along the road.*

Jesus' attitude in this story is extraordinary. All his greatness, his divinity we might say, is expressed here. Follow every detail of St Mark's narrative and you will find yourself discovering new aspects all the time.

We can distinguish four stages in this encounter, and all of them contribute to the miraculous healing:
- he stops, in verse 49;
- he says, 'Call him here' in the same verse;
- 'What do you want me to do for you?' in verse 51;
- 'Go; your faith has saved you,' in verse 52.

At each stage we can see the respectful love of Jesus, and we know from our own experience that this kind of love can work miracles.

The man's journey is also significant. Sitting at the side of the road, he is the model of all those who are marginalised, forced to beg for mercy while the great ones of the world pass by. But the faith which saves him is shown by his unconquerable spirit, his refusal to accept that he is destined to remain there for the rest of his life.

There are two groups of bystanders; the first – in verse 48 – scold the man for crying out. They are those who have grown to accept that his predestined place is to remain at the side of the road. Perhaps some of them were also beggars and they are genuinely angry that one of their number would want anything else for himself.

The second group of bystanders, mentioned in verse 49, are the opposite; they reassure the blind man, as if understanding how difficult it is for those who have been at the side of the road for a long time to throw off their cloaks and speak for themselves.

The climax of the story – 'he followed him along the road' – is very touching, and you might like to enter into the metaphor of walking as a symbol of what happens when the marginalised take their place in the movement of history.

* * *

Lord, send us leaders like Jesus who,
when they are surrounded by disciples and large crowds
and some blind beggar sitting at the side of the road
begins to shout for help,
will not continue walking but will stop,
and not merely throw a handout in his general direction
but call him to come forward
and stand in the centre of everybody;
and they will not take for granted
that they know what this man wants,
but will take the trouble to ask him
'What do you want me to do for you?'
And when the man has begun to see again
they will not take any glory for themselves
but will say to all that it was his own faith that saved him
so that he may take his place as a free member of the community
and follow them along the road.

Lord, there are many people sitting at the side of the road,
shouting to us to have pity on them,
but they often shout in strange ways:
- by behaving badly in the classroom;
- by taking drugs and alcohol;
- by sulking, remaining silent or locked up in their rooms;
- sometimes by insisting that they are happy to be at the side
of the road while others pass by.
Lord, like Jesus, we need to stop all that we are doing

so that we can hear them express their deep longing
to have their sight restored to them.

Lord, the people of the third world
have been a long time at the side of the road,
begging, while the wealthy nations in a large crowd
make their way to ever greater prosperity.
When these people begin to shout,
asking others to have pity on them,
many scold them as if they are wrong to shout,
as if it is their perpetual destiny
to remain at the side of the road and beg.
But you, Lord, have put in their hearts an unconquerable faith
that they too can take their places on the road to prosperity,
and this gift of faith will eventually save them.

Lord, when we have been a long time at the side of the road
it is not easy to stand in front of everyone
and express what we really want for ourselves.
We thank you for those who say to us
'Courage, get up, the Lord is really calling you.'

*'An Indian sat silently wrapped in his blanket. The leader asked him
what he thought of a particular point. No response; the man did not
even look up. He asked again; again, there was no response. Again –
and the man burst into tears. Eventually, comforted, he said, "This is
the first time in my life anyone has asked me what I think." Then he
proceeded to say what he thought for four hours.'*
Report from a church meeting in Latin America
Lord, we thank you
that Jesus is still leaving Jericho with his disciples
and walking along our roads.

Lord, we remember the day when, through your grace,
our sight was restored.
For many years, while other passed us by,
we sat at the side of the road,
    - lost in drink or drugs;
    - refusing to forgive someone who had hurt us;

- making money and success the goals of our lives.
There came a time when we knew that we were blind,
but we felt that we could do nothing about it.
Then came a day when we knew you had sent
a Son of David into our lives
– a Bible reading, a preacher, one of our children, a friend –
and we shouted to them to have pity on us.
There were loud voices within us
scolding us and telling us to keep quiet:
it was too late, people would never understand,
we were too far gone.
But we shouted all the louder
until eventually the moment came, and we knew it,
so that we threw off all our fears, jumped up and went to Jesus.
It all happened so simply: we just asked to be able to see again
and immediately we saw clearly what we had to do,
and we followed you along the road.
We thank you for the deep conviction
that the time of grace had come
for it was that conviction that saved us.

All Saints

Gospel Reading: Matthew 5:1-12

¹*Seeing the crowds, Jesus went up the hill. There he sat down and was joined by his disciples.* ²*Then he began to speak. This is what he taught them:*

³*'Happy are the poor in spirit; theirs is the kingdom of heaven.*

⁴*Happy the gentle; they shall have the earth for their heritage.*

⁵*Happy those who mourn; they shall be comforted.*

⁶*Happy those who hunger and thirst for what is right; they shall be satisfied.*

⁷*Happy the merciful; they shall have mercy shown to them.*

⁸*Happy the pure in heart: they shall see God.*

⁹*Happy the peacemakers: they shall be called sons of God.*

¹⁰*Happy those who are persecuted in the cause of right: theirs is the kingdom of heaven.*

¹¹*Happy are you when people abuse you and persecute you and speak all kinds of calumny against you on my account.*

¹²*Rejoice and be glad, for your reward will be great in heaven; this is how they persecuted the prophets before you.'*

On this feast day we are invited to reflect on St Matthew's version of the Sermon on the Mount, Jesus' long discourse which runs from chapter 5 to chapter 7. If the Sermon on the Mount summarises the teachings of Jesus' public ministry, the Sermon itself is summed up in the Beatitudes.

Doing *lectio divina* on the Beatitudes is a different exercise from reading a book on them. There have been many excellent books on the Beatitudes in recent years, one of the best (in my opinion) being *The Beatitudes – Soundings in Christian Tradition* by Simon Tugwell OP. No matter how helpful such books are, reading them is not the same as doing *lectio* on the Beatitudes. With a book our aim is to grasp the message of the Beatitudes; with *lectio divina* the aim is similar but the method different. We focus on the text, get to love it (perhaps for the first time) and let it lead us to love the Beatitudes. As a result the text engages us. Our response to it is not merely 'What a beautiful message!' but 'What a beautiful text!' and 'It has touched me deeply!'

The Jerusalem Bible version introduces each beatitude with

252

the word 'happy'. This is an unfortunate translation which the New Jerusalem Bible has corrected by returning to the traditional 'blessed'. Even with 'blessed' we need to give it its full biblical meaning. It includes being 'happy' (an aspect which was neglected in the past) but adds the notions of 'specially chosen by God' and 'a blessing for others'.

The Beatitudes are 'wisdom teaching', a biblical literary form that our church has tended to neglect in recent centuries. Jesus is reporting facts, not moralising. At no point does he say, 'You should do this.' He says, simply, 'People like this are blessed' and lets us draw our own conclusions. We respond by entering into the truth of the passage – not 'Jesus is telling me to do this', but 'This teaching is true.'

The wisdom is celebratory and our meditation must be the same. Each beatitude begins with an exclamation – 'How blessed!' I must modify the previous point therefore. Our response is not 'This teaching is true' but 'How true it is!' and even, 'How wonderful that it is true!'

Wisdom is universal by definition. The Beatitudes are teachings in human living, valid not for Christians only (still less for Catholics only) but for 'all men and women of good will', an expression used by all recent popes in their social teaching. We must make sure that our meditation leads to universal conclusions – 'All gentle people have the earth for their heritage', 'All who are pure of heart see God', and so forth.

As always with *lectio divina*, the text is intended to be in dialogue with our experience. The Beatitudes throw light on our experience and our experience explains the Beatitudes. Our response is not merely 'This is true' but 'This helps me to understand this parent, friend or teacher who touched my life very deeply' and in turn, 'This person helps me understand the Beatitudes.'

Referring to concrete experience is specially important with the Beatitudes which are expressed in biblical language that is foreign to us, e.g. 'poor in spirit', 'hunger and thirst for what is right', 'pure of heart', etc. Especially with such expressions, we need to start with our experiences of people and let them explain the meaning of the beatitude, e.g. 'My mother was the kind of person to whom the kingdom of heaven belongs, so being poor

in spirit means being like her'. Jesus himself is the prime example of the Beatitudes in practice. We should apply them to him,
basing ourselves on some incident reported in the gospels.

The Beatitudes constitute a whole. They are seven (in the
Bible, the number indicates perfection) aspects of the model
human being – for us Christians, the Jesus way of being human.

There is a movement between the seven so that the full picture of the ideal human being unfolds gradually, one beatitude
leading spontaneously to another, until we grasp the entire
teaching in its complex harmony.

It would be a mistake, however, to look for these connections
too quickly; our reflection would end up 'heady' rather than
'celebratory'. We take one beatitude at a time (any one), stay
with it for as long as we are comfortable and then allow the connections with others to emerge in our consciousness, so that they
are all contained in the one.

This will take time and we shouldn't hurry the process. At
any one stage in our lives we will find that one beatitude is particularly dear to us. We must be in no hurry to move to another.
Perhaps one lifetime is not long enough to love them all – and in
any case when we go to the Father we will see them as one.

In the Bible (as in all great religious traditions) we enter wisdom through paradox. Things that are usually opposed are reconciled at a higher level, giving us new insight – and new joy.

The Beatitudes are paradoxes and we must make an effort to
read them as such which is difficult because they have become
familiar and no longer surprise us. If a Beatitude does not surprise (even shock) us, it means that we have lost its meaning.

The paradox is in two 'movements' (like the movements of a
symphony).

   a) A main section brings together two 'opposites':
   - 'poverty of spirit' and 'possessing the kingdom';
   - 'gentleness' and 'having the earth for one's heritage';
   - 'mourning' and 'being comforted', etc.
The bringing together is simultaneous. We weaken the Beatitudes
when we make the second a 'reward' for the first.

The bringing together must be based on experience. The
question in each case is, 'When have I seen these two things
combined in one person?'

b) Having seen the combination, we exclaim 'How blessed!' (in the wide sense explained above).

The Beatitudes are generally interpreted as a teaching on the interior life, and so they are. This must be correctly understood however. According to biblical spirituality, our inner dispositions are reflected outwardly, not merely in one-to-one relationships but in every area of human living, including public life, international relations, etc.

Some commentators make a distinction between inward and outward looking beatitudes:

a) three are 'inward looking': poor in spirit, mourn, pure in heart;

b) four are 'outward looking': gentle, hunger and thirst for righteousness, merciful, peacemakers, being persecuted.

We must not make too much of this distinction however. All the beatitudes speak of inner dispositions which are reflected outwardly. What we must do is give the beatitudes their full scope, seeing them as ideals of human behaviour at every level:

- our relationship with God;

- one-to-one relationships as parents, friends, teachers, spiritual guides;

- leadership style in church or secular communities;

- relationships between communities within nations and nations within the human family.

Below are a few brief comments to help you start your meditation.

Verses 1 and 2 give the setting of the Sermon. They remind us that every gospel passage, even a long discourse like this one, is a story. It is never a text book reading, a disembodied 'voice' speaking to us from an indeterminate place. We read it as a story then, asking ourselves (from our experience as always) who has been the Jesus who 'began to speak' to us in this vein.

Verses 3 to 12 can be divided:

a) 3-10: a main section which proclaims the 'blessedness' of the Jesus way;

b) 11-12: a small section outlining its negative aspects.

Verse 3: This first beatitude summarises them all. We will experience this by seeing how it is lived in each of the others. The two sides of the paradox are:

a) 'poor in spirit' which means not being attached to anything less than the absolute;

b) 'theirs is the kingdom of heaven' means attaining the absolute; this can have as broad a meaning as we wish to give it, e.g. union with God, a wonderful human relationship, a harmonious community.

Verse 4:

a) We must make sure to relate 'gentle' to concrete experience; e.g. it must include being 'non-violent' in one form or another.

b) The 'earth' can be taken literally, giving the beatitude an ecological meaning but we can also interpret it of a community.

Verse 5:

With this beatitude especially we must not set a time lag between the two aspects of the paradox. Jesus' teaching is that only those who know how to mourn will experience true comfort.

Verse 6:

'What is right' is an unfortunate translation. The traditional 'righteousness' is better. It means God's plan of harmony for ourselves as individuals and for all communities, including the entire human family.

Verse 7:

We can interpret 'have mercy shown them' of the response of others, 'people will show them mercy'. Or we can take it as a Jewish way of saying, 'God will show them mercy'. In either interpretation it is a 'paradoxical' statement. We often think that the way to have people on our side is by inspiring them with fear, and believers tend to think that God is pleased with them when they take a hard line.

Verse 8:

We give a wide interpretation to both sides of the paradox. 'Pure of heart' means being free from every form of ego-centredness. 'See God' means being conscious of the divinity in every person and situation.

Verse 9 is paradoxical for the same reason as verse 7.

In verse 10 again 'right' is better translated as 'righteousness'.

Verses 11 and 12

Here again we must give a correct interpretation to the future tense. The contrast is not between present and future but between the inner peace of believers and the turmoil which surrounds them.

* * *

'When I was, he was not, now he is, I am not.' A Hindu sage
Lord, how true it is that when we are poor in spirit
your kingdom is ours.

'I can be saved only by being one with the universe.'
Teilhard de Chardin
Lord, forgive us that we look on the earth
as an enemy to be conquered.
Teach us to be gentle so that we will experience the earth
as a precious heritage that we come home to.

'If you love God the pain does not go away but you live more fully.'
Michael Hollings
Lord, forgive us that we are afraid to mourn
and so don't experience your comfort.

'The ideals which have lighted my way and time after time given me new courage to face life cheerfully have been kindness, beauty and truth. The trite subjects of life – possessions, outward success, luxury – have always seemed contemptible.' Einstein
Lord, forgive us that we no longer hunger and thirst
for your righteousness
and so are never satisfied.

'We don't possess the truth, we need the truth of the other.'
Bishop Pierre Claverie, French Dominican Bishop killed by fundamentalist Muslims in Algeria
Lord, lead us to the blessedness
of looking at others with compassion
and then experiencing their compassion for us.

*'Whether it is the surface of scripture or the natural form of nature,
both serve to clothe Christ, two veils that mask the radiance of his faith,
while at the same time reflecting his beauty.'*
John Scotus Eriugena
Lord, free your church
from all that takes away our purity of heart
and clouds our vision:
> - focusing on showing that we are superior to others;
> - trying to be popular with our contemporaries;
> - being concerned with increasing our numbers.

Lead us to purity of heart so that we may see you at work
in every person and every situation.

*'Once you have rid yourself of the fear of the oppressor, his prisons, his
police, his army, there is nothing they can do to you. You are free.'*
Nelson Mandela
Lord we thank you for peace makers;
they are truly your sons and daughters.

*'Truth must be protected at all costs but by dying for it, not by killing
others.'* Lactantius, 4th century
Lord, forgive us that we are afraid
of being abused and persecuted
and having calumny spoken against us.
Help us rather to rejoice and be glad
when these things happen to us,
and to know that we will have a great reward,
and that this is how they persecuted the prophets before us.

Thirty-first Sunday in Ordinary Time

Gospel Reading: Mark 12:28-34

28*One of the scribes came up to Jesus and put a question to him, 'Which is the first of all the commandments?'* 29*Jesus replied, 'This is the first: Listen, Israel, the Lord our God is the one Lord,* 30*and you must love the Lord your God with all your heart, with all your soul, with all your mind and with all your strength.* 31*The second is this: You must love your neighbour as yourself. There is no commandment greater than these.'* 32*The scribe said to him, 'Well spoken, Master; what you have said is true: that he is one and there is no other.* 33*To love him with all your heart, with all your understanding and strength, and to love your neighbour as yourself, this is far more important than any holocaust or sacrifice.'* 34*Jesus, seeing how wisely he had spoken, said, 'You are not far from the kingdom of God.' And after that no one dared to question him any more.*

This Sunday's passage consists mainly of abstract teaching, but the context is a story, and it would be good to enter into it. You can read it simply as a story of Jesus the teacher, and notice how he enters into a real dialogue with the scribe:
- verse 28, the scribe initiates the dialogue with a question;
- verses 29 to 31, Jesus answers the question with a clear but paradoxical answer, since the 'first' commandment turns out to be two;
- verses 32 and 33, the scribe takes up the dialogue by accepting the teaching of Jesus, but adds his own interpretation;
- verse 34, Jesus continues the dialogue by complimenting the scribe, and then invites him to go further, since he is still not at 'the kingdom' although he is 'not far'.

As you go through the verses you can focus on the scribe – evidently a humble person who grows in confidence through the dialogue – or on Jesus, the model of one who can walk with another into the truth.

You might prefer to concentrate on the content of the teaching in the passage. At one level there is the 'first commandment,' greater than any other, and in particular greater than any 'holocaust or sacrifice', which you can interpret either as ritual sacrifices or as the sacrifices involved in daily living. Remember the actual journey that you (or others) have made from putting other commandments higher that 'the first' to when Jesus brought you back to a correct hierarchy of values.

At a second level, there is the paradox which I mentioned earlier of a 'first commandment' which turns out to be two, although within the two (which are really one) there is an inner hierarchy. Don't leave this teaching abstract, but situate it in the context of a journey which leads there.

Finally, you might like to focus on the teaching on loving one's neighbour as oneself. Don't take it for granted that you have accepted it. Explore the meaning of 'as oneself'; let it shock and disturb you until you perceive as if for the first time that you had settled for a particular understanding of the concept of loving your neighbour, and see how these words modify it.

* * *

Lord, there was a time when we felt confused,
pulled in different directions.
as we tried to satisfy all our obligations.
We thank you for always sending us teachers like Jesus
who bring us back to basics.
They make us experience that loving you with all our hearts,
with all our understanding and strength,
and loving our neighbour as ourselves
is far more important than any holocaust or sacrifice.
At that moment we know
that we are on the right road to the kingdom
and we don't feel the need to ask any further questions.

Lord, we serve you in our private lives,
in church and in our prayer,
in our families, within our circle of friends.
But in the world of business, politics and international relations
we follow other gods.
Send us teachers like Jesus to remind us that you are one Lord,
that you are one and there is no other God,
and that in every area of life
we must love our neighbour as ourselves.

Lord, it is fairly easy to help our neighbours,
to give things that are left over and that we no longer need,
even to put ourselves to some trouble
so that they may have something to eat and clothes to wear.
But your commandment calls us to go further
and to love our neighbour as ourselves,
to experience that we need them as they need us,
that when we forgive them it is our own sins that we forgive,
and when we pity them it is because we ourselves need pity.

An Aboriginal Australian once said to a missionary:
'If you have come to help me, you are wasting your time.
But if you have come
because your liberation is bound up with mine,
then let us work together.'
Lord, we thank you for your commandment,
you must love your neighbour as yourself.

Lord, we pray that your church may enter into dialogue
with the learned people, the scribes, of our modern world,
not arrogantly, but like Jesus,
answering clearly the questions they put to us,
so that we can feel that we have spoken well
and that what we have said is true,
and so that listening to them in turn
we too may discover how wisely they speak
and how they are not far from the kingdom;
then there will be no more
of that constant questioning of one another.

Lord, there are often very wise people in our communities
who are shy to come forward, like the scribe in the gospel story.
They prefer to listen to others debating
and to observe how well the teacher is answering
before they will come up and put their own questions.
We thank you for teachers like Jesus
who can respond to them
and help them express in their own way
their understanding of the commandments,
and so find that they are on the right road to the kingdom.

Thirty-second Sunday in Ordinary Time

Gospel Reading: Mark 12:38-44

38*In his teaching to the crowds Jesus said, 'Beware of the scribes who like to walk about in long robes, to be greeted obsequiously in the market squares,* 39*to take the front seats in the synagogues and the places of honour at banquets;* 40*these are the men who swallow the property of widows, while making a show of lengthy prayers. The more severe will be the sentence they receive.'* 41*He sat down opposite the treasury and watched the people putting money into the treasury, and many of the rich put in a great deal.* 42*A poor widow came and put in two small coins, the equivalent of a penny.* 43*Then he called his disciples and said to them, 'I tell you solemnly, this poor widow has put more in than all who have contributed to the treasury;* 44*for they have all put in money they had over, but she from the little she had has put in everything she possessed, all she had to live on.'*

Jesus is teaching in Jerusalem, the centre of the Jewish religion, the heart of the opposition to all he stood for. Remembering this context will give an added dimension to our meditation.

The passage is in two sections:
- verses 38 to 40,
- verses 41 to 44, the touching story of the widow.

In verses 38 to 40 we see first the simple fact that Jesus spoke out courageously in Jerusalem – a model not merely for the church but for all his followers. Then there is the content of his teaching – the tendency for all of us religious people to seek public approval (usually an unconscious tendency brought to light by a Jesus person). Follow St Mark in making a connection between that tendency and swallowing the property of widows in verse 40.

We must be careful to interpret verses 42 to 44 correctly. Jesus is not pointing out the difference between people who can give plenty and people who can give very little, as the passage is often interpreted. He is pointing out the difference between giving what we have left over and giving all that we have.

You might like to focus on Jesus again in this section – for example, on the fact that he noticed the widow. What kind of person does this show him to be?

You might also like to see if you can make a connection between the two sections of the passage, based on your own experience.

* * *

Lord, people today set great store on show;
    - the wealthy and powerful are much sought after;
    - when people give donations to charity it is written up in the
    papers.
We pray that the church may continue
to judge things like Jesus did.
When we sit down opposite a treasury
and see those who are putting in a great deal
we may notice, like Jesus did, the poor widow
who comes and puts in two small coins,
the equivalent of a penny.
Give us the courage then
to call people and to say plainly to them
that the poor widow has put in more
than all who have contributed to the treasury,
for they put in what they had over,
but she, from the little she had, put in everything she possessed,
all she had to live on.

Lord, if the property of defenceless people
is so often swallowed up in society today
it is because we are putting too much store on public acclaim,
on who is wearing long robes,
and being greeted obsequiously in the market squares;
on who takes the front seats in church
and places of honour at banquets.
Lord have mercy.

Lord, we remember with gratitude
a time when we were not succeeding
    - at school, no matter how much we tried we could not get
    our sums right;
    - in our family, a brother or sister just kept getting on our
    nerves;
    - at work, others finished their tasks long before we could.

We thank you that at that moment you sent Jesus to us
– a teacher, a parent, a supervisor,
someone who understood
that even though we did not have much to show
we were giving more than all the others
because from the little we had we were giving everything.

Lord, Jesus was such a balanced person.
He pointed out the faults of the powerful,
those who made a show of lengthy prayers
and at the same time swallowed the property of widows.
But he was also constructive.
By praising the poor widow
who gave everything she possessed,
he showed us all the way we could go.

Lord, when we find people using lengthy prayers
to cover up the fact
that they are swallowing the property of widows
we are more severe in our judgment of them,
now we know that Jesus felt the same way.

*'A society that does not value women turns likewise a deaf ear to its
children; in other words, it cuts off its own future.'*
Jeanne Henriquez of Curaçao
Lord, we pray that like Jesus
we may always notice the women of our society
who give themselves unreservedly to bringing up their families.
From the little they have, they put everything they possess,
all they have to live on.

*'A young woman asked an old woman, "What is life's hardest bur-
den?" And the old woman replied, "To have nothing to carry".'*
A Jewish tale
Lord, we feel sorry for people who only know
about giving what they have left over.
They do not know the joy
of giving everything they possess to a cause they believe in.

Thirty-third Sunday in Ordinary Time

Gospel Reading: Mark 13:24-32

24*Jesus said to his disciples, 'In those days, after that time of distress, the sun will be darkened, the moon will lose its brightness,* 25*the stars will come falling from heaven and the powers in the heavens will be shaken.* 26*And then they will see the Son of Man coming in the clouds with great power and glory;* 27*then too he will send the angels to gather his chosen from the four winds, from the ends of the world to the ends of heaven.* 28*Take the fig tree as a parable; as soon as its twigs grow supple and its leaves come out, you know that summer is near.* 29*So with you when you see these things happening: know that he is near, at the very gates.* 30*I tell you solemnly, before this generation has passed away all these things will have taken place.* 31*Heaven and earth will pass away, but my words will not pass away.* 32*But as for that day or hour, nobody knows it, neither the angels of heaven, nor the Son; no one but the Father.'*

This is the final teaching of Jesus' public ministry. The language is very symbolic but through our meditation we will be able to enter into it and really enjoy it.

The whole passage is under the heading that this is what Jesus said to his disciples. We can begin by asking ourselves who was the person who spoke to us in this way? It could be anyone; often we find that it was someone we had never thought of as having been sent to us by God. Now we can recognise that he or she (or perhaps they) were truly a 'divine' person.

Perhaps it was one of our children; a person in our neighbourhood we had thought little of; or someone from another faith we had tended to look down on. Now we recognise that they were sent to us by God, sent by him to stir us up. They remind us of deep lessons we could learn from the evil we see going on all round us. It was a 'time of distress', many things had gone wrong for us, but life teaches us that times like that also contain an important message for us. Now we can see this more clearly than ever before.

We can divide the passage into three sections. They are connected of course, but the language is very symbolic and it would be better to focus on one at a time, allowing each to touch us very deeply.

Let's take verses 24 to 27 first. They tell us of the breakdown of stable parts of our surroundings. Things we had taken for granted we couldn't do without; now life has taught us that we can well survive without them.

Two things happening at the same time however:
- the scattering of what at first seemed so important that we thought we could never survive without it,
- the gathering of God's faithful.
While areas were being destroyed which we thought we couldn't do without, God's faithful ones, his true citizens, were now being gathered into one community, a very happy zealous community. It was the kind of community that many of us outside are not involved in, but we know now that it was really a true and easily verifiable community.

This is a teaching about the end of the world. We must however start by letting it remind us of other experiences, times when things whose disappearance we believed would mark the end of our little world actually disappeared – and yet we survived! Things that we had thought were destined to last forever turned out to be just temporary. We had taken things for granted – now we are taught by life that it was merely our little 'private world' which has come to an 'end'. The ancient order has truly passed away and we are now well and truly into a new one. It is one that we hadn't prepared ourselves for; it's advent took us by surprise.

These experiences occur both for communities and for individuals. There were times when we thought that, provided we were faithful to certain circumstances our life, our community would be fine. Now we know how inaccurate our little prejudices were.

In verses 28 and 29 we read the parable of the fig tree. It speaks to us about life and how it turns out for us. Even in an atmosphere of winter, a small sign of hope was present among us. We can look back now and see how it was there – even though we didn't recognise it at the time. Now we can see it for what it really is.

In verses 30 and 31, Jesus gives a sense of urgency to the parable. He assures us that whatever happened to him, his words will not pass away – they will last forever. This was a true prophecy in the time of Jesus; in what sense can we say that it is always true when it happens to us today?

We need to put our views of life forward with the same sense of self-confidence, the sense that this is really what God wants us to say to others. We ourselves are significant.

We had not seen the connection between the commandment and God's pleasure in what we do. As we read it here, it is a statement made by Jesus to us. We must now ask ourselves to what extent can we Christians speak with similar confidence about our own statements to the world of today? They are our own ideas of what is right and what is wrong. We do not say them with the confidence that this is really what God wanted us to say to our people and indeed to the whole world.

Verse 32 can stand by itself as a powerful statement of faith in God's future. Only the Father knows what was really happening to us. The angels did not and neither did the Son. We can often think of similar surroundings now. We tended to look to the angels or to the Son to give us a correct answer but find none from them. We must therefore have confidence to say what we truly believe in.

* * *

Lord, we remember with gratitude
the times of crisis in our lives:
    - a spouse proved unfaithful;
    - we lost our job;
    - we fell into a serious sin;
    - we learned we were seriously ill;
    - we lost someone dear to us.
Our world fell apart in those days, after that time of distress.
The sun was darkened, the moon lost its brightness;
the stars came falling from heaven,
and the great powers of heaven were shaken.
But you did not abandon us;
in the midst of all that turmoil we received a great grace
    - we understood for the first time the meaning of faith;
    - we discovered inner resources we didn't know we had;
    - friends rallied around us.
We experienced your saving power coming in the clouds

with great power and glory
and sending your angels to gather us,
your chosen ones who had been scattered to the four winds,
from the ends of the world to the ends of heaven.

'The more solitary I am, the more affection I have for all my brothers.'
Thomas Merton
Lord, when we are driven by our egos
we put people into categories:
rich and poor, saved and sinners,
developed countries and third world countries.
When we enter into our nothingness before you,
letting the stars we aspire to fall from heaven
and the great powers to be shaken,
we experience your angels gathering together all those people
whom in our willfulness we had scattered to the four winds.

*'If we listen attentively we shall hear, amid the uproar of empires and
nations, a faint flutter of wings, a gentle stirring of life and hope.'*
Albert Camus
Lord, we thank you for those people who,
when everyone else sees only deep winter,
perceive that the twigs of the fig tree have become supple,
and therefore summer is near,
a new era is coming, is at the very gates,
and that before this generation has passed away
new and wonderful things will have taken place.

Lord, prayer is trusting totally in your love,
knowing with unshakeable confidence
that heaven and earth will certainly pass away
but your love for us will not pass away.

Lord, the freedom which Jesus bequeathed to us
enables us to do our best
without having to worry about when or where it will bear fruit.
Like Jesus, we are quite content to acknowledge
that as regards the day and the hour of success, no one knows it,
no one but you, our loving Father.

'The dark period is over and Europe is on the threshold of a new era.'
Pope John Paul II in Hungary, August 1991
Lord, we thank you that we have seen stars fall from heaven
and great powers shaken.
Your chosen ones who were scattered to the four winds
are being gathered to build a new future.

Thirty-fourth Sunday in Ordinary Time
The Feast of Christ the King

Gospel reading : John 18:33-37

³³*Pilate asked Jesus, 'Are you the king of the Jews?'* ³⁴*Jesus replied, 'Do you ask this of your own accord, or have others spoken to you about me?'* ³⁵*Pilate answered, 'Am I a Jew? It is your own people and the chief priests who have handed you over to me; what have you done?'* ³⁶*Jesus replied, 'Mine is not a kingdom of this world; if my kingdom were of this world, my men would have fought to prevent my being surrendered to the Jews. But my kingdom is not of this kind.'* ³⁷*'So you are a king then?' said Pilate. 'It is you who say it,' answered Jesus. 'Yes, I am a king. I was born for this, I came into the world for this: to bear witness to the truth; and all who are on the side of the truth listen to my voice.'*

In today's feast we celebrate Jesus under the title of King. These days, of course, we don't have too many kings around but we do have 'leaders' – so today we can call him a 'perfect leader'. He is the kind of leader we all want to be, the kind of leader we want for ourselves and for others.

We know that Jesus exercised a special kind of leadership. His example must therefore invite us to a deep reflection on how we exercise leadership. Is our way of exercising it true or false? How do other people do it? What is the true form of leadership as it is understood in the world of today? This is clearly the importance of this feast for us and for the world in which we live.

To help us in this meditation on leadership, the church invites us, in this year B, to reflect on St John's account of the confrontation between Jesus and Pilate. What we have here is only a short extract of a long and very wonderful scene. It is still long enough, however, for us to really enter into the extraordinary interplay between these two men.

It is a meeting between two people who know what kind of leadership they are about. We often find ourselves in this kind of situation today and so we can really meditate on it.

- Jesus is the ideal we are all looking to be like;

- Pilate represents the kind of leadership we are anxious to get away from.

We have played both parts at different times in our lives and we must be able to see how we can fit into each; we will then be able to measure how we are like them, and draw our conclusions. So this meditation will lead us to two things:

- to make an act of thanksgiving for the times when we have exercised leadership as Jesus wants us to;
- to make an act of humble repentance for the times when we have done it all wrong, when we have been more like Pilate than like Jesus.

We remember those who stood up proud and self-confident in the presence of rulers who were considered powerful in the eyes of the world but in fact were not. We think of people like

- the great popes and saints of our church's history
- the great women in the history of our church who have objected to the accepted ways of behaving and done wonderful things on their own;
- people of different faith traditions who we know are among us today;
- the many strong men and women in the world today.

Naturally Jesus himself is a powerful challenge to the church of our time – the universal church and local church communities. He also reminds us of communities of people who in the face of very opposed values share a common faith, in themselves, and in the real values of the world they live in.

We need to go more deeply into this aspect of what Jesus claimed for himself. Note his total self-confidence. He says, 'My kingdom is not of this kind.' It is a tremendous act of self-confidence. He is claiming his kingdom and declaring it to be different from that of Pilate. Let us learn to recognise how separate we are from many in our society.

Jesus in his nothingness was totally self-confident, while Pilate was afraid. This comes out more clearly in a later passage but we already see it here. Pilate was afraid, anxious to set Jesus free, but Jesus was not afraid. Jesus knew what kind of leadership he was offering and how different it was from that of Pilate. We too must be very conscious of what is special in our kind of leadership and how it separates us from the rest of humanity today.

Often in our lives we are like Pilate. As we sit on our thrones and call people into our presence to pass judgement on them, it is they who question us. They ask us, are we speaking from the truth of ourselves or just mouthing what others have told us? Jesus knew what was happening in the world, how different his style was from that of other leaders. He chose it with no reference to what others said or taught.

* * *

'Teach us to love as you did and to see others as you did.' Gandhi
Lord, remind us that the values of Jesus cannot be imposed.
It is never a matter of fighting battles,
with followers preventing their leaders
being surrendered into the hands of their enemies.
Our kingdom is different, it is not of this kind.

'The springs of war are in the invincible world and it is there that we must deal with it, remembering that those most responsible for its sins and horrors lie in the power of those who are our neighbours and they need our help.' Evelyn Underhill
Lord, give us the power which comes from knowing
that we were born for a purpose.
We come into the world to bear witness to certain principles,
and therefore we don't have to worry
about who approves or disapproves of them.
We know that those who are on the side of these principles
listen to our voice and will be touched by them.

Lord, nowadays anybody who has something to sell
spends a lot of time and money making it look good,
covering up whatever aspects are not attractive.
Forgive us that we try to do the same with the message of Jesus.
Remind us that like Jesus we have come into the world
to bear witness to the truth
and that whoever listens to the truth will listen to our voice.

'God has created me to do him some definite service. I may never know it in this life but I shall be told it in the next.' Cardinal Newman
Lord, once we know that like Jesus
we have come into the world for a purpose,

we need not be afraid of others,
even if they are governors
and can summon us to enter into their praetorium.

*'God communicates himself to all persons, redeems them and stamps
their being with an orientation towards sharing his own life.'*
Karl Rahner
Lord, we thank you that you have planted your truth
in the heart of every human being.
We know that we are followers of Jesus
when those who are on the side of truth recognise our voice.

*'Lord, look through my eyes, speak through my lips, walk with my feet.
Then my poor human presence will be a reminder – however weak – of
your divine presence.'* Helder Camara
Lord, help us to walk with Jesus in our daily surroundings,
so that we may be sure that you are there to walk with us.